Perfect T

SOUTH AFRICA

Travel with
**Insider
Tips**

MARCO ⊕ POLO

Contents

 TOP 10 4

That South Africa Feeling 6

For chapters: See inside front cover

TOP 10

Not to be missed!

Our TOP 10 hits – from the absolute No. 1 to No. 10 – help you plan your tour of the most important sights.

⭐ THE KRUGER ➤ 140
One of the largest game reserves in the world (left, two springboks) offers unparalleled game drives through the wilderness – it is the county's premier national park.

⭐ CITY CENTRE (CAPE TOWN) ➤ 50
Known as the Mother City it is often rated as one of the most beautiful cities in the world and it is where the cultural diversity of the Rainbow Nation is at its most colourful.

⭐ GARDEN ROUTE ➤ 70
The southern coast between Cape Town and Port Elizabeth boasts numerous nature reserves, wonderful bathing beaches and some outstanding restaurants.

⭐ UKHAHLAMBA-DRAKENSBERG PARK ➤ 94
The soaring "dragon mountain" peaks form the border with Lesotho and the area is popular for outdoor pursuits – and one of the most scenic landscapes in the country.

⭐ PILANESBERG NATIONAL PARK ➤ 158
Occupying an extinct volcano north of Sun City, this is a wonderful place to encounter many of the animals that have been relocated to the reserve.

⭐ PANORAMA ROUTE ➤ 142
This route in Mpumalanga takes in some of the most dramatic scenery in the country. It winds through the Drakensberg escarpment – which drops off to afford some spectacular viewpoints – and includes the magnificent Blyde River Canyon.

⭐ ZULULAND & MAPUTALAND ➤ 98
A region of lush rolling hills famed for its great warriors and, in the north, vast wetlands – with forests, lakes and lagoons – border endless, pristine beaches with fine sand.

⭐ PRETORIA ➤ 118
The capital of South Africa offers interesting museums and heritage sites including the impressive Victorian parliament buildings.

⭐ SOWETO ➤ 122
Nobody knows exactly how many people live in South Africa's townships. A visit to Soweto is a must for anyone who wants to understand the country's history.

⭐ DURBAN ➤ 100
A city with an unmistakeably Indian feel, its wide sandy beaches and hotel-lined seaside promenade make it a popular summer holiday destination.

THAT
SOUTH AFRICA

Experience the country's unique flair and find out what makes tick – just like the South Africans themselves.

BRAAI AND BEER

The South African *braai* (barbecue) is more than just cooking meat outdoors on an open fire; it is integral to the South African identity, a social part of every event, excursion or gathering. The word *braai* includes building the fire, stoking the embers, grilling the meat and the actual socializing. On weekends a *braai* will often start at noon with the preparation of the fragrant wood fire, once it is lit then it is time for the first beer. Next the meat is marinated (using a secret recipe) and the vegetables are either added to a cast-iron *potjie* pot or wrapped in foil and tossed in the embers. Another beer and then it is time for the meat and the spirals of *boerewors* (sausage) to be cooked to perfection over the bed of glowing embers. A *braai* is not just about eating, it is not just about a fire but rather it is about people and community – *braai* is a way of life.

HOME IS WHERE THE HEART IS

Needless to say there are still townships in post-apartheid South Africa but the government has done a lot

Street art in Johannesburg's Soweto (short for South Western Township)

FEELING

to maintain and improve them. There are now tarred roads, electricity supplies and sewer systems – entirely new settlements have emerged. However, many South Africans who have done well for themselves do not want to leave the townships. It is their home, the place of their youth, the place of their family and friends. So, along with makeshift shacks, you'll also see some spacious mansions with several luxury cars in the garage.

That South Africa Feeling

A DAY AT THE MALL

There is a strong mall culture in South Africa and mall parking lots are always full. A trip to the mall is often a family outing as malls offer more than just shops. They are entertainment centres that provide everything needed for a successful day out – restaurants, cafés, cinemas, playgrounds, even flea markets and picnic areas. Everyone takes their time, strolling along, browsing the shops and enjoying themselves in a safe environment – the actual shopping is not that important.

SPORT UNITES

South Africans are passionate about sport and the national rugby team – the Springboks – are one of the best in the world and the pride of the nation. If you don't have time to attend a stadium game, visit a sports bar and watch the action with friends or the locals. Football and cricket are also hugely popular, for a long time cricket and rugby were white-dominated sports and football was predominantly black. After returning to the international sporting world after apartheid and the success of the World Cup in 2010 it seems that the *vuvuzelas* have blown away racial barriers and redefined sports for the Rainbow Nation.

NATURE RESERVES

In 1846, the Cape Colony passed the first Nature Conservation Act; a lot has happened since then. South Africans are proud of their many small nature reserves, which are just as popular as the world-famous national parks. They are enjoyed across society: school children learn about the flora and fauna, families have picnics, tough men test their 4×4s, birdwatchers are kept busy, and photographers wait for the ultimate wildlife shot.

CELEBRATING FAITH

While church worship in the white community is a traditional, reserved affair, church services in the black community are vibrant and exuberant. Sunday is a holiday in the truest sense of the word, services are a joyous celebration with the choir singing rousing songs and the congregation joining in for the chorus – and visitors are always warmly welcomed.

Thunderstorm clouds over the Kalahari Desert

The Magazine

A WORLD
IN ONE COUNTRY

South Africa's appeal lies in its natural beauty, with a wealth of varied landscapes spread across nine provinces. It's also a melting pot of origins, cultures, languages and beliefs.

Western and Eastern Cape Provinces

The highlight of Western Cape province is Cape Town, inarguably one of the most beautiful cities in the world. The city is home to a cosmopolitan ethnic mix including Cape Coloureds – a distinct community descended from Malay slaves, White colonists and the indigenous San and Khoi peoples. Other attractions in the province include pretty winelands, the Garden Route, and fine beaches, where whales, dolphins and sharks swim along the coast. To the north of the province are the sun-baked plains of the vast and empty Karoo with its quirky 19th-century towns. The Eastern Cape is dominated by the Wild Coast: a largely rural and richly green region dotted with colourful *kraals* (villages) of the Xhosa people and backed by near-deserted swathes of beach.

KwaZulu-Natal and Gauteng

Durban and a string of resorts line the subtropical Indian Ocean coast of southern KwaZulu-Natal, while to the north is the iSimangaliso Wetland Park, where hippos and sharks share the same ecosystem. Offshore, coral gardens teem with colourful marine life. The coast has a rich cultural heritage as the heartland of the Zulu people and home to a vibrant Indian community

who first came to the region to work on sugar plantations. The province has superb game reserves and is home to more rhino than anywhere else in the world. Inland, the hilly KwaZulu-Natal Midlands, studded with the intriguing 19th-century battlefield sites, rise toward the uKhahlamba-Drakensberg Park – a UNESCO World Heritage Site of imposing jagged mountains, green valleys and excellent hiking. The park's San rock art sites are one of South Africa's greatest cultural treasures.

Gauteng, the smallest but most densely populated province in the country, is home to the rather staid capital Pretoria (now part of Tshwane municipality), as well as vibrant Johannesburg. Gauteng has thrown up a rare wealth of early hominid fossils, and its most important palaeontological sites are now protected in a World Heritage Site known as the Cradle of Humankind. Today, Johannesburg – more affectionately known as Jozi – witnessed some of the most important events in the struggle against apartheid and you can meet the people in the lively townships and visit the excellent museums to find out more. Shopping in the giant mega-malls, eating at award-winning restaurants and enjoying the nightlife are other urban highlights.

The North and Northwest

Mpumalanga and Limpopo contain the vast Kruger National Park and offer South Africa's best opportunities to see the Big Five: lion, leopard, buffalo, rhino and elephant. The northwest of South Africa, comprising the Free State, Northwest and Northern Cape provinces, is an arid region of sparsely populated farmland, giving way to the parched Kalahari grasslands in the far north. There are a few little-visited game reserves worth the effort of getting to; Kimberley and Bloemfontein have interesting historical pasts, and the lavish resort of Sun City is hidden in the bush of the adjacent Pilanesberg National Park.

The Valley of Desolation, Karoo Nature Reserve, Eastern Cape province

From **DIVIDED** to **UNITED**

**South Africa's recent history has been overwhelmingly domi-
nated by apartheid – "being apart" in Afrikaans. After apartheid
ended, Nelson Mandela (1918–2013) proclaimed the country,
"a rainbow nation at peace with itself and the world".**

And does the new South Africa reflect this statement? When the weather
is fine, some of the country's large cities – spruced up with a lot of modern
chrome and glass designs – look like massive amusement parks where
everyone seems to have only two goals: fun and consumerism. Is this what
remains of the vision that Nelson Mandela had of the country in 1994? At
his presidential address Mandela said: "We enter into a covenant that we
shall build a society in which all South Africans, both black and white, will
be able to walk tall, without fear in their hearts, assured of their inalienable

A new generation looking ahead to the future (on the Moses Mabhida Stadium viewing platform, Durban)

right to human dignity – a rainbow nation at peace with itself and the world". Thus ended the apartheid chapter of the country's history – politically at least. All that remained was for Mandela's vision to move people's hearts.

Resistance...

...against the white minority began as far back as the 19th century. In 1912, black intellectuals and politically minded individuals founded the South African Native National Congress in Bloemfontein. Later, in 1923, the name was changed to the African National Congress (ANC). It was founded to fight against racism and ethnic rivalries, for the political rights of the black majority and the improvement of their living conditions.

The Magazine

Not only were black people denied the right to vote, but from 1913 they also had to live exclusively in designated areas of townships and homelands. Up until the Second World War, the ANC, which was rather urban and medium-sized, was content with petitions, protests and meetings. In 1944, with the participation of Nelson Mandela, the ANC Youth League was formed, calling for tougher methods. The goal was no longer integration into the white political system, but liberation from this system. After increasingly repressive apartheid laws were passed from 1948 onwards, the ANC responded with strikes, civil disobedience and protest marches. Its membership rose rapidly to more than 100,000. In 1955 several organizations joined forces with the ANC. They adopted the Freedom Charter for a non-racial, democratic South Africa, which remained the ANC's core policy document until the 1990s.

Tensions

There were also tensions within the ANC. The Pluralists demanded equal rights, while the Africanists, contrary to the policy of the ANC at the time, were striving for a South Africa free from white rule. In 1959, the Africanists split from the ANC and founded the Pan Africanist Congress (PAC). In 1960, the ANC and the PAC planned large campaigns against the hated pass laws. On 21 March, the PAC called for a peaceful demonstration in front of the Sharpeville police station. The police, feeling threatened, shot into the crowd and killed 69 demonstrators. The international community reacted with horror and outrage. Throughout the country, strikes and demonstrations took place, at the cost of more lives. The government reacted harshly. On 8 April 1960, they banned

> "I have cherished the ideal of a democratic and free society" (Nelson Mandela)

the ANC and the PAC, who then continued their work underground and in exile. Both parties formed military wings. The ANC's wing was Umkhonto we Sizwe (Spear of the Nation) headed by Mandela, who, after the banning of Luthuli and the condemnation of Sobukwe, became the president of the ANC and leader of the movement. Although the organization completed a few spectacular attacks, it was nearly destroyed in 1963 when Nelson Mandela (who was arrested in 1962 and sentenced to five years imprisonment) was sentenced to life imprisonment for sabotage after warfare documents were found at the Umkhonto we Sizwe headquarters. For some time, it seemed as if the government had broken the resistance of black people. Activists were imprisoned (often without trial) and many died in police custody. Executions reached record highs. Early in the 1970s new organizations emerged, including those who wanted to create a "black consciousness" along the lines of the Black Panther movement in America. When the government wanted to introduce Afrikaans (the language of the white oppressors) as the language of instruction in schools, 20,000 Soweto pupils demonstrated on 16 June 1976. The police responded with gunfire, killing two unarmed youths. There were bloody unrests all over the country. This time the government did not manage to bring the situation under control again until the end of 1977. The government ruthlessly suppressed opposition organizations; in 1977 the leader of the Black Consciousness Movement, Steve Biko, died in prison from injuries sustained during torture.

A Noble Peace Prize

In early 1990, President FW de Klerk (the "Gorbachev of Africa") went against his own party and the white far-right and legalized struggle organizations such as the ANC, the PAC and the Communist Party. He also released Nelson Mandela from prison began negotiations to form a new transitional government. For their efforts to end apartheid and lay the foundations for democracy, Mandela and de Klerk received the Nobel Peace Prize in 1992. Following South Africa's first free parliamentary elections in April 1994, the ANC emerged as the strongest party with 62 per cent of the vote. Nelson Mandela remained in office as president until 1999 and died on 5 December 2013 from a lung infection. In the 2014 election, the ANC again confirmed its absolute majority with 62 per cent of the votes.

On the right track? Mandela's vision continues to be both the county's challenge and its mission

Game PLAN

South Africa's diverse network of national parks and game reserves is certainly its main attraction, offering some of the most exciting safari experiences on the continent. These reserves encompass every possible landscape from desert and forest to mountain and coast, and they collectively harbour a full range of southern African animals.

Several South African reserves are home to the Big Five: lion, leopard, buffalo, rhino and elephant. This is a term that originally described the five animals most feared by professional hunters, and capturing this legendary quintet on camera is a prime goal of most modern photographic safaris. To bump up the Big Five to the Big Seven you need to add the great white shark and the southern right whale to the list, both species can be seen in the marine reserve section of the Addo Elephant Park. Other interesting animals to photograph are cheetah, giraffe, hippo and zebra, and there is a range of other species of mammals, reptiles and birds that deserve equal attention. Many parks and reserves are run by government or provincial administrations, and are economical to visit by self-driving and staying in park chalets or campsites. Most offer additional guided game drives or walks. The increasing number of private game reserves is making a huge

Numbers of cheetah, an endangered species, are bolstered by breeding programmes

impact on the environment, and many of them are reintroducing animals in areas where they had previously become extinct. With a bigger budget, you can stay at these lavish all-inclusive game lodges or beautifully positioned tented camps for an unsurpassed wilderness experience. By the way, the "tents" on offer at the exclusive lodges are often luxurious suites with stylish décor and all the amenities.

When to Visit

In both the public and private parks and reserves, the main activity is game drives, which are best undertaken in the early morning or late afternoon when the animals are at their most active and make their way to waterholes and rivers. Spotlight safaris after dark offer the opportunity to spot the nocturnal creatures. The climate varies around the country but as a rule of thumb the dry season, when the animals are concentrated around waterholes and the grass is short, is the best time for game viewing. The wet season does have its advantages as the animals will be in good condition after feeding on the new shoots and there's the opportunity to witness breeding or calving.

One lifetime would not be enough to discover all the natural wonders on offer in these parks; the social life of the elephants, the interplay between flowers and insects, the survival and the battle between the species, the ups and downs, the annual display of wild flowers in the seemingly barren soil, and the whales that make their way to the coast. Each climate zone in South

Elephants at Addo Elephant National Park, Eastern Cape Province

Africa has its own wildlife and tells its own natural history. Even the arid Karoo has its own diverse animals and plants, although they are not as obvious as those in the tropical areas along the Indian Ocean, where the trees are dense with lush creepers and crocodiles bask in the sun. Botanists classified the Cape's rich and unique vegetation as the Cape Floral Kingdom, the smallest and most diverse of the world's six floral kingdoms. No less impressive are the bizarre succulents in the country's semi-desert region.

Greater Kruger National Park
The provinces of Limpopo and Mpumalanga offer access to the Kruger National Park, which harbours more mammal species than any other sanctuary in Africa. A number of private reserves adjoin the Kruger, and now that fences have been taken down and animals can move freely between the park and the private reserves, the region is promoted as the Greater Kruger National Park. The Kruger is also a component of the Great Limpopo Transfrontier Park encompassing protected areas in Zimbabwe and Mozambique. There are other smaller reserves such as the Rhino and Lion Nature Reserve on the outskirts of Johannesburg.

KwaZulu-Natal and Northwest Provinces
KwaZulu-Natal has the country's highest concentration of reserves, and these cover a wide variety of habitats. Hluhluwe-iMfolozi National Park is home to the largest concentration of rhino in the world, while the iSimangaliso Wetland Park harbours crocodiles and hippos. The little-visited waterlogged reserves along the Mozambique border have an array of wildlife from

elephants to turtles. The uKhahlamba-Drakensberg Park offers unparalleled attractions for hikers and birdwatchers.

Northwest Province is home to the Pilanesberg National Park, an area of former farmland that has been restocked with animals from all around the country. The nearby Madikwe Game Reserve lies on a game transition zone on the edges of the Kalahari. Both are home to the Big Five.

The Cape Provinces

The Eastern Cape parks include the Mountain Zebra National Park and Addo Elephant National Park, while the coastal parks such as Tsitsikamma are rich in marine life. Also in this province, private game reserves such as the critically acclaimed Shamwari and Kwandwe are re-establishing wildlife that hadn't been seen in the region for many years.

The Northern Cape is best known for the remote Kgalagadi Transfrontier National Park that stretches into neighbouring Botswana. Kgalagadi is home to hardy desert-adapted animals such as gemsbok and black-maned lions.

The Table Mountain National Park in the Western Cape is scenically beautiful and includes the mountain chain that stretches from Signal Hill to Cape Point along the Cape Peninsula.

WHERE TO WATCH

- **National Parks:** South African National Parks; www.sanparks.org
- **KwaZulu-Natal Game Reserves:** Ezemvelo KZN Wildlife; www.kznwildlife.com
- **Western Cape Game Reserves:** Cape Nature; www.capenature.co.za

For sightings of hippo, head to the iSimangaliso Wetland Park, KwaZulu-Natal

Grape Expectations

After his arrival in Table Bay in 1652, the first Commander of the Cape, Jan van Riebeeck planted the first vine – thought to have been a French Muscat. By 1659 he was able to write in his diary, "Today, so praise be to God, wine was pressed from Cape grapes for the first time."

So winemaking in South Africa took root. Commander Simon van der Stel, who succeeded Van Riebeeck, continued where his predecessor left off, establishing his own estate, Groot Constantia, in 1699. A group of Huguenot Protestants, already experienced winemakers, settled in South Africa in the 1680s, having fled persecution in their native France, and laid down the vines around Franschhoek (French Corner). Wines made here were much sought after in Europe, with Napoleon and Frederick the Great of Prussia among their admirers. In the early days, wine was produced for the benefit of the ships passing the Cape en route from Europe to the East Indies. Wine kept better than water on long sea voyages, and it was also believed that young red wine could stave off scurvy. Today a wide range of grape varieties are grown throughout the Western Cape and as far north as the Orange River Valley.

Barrels of maturing wine at Chamonix Wine Estate, Franschhoek

Bountiful vineyards near Robertson, in the Western Cape Province

White Wine

The top white wine grape is **Chenin Blanc** (also called Steen in South Africa) a variety that has its origins in the Loire Valley in France. Its naturally high acidity produces fresh, lively wines, but its share has declined by 40 per cent in recent decades. Currently in vogue are **Colombard**, **Chardonnay** and **Sauvignon Blanc**, rather rare is the "real" **Riesling**. **Muscat d'Alexandrie** (Hanepoot) is cultivated for fortified sweet wines while the **Sultana** variety is mainly used for table grapes and brandy.

Red Wine

South Africa has followed the global trend towards the increased consumption of red wine. Production of international varieties has increased sharply but even the **Pinotage**, a cross between Pinot Noir and Cinsaut/Hermitage which is unique to South Africa, has tripled its share. The best red wines are from Bordeaux grapes and include **Cabernet Sauvignon**, **Shiraz**, **Merlot**, **Cinsaut** (for fresh table wine), **Cabernet Franc** and **Pinot Noir**.

INSIDER INFO

Up to a billion litres (220 million gallons) of wine is produced in South Africa every year on more than 600 wine estates. Most South African wines aren't labelled by region, but rather by grape variety and style. The grape itself, and the reputation of the winery that made the wine, are the two things to watch for – region is of lesser value. For something special at virtually no price at all, order a bottle of local Méthode Cap Classique (MCC) bubbly such as Krone MCC from the Twee Jonge Gezellen estate.

Into the
DEEP

With almost 3,000km (1,860mi) of coastline there are plenty of opportunities to get wet and wild in South Africa. Most people believe that the Atlantic and Indian oceans come together at Cape Point, but they actually meet at the southernmost point of Africa at Cape Agulhas. Although the Cape has some beautiful beaches, the Atlantic is too cold to swim in, but the Indian Ocean is warm and this coast, especially in KwaZulu-Natal, is popular for beach holidays.

Surfing

South Africa is a top surfing hotspot and experienced surfers will have already heard of Dungeons near Cape Town, one of the biggest waves in the world, and Supertubes in Jeffrey's Bay – also known as the Perfect Wave, and the best right-hand point break in the world. Serious surfers should head for Durban or surf central, Jeffrey's Bay. There's a small danger of encountering a shark – always adhere to local advice about where to surf.

THE GREATEST SHOAL ON EARTH

From May to July millions of sardines migrate from the cool waters of the Cape, collect in giant tightly packed shoals along the Eastern Cape and then move northward before dispersing into the vast blue yonder beyond Durban. They are attracted by plankton close to the shore and are followed closely by predators such as sharks, dolphins, thousands of seabirds, and of course fishermen. Known as the Sardine Run, the event is likely triggered by changes in the water temperature.

Scuba Diving

The mixing of the two oceans provides the coast with diverse marine life. Popular spots are the coral gardens in Sodwana Bay

Surfers catching the waves at Cape Town's Llandudno Beach

and the Aliwal Shoal in KwaZulu-Natal where sightings of reef sharks, turtles and stingrays are common, and sites around Port Elizabeth where you may also spot dolphins. Whales-watching, wreck and lagoon dives around Knysna, and kelp forest and wreck dives around the Cape are also recommended. Gansbaai near Hermanus is the spot to try cage-diving with great white sharks, or dive in the shark tank in Cape Town's Two Oceans Aquarium.

Whale-watching

Whales can be seen all along the coast but the self-proclaimed Whale Coast around Hermanus and Walker Bay is considered one of the world's best spots for land-based whale-watching in season. Southern right whales make their way from Antarctica up the coast between July and November and many come into Walker Bay where you can see them blowing and breaching from as little as 50m (55 yards) away. Humpbacks migrate between May and December and can be seen from boat-based whale-watching trips off the coast of the Garden Route and KwaZulu-Natal.

Sporting CHANCE

South Africa is a sports mad country and fans, even those that aren't athletes, are passionate about supporting and watching the many sporting events that take place throughout the country all year round.

Football (www.safa.net) is the most popular sport in South Africa and each game is an incredibly loud spectacle, as visitors to the 2010 FIFA World Cup found out for themselves when they were surrounded by *vuvuzela*-blowing, cheering fans. This was the first time this global event was held on African soil. The national team, nicknamed Bafana Bafana (meaning "our boys") tends to perform quite erratically, though it did win the 1996 Africa Cup of Nations, and it has qualified three times for the FIFA World Cup; in 2014 they failed to qualify. The main domestic competition is the Premier Soccer League, which is currently dominated by the Bidvest Wits from Braamfontein and Cape Town City FC.

In contrast to football fans, the stands at rugby matches are more sub-dued. The greatest moment in South African **rugby** (www.sarugby.co.za) came in 1995, when after years of being ostracized from world sport during apartheid, the Springboks hosted and won the Rugby World Cup, beating New Zealand's All Blacks 15–12. An excited Nelson Mandela presented the cup to the team's captain, Francois Pienaar, a white Afrikaner. Mandela donned the same "boks" green-and-gold number six jersey as Pienaar and the two embraced in a gesture of racial reconciliation that melted the hearts of South Africans everywhere.

Cricket (www.cricket.co.za) is the third most popular sport in South Africa. For more than 20 years during apartheid, South African cricket, like rugby, was largely isolated from the rest of the world. However, once the South African team, the Proteas, were allowed to play internationally

Left: A cricket game in Cape Town

Below: Participants in the Cape Town Cycle Tour, which is held every year on the second weekend of March

again, the country soon established itself as one of the world's leading cricketing nations. South Africa hosted the World Cup in 2003, which, unfortunately for local fans, was won by Australia. The team currently holds the record for the highest successful run chase in a one-day international (438–9 in 49.5 overs) against Australia in 2006, considered by many to be the greatest one-day match ever to have been played.

South Africa is also a land of **golfers** (www.saga.co.za). With its more than 500 courses, ideal climate and scenic charms, the country attracts players from all over the world. One of the most important events that draw world champions is the Nedbank Golf Challenge that takes place in December at Sun City (www.nedbankgolfchallenge.com). The classic South Africa tournament is the Sunshine Tour with the South African Open, the Dunhill Championship and the Joburg Open, which is held throughout the year mainly in South Africa, but also in Namibia, Zambia, Swaziland and Zimbabwe (www.sunshinetour.com).

Other Sports

The country is a great destination for **cycling** fans. The tough Cape Epic (www.cape-epic.com) is a major fixture on the international mountain bike calendar. It takes place late in the South African summer (March) and over 1,000 cyclists from all over the world come take part in this "Tour de France of mountain biking". Teams of two have eight days to complete the 800km (500mi) route with altitude climbs totalling 15,000m (49,200ft). The course route is changed yearly and is also open to amateurs. The Cape Town Cycle Tour (www.cycletour.co.za) is open to all amateurs. Every March, more than 35,000 participants cycle the 109km (68mi) route, making this one of the country's largest and most popular sporting events.

South Africa also offers a top selection of **marathons** such as the Two Oceans Marathon (56km/35mi and 21km/13mi half marathon), which takes place on Easter Sunday and winds (with a 500m/1,640ft altitude climb) along the scenic Indian and Atlantic coasts of the Cape Peninsula. The popular marathon draws some 15,000 participants. The Comrades Marathon in June follows a 90km (56mi) route between Durban and Pietermaritzburg (the direction changes each year) and participants must complete the race in under twelve hours.

South Africans love water and there is an incredible array of **water sports** and activities on offer. In February (with temperatures up to 40°C/104°F) you can tackle the Dusi Canoe Marathon on the Msunduzi River from Pietermaritzburg to Durban – one of the most prestigious canoe competitions in the world. It started in 1951 as a one day race but now takes place over three days when 2,000 participants paddle (and carry) their canoes a distance of 125km (77mi). The record time stands at eight hours. In July, Jeffrey's Bay (www.worldsurfleague.com) hosts the J-Bay Open, which attracts the world's top pro surfers. Breaks such as the famous Supertubes are legendary. The Midmar Mile (www.midmarmile.co.za) on the Midmar Dam near Pietermaritzburg has earned a World Record (2009) for the largest open water event; almost 14,000 swimmers completed that race. Since 2012 the National Open Water Swim Competition has been taking place in April on the Albert Falls Dam.

Adventure sport in a setting of natural beauty: abseiling in the Featherbed Nature Reserve in Knysna, Western Cape

eGoli

Place of Gold

The province of Gauteng means "Place of Gold" in Sesotho, while the isiZulu name for its capital Johannesburg, eGoli, means "City of Gold".

The name is no coincidence; in 1886 the world's richest gold deposit was discovered on the Witwatersrand, 50km (30mi) from the capital of Pretoria. A reef 430km (267mi) long and 24km (15mi) wide was quickly identified, which instantly drew prospectors from across the globe. Before a year had passed, 20,000 people had settled on claims and by 1889 more than 19,595kg (630,000oz) of gold had been mined.

"there are still more than 40 working gold mines in South Africa with gold ore reserves estimated at 6,000 tonnes"

Birth of a New City

A shanty mining camp of wagons and tents called Ferreira's Town rapidly grew on the bare veld. The Pretoria government laid out a plan for a formal town immediately north of the main gold reef and named it Johannesburg after two government commissioners – Johannes Meyer and Johann Rissik.

A Golden Legacy

Today South Africa produces five per cent of all the world's gold. About 95 per cent of the country's gold mines are underground, reaching depths of over 3.8km (2.35mi): the deepest gold mines in the world. Johannesburg's 3,293m-deep (10,800ft) Shaft No 14 opened in 1897 and closed in 1971,

A reminder of Johannesburg's mining heritage: a toxic gold mine dump outside the city (above) and Gold Reef City (below) a theme park on the grounds of Crown Mines with its historic shaft, one of the richest and deepest the world

during which time it produced 1.4 million kg (3.08 million lb) of gold. Today the tourist attraction of Gold Reef City is based at the shaft where you can go underground to depths of 220m (722ft) (► 125). This was the last operating mine in the city centre itself, but there are still 40 working gold mines in Gauteng and South Africa has enormous gold ore reserves, estimated at 6,000 tonnes.

Today the classic view of Jo'burg – pale-yellow mine dumps in the foreground and skyscrapers in the background – will be retained, as while most dumps are being cleared for development, some are being preserved as a reminder of the history of a city founded on gold.

THE OTHER GEORGE HARRISON

In 1886 a sleepy farm on the Transvaal veld was rudely awakened when Australian miner George Harrison smashed a rock with his hoe and yelled "gold!" The area was pronounced open to diggings and drew prospectors from all over the globe. Strangely, Harrison is believed to have sold his claim for only £10, left the area and was never heard from again.

LOOK WHO'S TALKING

First-time visitors to South Africa are often surprised by the country's linguistic diversity.

Most South Africans can speak more than one language, usually Afrikaans and English or either one of those and an indigenous language. After the end of apartheid the official languages of English and Afrikaans were

SOUTH AFRICAN SLANG

Aita! Common greeting in the townships

As well Also, me too, (accent on "as")

Babalaas Hangover

Bokkie Refers to a girlfriend or girl

Braai Barbecue and very popular South African way of socializing

Bru Brother, mate, buddy

Cooldrink Soft drink

Cuz Cousin, mate, friend; used in Durban; similar to Bru

Dop To drink alcohol; a doppie is an alcoholic drink

Dorp Afrikaans for small town/village

Eish Zulu expression used for surprise, bewilderment or shock

Howzit Famous South African greeting short for "How is it?"

Izzit? Is that so?

Ja well no fine Expresses that a person is not really fine

Jol Party, good time

Just now Will do something later; "now now" means immediately

Lekker Nice, lovely, good

Lightey Youngster

Madiba Nelson Mandela's clan name, which has become universally used as an affectionate nickname

Oke Guy, bloke

One time Nice one

Shame Expression of sympathy

Sis Yuck

Skrik Afrikaans for fright

Strue's Bob I kid you not It's the gospel truth

The Magazine

FANAGALO AND TSOTI TAAL

Fanagalo is based mostly on isiZulu, with a peppering of English, Dutch, Afrikaans and Portuguese words, this was spoken in the gold mines in the early days as communication between white supervisors and migrant African labourers from other regions of southern Africa. It was considered insulting to use this pidgin language anywhere but underground.

Tsotsi Taal, a mixture of Afrikaans, English and African words, was developed to communicate across different languages in the townships, and is sort of gangster rap – *tsotsi* means "thug" while *taal* means "lingo", and is commonly used in Kwaito music (South African rap). The brilliant South African-made movie *Tsotsi* which won Best Foreign Film at the 2005 Academy Awards, was filmed in Tsotsi Taal and most of it was shot in Soweto.

expanded to include nine indigenous languages, making a total of eleven official languages. In addition to Afrikaans (the mother tongue of most coloureds) and English (spoken by almost 40 per cent of whites and most Asians) there is also isiZulu, isiXhosa, Sepedi, Sesotho, Setswana, Xitsonga (Tsonga), siSwati, Tshivenda (Venda) and isiNdebele. Tsonga has affinities to two of the language groups while the Venda have their own language. Afrikaans emerged from the dialects of the Dutch immigrants who arrived in the 17th century. Through contact with African and Khoisan languages, German, English, French, Portuguese and Malay, new words were added and other words changed their meaning. This also applied to pronunciation, spelling and grammar. Afrikaans is spoken by more than 80 per cent of coloureds and almost 60 per cent of whites, while isiZulu is spoken by more than 10 million people of whom 8 million live in KwaZulu-Natal and 2 million in Gauteng.

Opposite page: A Ndebele woman in her village in Mpumalanga. The Ndebele (like the Zulu, Xhosa and Swazi) belong to the Nguni language group

Left: A Zulu healer (*sangoma*) in the DumaZulu Traditional Village, KwaZulu-Natal. The Nguni languages contain characteristic tongue-clicking sounds

31

SAN
CULTURE

The San, also known as the Bushmen by the first settlers in the Cape, are nomadic hunters and gatherers that once roamed southern Africa. They carried little more than what they wore on their backs, lived in the caves and shelters and spoke a unique language using click consonants.

When the white colonization of South Africa began in the 17th century, the San (a collective term) had already had several waves of tribes invading their homeland. Every new invasion drove the San to retreat further into inhospitable areas. The San are now considered the descendants of the original population of southern Africa.

Their extensive knowledge of the mysteries of nature has resulted in unique abilities, which enable them to survive even in the most arid lands. Men traditionally hunted with poison arrows and traps, while

San men demonstrating their hunting techniques at !Xaus Lodge, Kgalagadi Transfrontier National Park

the women were responsible for gathering edible plants and bulbs. Today, these fascinating people live on the margins of society, often beset by unemployment, alcoholism, tuberculosis or HIV/Aids. It seems that there is no longer any place for hunters and gatherers in our modern society. Some San manage to continue their traditional life at tourist lodges or in nature reserves. In this context, a pilot project has been started at !Xaus in the Kgalagadi Transfrontier National Park (www.xauslodge.co.za). The state has returned land to two of the local San communities who have built a tourist lodge that now provides them with a sustainable income.

There is also a living museum village where visitors can see craft demonstrations, learn about medicinal plants, how the San hunt, their tracking techniques and animal behaviour. The San here wear traditional clothing but only because it makes for a good photo opportunity. However, a project such as this does play an important and valid role in San culture as it is the only way that their knowledge, normally passed down through many generations in an oral tradition, is being preserved. This knowledge – especially their remarkable abilities as trackers – has even been used by researchers from the University of Cologne, and the Neanderthal Museum in Mettmann, to interpret the footprints and traces of early hunters in the remote caves of the Pyrenees in France.

FESTIVALS

South Africa has a wealth of annual festivals across the country, celebrating anything from the arts to oysters, and offering entertainment for the whole family.

Festivals unique to South Africa include the **Clarens Craft Beer Festival** in the Free State (end of March; www.clarenscraftbeerfest.com), offering over 70 different craft beers, and the **Prince Albert Town and Olyf & Kos Mark** (end of April; http://princealbert.org.za), which showcases food and oil made from olives, as well as local Karoo lamb and ostrich. At the **Knysna Oyster Festival** (early July; www.oysterfestival.co.za) enjoy oysters straight from Knysna Lagoon, learn how to cook them or join an oyster-eating competition. The festival also includes street markets, a marathon and cycle race. The **Hermanus Whale Festival** (late September or early October; www. whalefestival.co.za) is packed with entertainment and is the best time of the year to join the Whale Crier on Hermanus's cliff tops to watch whales splashing around in Walker Bay.

JOIN THE PARTY
- **Arts Alive** Johannesburg, September; www.arts-alive.co.za
- **Cape Town Jazz Festival** (above) end of March; www.capetownjazzfest.com
- **Oppikoppi Bushveld Festival** Northwest Province, August; www.oppikoppi.co.za
- **Sasol Scifest** Grahamstown, end of March; www.scifest.org.za
- **Pink Loerie Mardi Gras** Knysna, end of April to early May; www.pinkloerie foundation.com
- **National Arts Festival** Grahamstown, end of June to early July; www.national artsfestival.co.za
- **Joy of Jazz Festival** Johannesburg, end of August; www.joyofjazz.co.za
- **Splashy Fen Music Festival** Underberg, Easter; www.splashyfen.co.za

Finding Your Feet

First Two Hours

Scheduled international flights arrive at the three gateway airports listed below, from where there are onward domestic and regional flights. They offer food courts, banks and exchange bureaus, cell phone, wireless and SIM card rental desks and postal services. Long-distance buses link South African cities with cities in Zimbabwe, Mozambique, Botswana, Namibia, Swaziland and Lesotho. Namibia and Mozambique are also linked by rail, while cruise ships dock in Cape Town and Durban harbours.

Ground Transport Fees
R under R100   **RR** R100–R300   **RRR** over R300

Arriving in Johannesburg (JNB)

- **OR Tambo International Airport** (formerly Johannesburg International) is the main point of entry into South Africa. It lies 24km (15mi) from the city centre and 35km (22mi) from the northern suburbs (tel: 086 727 7888; www.airports.co.za).
- Metered **taxis** (RRR) are found outside the arrivals hall and take 45 minutes to 1 hour to hotels in the northern suburbs.
- To book one of the cheaper **shuttle buses** (RRR) to the northern suburbs call Magic Bus (tel: 011 548 0800; www.magicbus.co.za) or you can go to the desks in the arrivals hall. The most convenient way to get to Johannesburg and Pretoria is with the safe and modern **Gautrain** (RR). To do this, you must first purchase a rechargeable **Gautrain Gold Card** for R15 (http://join.gautrain.co.za) and then the applicable destination option such as Sandton or Pretoria (RR).
- **Car rental** desks in the Parkade Centre include Avis, Budget, Europcar, Hertz, Imperial and Tempest/Sixt.

Tourist Information

- **Gauteng Tourism Authority** has a desk in the international terminal (tel: 011 390 3602/14; www.gauteng.net; daily 8–10).

Arriving in Cape Town (CPT)

- **Cape Town International Airport** is the second major point of entry to South Africa for international visitors. It lies 22km (14mi) east of the city centre along the N2 highway (tel: 082 727 7888; www.airports.co.za).
- Metered **taxis** (RRR) can be found outside and take 30–45 minutes into the city centre.
- **Shuttle buses** (RR) can be arranged in international arrivals from Citi Shuttles (tel: 086 111 4557; www.citishuttles.co.za) or pre-arranged through the Backpacker Bus (tel: 082 809 9185; www.backpackerbus. co.za).
- **Car rental** desks in the international and domestic arrivals terminals include Avis, Budget, Europcar, Hertz, Imperial and Tempest/Sixt.

Tourist Information

- **Cape Town Tourism** has a desk in international arrivals (tel: 021 934 1949) and at The Pinnacle, corner of Berg and Castle streets (tel: 021 487 6800; www.capetown.travel; Mon–Fri 8–6, Sat, Sun 9–1).

Arriving in Durban (DUR)

- **King Shaka International Airport** opened in 2010 and is about 35km (20mi) north of the city centre (tel: 086 727 7888; www.airports.co.za).
- **Taxis** (RR) wait outside the terminal for transfers to the city centre.
- **Shuttle buses** (RRR) can be called from King Shaka Airport Shuttle Service (tel: 086 661 1707; www.kingshakashuttles.co.za).
- **Car rental** desks in the international and domestic arrivals terminals include Avis, Budget, Europcar, Hertz, Imperial and Tempest/Sixt.

Tourist Information

- **Durban Tourism** has a small desk in domestic arrivals (tel: 031 304 7500; 7am–9pm) and downtown (90 Florida Road; tel: 031 322 4146; www.durbanexperience.co.za; Mon–Fri 8–5, Sat, Sun 9–1).

Getting Around

South Africa has an excellent network of transport and highways, and you can travel between regions quickly and easily.

Domestic Air Travel

There is an efficient network of domestic flights linking the main cities, none of which are more than two hours' flying time apart. Good deals can be had if you book early through the websites. Some of the private game reserves and lodges can arrange flights to their own airstrips.

- British Airways' (BA) African operator, **Comair** (www.comair.co.za): British Airways links larger domestic cities and destinations in other southern African countries;
- **Kulula** (www.kulula.com) is also owned by Comair; it is a no-frills airline linking major domestic cities and other African cities on a code share agreement with BA.
- No-frills airlines **Mango** (www.flymango.com) and **FlySafair** (www.flysafair.co.za) have competitive fares.
- **Federal Air** (tel: 011 395 9000; www.fedair.com) operates daily flights between Johannesburg and all the top game lodges in and around Kruger National Park.
- **South African Airways** covers the whole country and other southern African cities in conjunction with their subsidiaries SA Airlink and SA Express; www.flysaa.com.

Trains

- Passenger services connecting Johannesburg to Cape Town, Durban and Musina (Limpopo Province) as well as Cape Town to Queenstown are operated by the **Passenger Rail Agency of South Africa** (PRASA; www.prasa.com) under the name of **Shosholoza Meyl**. Services are reasonably comfortable and affordable but slow. There are sitting and sleeper compartments, and on the Johannesburg-Cape Town and Johannesburg–Durban route there is also the option to transport private motor vehicles. Fast food can be bought in the dining car. Online booking, enquiries and reservations are best directed to tel: 086 000 8888 or www.shosholozameyl.co.za.
- PRASA operates **Premier Classe** along the same routes (tel: 011 773 9247). Considerably more upmarket than the regular train, it has good

Finding Your Feet

food and service. Compartments sleep 2–4 (tourist class) and 1–2 (premier class) and quality meals are served in the dining car.

■ South Africa's famous **Blue Train** (www.bluetrain.co.za) has scheduled departures between Pretoria and Cape Town via Johannesburg (and charter routes between Pretoria and Hoedspruit/Kruger National Park), and there are other special excursions throughout the year. Spacious suites with baths and digital entertainment help it live up to its reputation as a 5-star hotel on wheels. A similar luxury train, **The Pride of Africa**, operated by Rovos Rail (www.rovos.com), also runs luxury trips to Mpumalanga and to several countries to the north of South Africa.

■ Spoornet also operates **Metrorail** (www.metrorail.co.za) in the bigger cities: an overland rail network linking the city centres with the suburbs used by commuters. It's not advised for visitors to use these because of the high risk of crime.

■ Gauteng's **Gautrain** (www.gautrain.co.za) is a high-speed rail link connecting OR Tambo International Airport to the upmarket suburb of Sandton and links to central Pretoria and Johannesburg.

Buses

■ A number of companies run **long-distance bus** services with toilets, air-conditioning and on-board refreshments. Four main operators cover dozens of daily routes. Among them are **Greyhound** (tel: 011 611 8000; www.greyhound.co.za); **Intercape** (tel: 021 380 4400; www.intercape.co.za); **Intercity Express** (tel: 087 150 1895; www.intercityexpress.co.za); and **Translux** (tel: 011 774 8304; www.translux.co.za). Some distances are long, however, and many buses travel overnight and could deposit you at your destination at an inconvenient hour. Consider too, that if you book early enough online, airfares with the no-frills airlines are comparable to bus tickets. Bus tickets can be booked online through South Africa's nationwide reservations service **Computicket** (www.computicket.co.za).

■ The jump-on-jump-off **Baz Bus** (tel: 086 129 9287; www.bazbus.com) picks up and drops off at backpackers' hostels. It's cheaper over short distances than regular bus companies and doesn't arrive in the middle of the night. It runs along the coast between Cape Town and Durban and between Durban and Johannesburg – with short detours to visit tourist attractions.

■ The cities operate **local buses** along major roads with clearly signposted stops. In Johannesburg these are run by **Metrobus** (www.mbus.co.za); in Cape Town **Golden Arrow** (www.gabs.co.za) and in Durban **Muvo** (www.muvo.co.za). A short journey will cost less than R10.

Taxis

■ **Taxis** cannot be hailed on the street and must be ordered by phone; any hotel or restaurant can do this and they turn up quickly. They are metered but not cheap; expect to pay around R75 for 3–4km (2–3mi). Larger groups and wheelchair users should ask for a Toyota Venture, which has extra seats. It is usual to tip taxi drivers 10 per cent.

■ **Minibus taxis** are a popular form of local transport and are hailed down at the side of the street. Like the Metrorail, however, they are not advised for visitors as there is the danger of theft and are often driven recklessly.

Driving

■ Driving is the easiest and most flexible way of getting around South Africa. The major cities are linked by a network of excellent **highways**.

The N1 runs from the Zimbabwe border in the north to Cape Town via Johannesburg, Pretoria and Bloemfontein. Durban is linked to Johannesburg by the N3 and to Cape Town by the coastal N2 via East London, Port Elizabeth and the Garden Route. Maputo in Mozambique is linked to Gaborone in Botswana via Johannesburg by the N4, while the N7 runs up the western coast and links Cape Town with Windhoek in Namibia. Tolls are charged so keep some cash handy.

- There's a comprehensive network of **other roads** across the country. Almost all are tarred but in some rural areas they are unsealed, though usually in good condition. Roads in **Kruger National Park** are mostly tarred and suitable for a normal car.
- When **driving in cities**, be aware of where the trouble spots are – inner city areas, townships, neglected neighbourhoods – where it's not advised to drive. Carry a good map and cell phone, and if driving at night keep doors locked and windows up.
- Almost all hotels, tourist attractions and shopping malls have adequate **parking**. If parking on the street, make use of **car guards** who are usually identified by a badge or work vest and pay them R2–R5 on your return for watching your vehicle. Always lock your vehicle and never leave anything on display.
- In the event of a roadside breakdown contact your car hire company.

Driving Essentials

- Drive on the **left-hand side** of the road. Overtaking is on the right but on the highways be careful of other cars overtaking on the right.
- Drivers must be **18**, though to hire a car you'll need to be aged over 21 or over 25 depending on the rental company.
- **Four-way stops** are common and are indicated by red stop signs. Whoever gets to the junction first (including pedestrians) has right of way, then the others get their respective turns.
- At traffic lights, a **flashing green** arrow lets you turn across or off a highway while straight over is still on red. Traffic lights in South Africa are known as **robots** and roundabouts as **traffic circles**.
- **Speed limits** are 60kph (37mph) on urban roads, 80–100kph (50–62mph) outside built up areas, and 120kph (74mph) on highways. Speed traps and cameras are common.
- In urban areas **petrol stations** (gas stations) are plentiful and are open long hours but in remote parts remember to fill up when you can. Some **petrol stations** only accept cash **and not credit cards**, although most have ATMs.
- **Road signs** are in English and Afrikaans.
- All roads are numbered. **National highways** are denoted with an N, **municipal highways** with an M, other **major roads** with an R, and **minor dirt roads** with a D.

Car Rental

Anyone over 21 (25 with some companies) can hire a car with their licence from their home country as long as it's in English. Holders of licences in other languages will need an **International Driving Licence**. Additionally you'll need your **passport** and a **credit card**. All the **international car hire companies** have offices at the airports and in the cities where you can hire a car immediately. Most will let you return the car to other cities but this must be agreed in advance and will attract a surcharge.

Accommodation

Hotels

Large **international chains** such as Holiday Inn, Hilton and Inter-continental are well represented and there's a growing crop of luxury and boutique hotels set in stunning locations. **Protea Hotels** (www.proteahotels.com) manage a range of 3- to 4-star individually designed hotels, while the modern **City Lodge** chain (www.citylodge.co.za) is popular with business travellers. Smaller towns usually feature at least one 2- to 3-star hotel.

Bed-and-Breakfasts

Even the smallest town has a private home with rooms available. A home-away-from-home atmosphere is usually the norm and most are owner-operated. If you prefer more anonymity, some have separate entrances or rooms in garden cottages. A Continental or full English breakfast is included. Visit www.bnbfinder.co.za.

Guest Houses

Some guest houses are in period homes or historic buildings, and in most a great deal of thought has gone into the furnishings; extras can include swimming pools or air-conditioning. Breakfast is included in the rates, and in some, evening meals are available on request. Contact the **Guest House Association of South Africa** (www.ghasa.co.za).

Backpacker Hostels

Hostels are found in the popular destinations, especially along the coast. They offer dormitory-style accommodation and double rooms. Facilities are likely to include a kitchen, pool or garden, and the management can usually arrange activities and transport within the local area. Some rent out surfboards or mountain bikes and arrange their own excursions. Information is available at Backpacking South Africa (www.btsa.co.za). *Coast to Coast* (www.coastingafrica.com) is an annual guidebook to South Africa's hostels available free from the hostels.

Self-catering

Self-contained flats, cottages or chalets are widely available and for groups or families, rates are economical. Some are individually located, or are in blocks of flats; others are in large resorts with campsites and recreational facilities. Most towns have municipal campsites which usually also have a few chalets.

National Parks Accommodation

Self-catering cottages, chalets and campsites can be found in the **restcamps** of the larger national parks and reserves such as Kruger or the uKhahlamba-Drakensberg. There's usually a central block where reception, a shop, and perhaps a swimming pool or restaurant are located. At some, additional game drives and walks are on offer. In the smaller game reserves a couple of cottages may be available but with few facilities and you'll have to take everything such as linen with you.

Parks accommodation is managed by **South African National Parks** (www.sanparks.org), **Cape Nature** (www.capenature.co.za), or **KZN Wildlife** (www.kznwildlife.com), and should be booked well in advance especially during local school holidays.

Luxury Game Lodges

These are usually located in **private game reserves** and are all-inclusive of meals and game drives and some have extras such as a spa. The highlight is to sleep in close proximity to the wildlife in luxurious surroundings. Some are isolated and accessed by light aircraft.

Finding a Room

■ It's advisable to **reserve your room in advance**, particularly in the parks, and on the coast during the long South African school holidays in December.

■ In the parks always enquire about room availability at the gate first to avoid travelling long distances before finding out that there's no room to stay at a restcamp.

■ **The Portfolio Collection** offers a wide range of accommodation in all price categories (www.portfoliocollection.com).

Room Rates

Rates vary tremendously from around R100 for a dorm bed in a back-packer's hostel to over R10,000 in a super-luxurious game lodge. In most places rates stay the same throughout the year. The exception to this is on the coast where prices increase dramatically during summer. Some establishments offer a discount for **booking online**.

Accommodation Prices

Expect to pay in high season per double room per night:

R under R1,500   **RR** R1,500–R2,500   **RRR** over R2,500

Food and Drink

Local Produce

The climate is ideal for agriculture and just about every imaginable fruit and vegetable is grown. Prime steak, Karoo lamb and game meat, such as ostrich or kudu, is very good. Local meaty products include biltong (dried salted meat) and *boerewors* (a coarse, fat sausage). *Pap* is a stiff maize porridge that is a staple all over Africa, while *bobotie* is a spicy local version of shepherd's pie with a savoury custard topping. Seafood is plentiful along the coast, and most menus feature "linefish" (catch of the day).

Ethnic Cuisine

In Cape Town you will find restaurants serving Cape Malay cuisine: dishes cooked in spices and dried fruit; while Durban is famous for its Indian food, especially bunny chow – half a loaf of bread with the middle scooped out and filled with curry. One of the most popular and social ways to eat in South Africa is the *braai*; most households have one, and every weekend friends meet to cook over the coals.

Finding Your Feet

Restaurants

Many restaurants enjoy lovely settings or fine views and almost all have outside seating, although a cosy interior is preferable in winter. South Africa doesn't have pubs as such, so most restaurants double up as bars, too. There are a number of chain establishments that lack individuality but are good value. South Africans are fairly casual when dining out and generally nowhere requires a jacket and tie.

Cafés

Cafés are **open throughout the day** and focus on breakfasts, coffees and light meals, although they still offer a full range of alcoholic drinks. Some close earlier in the evening than the restaurants while others pump up their menus and become full-on bars as the day wears on. In a potentially confusing quirk of South African English the term café is more often used to describe a small convenience store than a place to eat.

Practicalities

- **Chain restaurants and cafés** are open for breakfast until 10pm, while most **restaurants** open from noon until midnight, though some close for a couple of hours between lunch and dinner. Some close one day a week, usually Sunday or Monday. In the smaller towns, hours are shorter and kitchens usually close by 9pm.
- It's always a good idea to **make a reservation** at the popular places but apart from weekends you shouldn't have to wait too long for a table.
- Almost all establishments accept **credit cards**.
- **Service** is generally of a high calibre. Tables usually have a dedicated waiter and, as tip money makes up a substantial part of their income, a voluntary tip of 10 to 15 per cent of the bill is the norm.

Where to Eat

There's a thriving restaurant scene and there are several sources of information. Once in South Africa look out for the annual *Eat Out* magazine (www.eatout.co.za), or visit www.dining-out.co.za or www.restaurants.co.za.

What to Drink

- **Wine** is available and, as it's produced in the Cape Winelands, there's a wide choice of affordable labels. The most widely available white wines are Chardonnay, great with fish and seafood, and the crisper, fruitier Sauvignon Blanc, which perfectly complements spicy Cape Malay dishes and curries. Of the reds, the full-bodied Cabernet Sauvignon and the more keenly priced Pinotage are the most popular.
- South African Breweries produce a range of good bottled lagers, and look out for Windhoek Lager from Namibia. Few places have beer on tap and British-style ales are not available.
- There's a full range of **spirits**, including several home-grown brandies and South African Amarula, a cream-based liqueur made from the fruit of the Marula tree.
- **Supermarkets** are legally only allowed to sell wine. Other alcohol is sold in **bottle stores**, usually next to the supermarkets. No alcohol is sold from shops on Sundays.

Restaurant Bests
Best for the view: Bientang's Cave (➤86)
Best pub: The Occidental Bar (The Ox) (➤171)
Best for an African set menu: Gold Restaurant (➤62)
Best deli: Giovanni's (➤62)
Best for game meat: The Carnivore (➤117)
Best local restaurant chain: Harrie's Pancakes (➤150)
Best for steak: The Butcher Shop and Grill (➤132)
Best for seafood: Baia (➤61)
Best for Indian: Bukhara (➤61)
Best for people watching: Moyo (➤132)

Restaurant Prices
Expect to pay for a two-course meal per person excluding drinks:
R under R150   **RR** R150–R300   **RRR** over R300

Shopping

Opening Hours
■ Shops in **malls** including supermarkets are generally open 9am to 6pm. Restaurants, cinemas and other entertainment stay open until 11pm. Outside of the cities, smaller malls close on Sundays.
■ There are **markets** all over the country selling crafts, clothing, gifts and food and many make a good day out with entertainment and activities. These are usually held at the weekends from 9am to 4pm.

Payment
■ Almost all shops take **credit cards**, although Visa and MasterCard are far more widely accepted than other brands. In markets and smaller shops you'll need cash.
■ International visitors can **reclaim the 14 per cent VAT** on all purchases taken out of the country. This is done at the airport on departure and you will need to show your passport and air ticket as well as VAT receipts of purchases. Visit www.taxrefunds.co.za for more information.

What to Buy
■ **African crafts, art and curios** such as wooden or tin sculptures, masks, cloth and beaded jewellery from all over the continent can be found in South Africa. Look out for items made by local people.
■ **Fashion** is comparable to Europe and North America and there are a number of quality chain stores and shops.
■ South Africa is well known for its **wine**, and the ideal place to purchase wine is in the Cape Winelands.
■ Taking home **wildlife souvenirs** sourced from rare or endangered species is highly unethical as it encourages poaching. In addition, it is likely to be illegal in your home country or to require a special permit.

Entertainment

The arts and nightlife in the cities cover a broad range of genres, from theatres and casinos to traditional dancing and township jazz. In the rural areas, however, entertainment is limited to drinking in a local bar. For listings and online booking, visit Computicket (www.computicket.com).

Nightlife

- There's a multitude of venues for **live music** from rock concert-accommodating stadiums to hot dance clubs and small intimate bars. Cape Town's Kirstenbosch Botanical Gardens (www.sanbi.org) hosts a range of outdoor concerts over summer. Cape Town has a jazz festival in March and Johannesburg has one in August. There are several multi-day **music festivals** across the country with camping and fringe activities, the best known being Splashy Fen (www.splashyfen.co.za) and Oppikoppi (www.oppikoppi.co.za).
- **Theatres** range from large civic centres showing Broadway-style musicals and performances by international ballet troupes, to community theatres offering serious plays. There are also small supper theatres which feature solo shows and comedy.
- **Dance** is showcased during Johannesburg's FNB Dance Umbrella (www.danceforumsouthafrica.co.za) in February and the Arts Alive festival (www.arts-alive.co.za) in September.
- The cities have numerous late-night bars and **nightclubs** varying from fashionably smart to student grunge. Most attract an entry charge of around R50 and open until at least 2–3 in the morning. As well as mainstream dance music, jazz and Kwaito (South African hip-hop) are popular too. Check national and local newspapers for listings.
- The many large **casino** resorts also have cinemas, show bars and a selection of nightclubs.
- While rural South Africa is fairly conservative in its attitude, there are many **gay and lesbian** venues in the three liberal big cities.

Festivals

Hundreds of festivals with entertainment for the whole family take place throughout the country every year celebrating just about everything – the arts, food and drink, science, even oysters and whales (➤ 34).

Outdoor Pursuits

- With rugged coastlines and lofty mountains, South Africa was made for **hiking**. Visit www.hosavosa.co.za or http://greenflagtrails.co.za. for details of more than 300 hiking trails.
- You can get adrenalin high on a number of **adventure sports** including the biggest bungee jump in the world at Bloukrans Bridge, shark cage diving, parasailing, kitesurfing, sandboarding, surfing, abseiling or white-water rafting.
- South Africa stages two big **cycling events**, which attract thousands of participants. The Cape Town Cycle Tour in March (www.cycletour.co.za) is the world's largest timed cycling event and it winds its way around the Cape Peninsula. The Momentum 94.7 Cycle Challenge (www.cyclechallenge.co.za) in November rides through Johannesburg's northern suburbs.

Cape Town & Around

 Little Treats

Outdoor Party
Join the Capetonians that flock to **Mzoli's Place** in Gugulethu township for the buzzing atmosphere, delicious *braai* and live music. Just hop into a taxi – all the drivers know the way.

Street Music
Cape Town is a hub of exciting music and its street musicians are legendary – you are sure to find some at Greenmarket Square or on Long Street.

Colourful History
The changing of the guard parade in the **Castle of Good Hope** (➤ 50) provides a vivid glimpse of local history.

Getting Your Bearings

Hugging majestic Table Mountain and surrounded by the wild Atlantic Ocean, Cape Town is inarguably one of the most beautiful cities in the world. An absolute must is a sightseeing trip around the Cape Peninsula, with its magnificent beaches, and a tour of the scenic Winelands area.

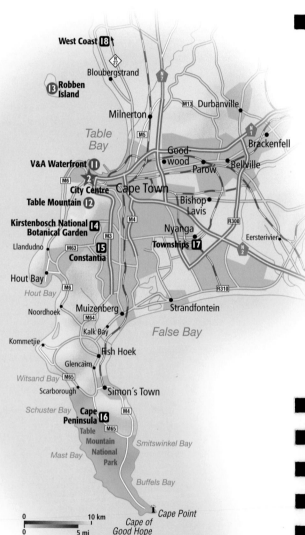

West Coast **18**

Bloubergstrand

13 **Robben Island**

Milnerton

Durbanville **M13**

Table Bay

M5

Good-wood

Brackenfell

Bellville

V&A Waterfront **11**

Parow

2

M6

City Centre

Cape Town

Table Mountain **12**

Bishop Lavis

Kirstenbosch National Botanical Garden **14**

M4

Nyanga

R300

M3

Eersterivier

Llandudno

M63

15

Constantia

Townships **17**

Hout Bay

M6

Hout Bay

Noordhoek

Muizenberg

M64

Strandfontein

R310

Kalk Bay

False Bay

Kommetjie

Fish Hoek

Glencairn

Witsand Bay **M65**

Scarborough

Simon's Town

Schuster Bay **Cape Peninsula** **16** **M4**

Table Mountain National Park **M65**

Smitswinkel Bay

Mast Bay

Buffels Bay

Cape Point

0   10 km

0   5 mi

Cape of Good Hope

Getting Your Bearings

The coastline at Cape Point

Its location also makes Cape Town one of the most fascinating cities in the world. The heart of Cape Town is the City Bowl, which lies between Table Bay and the harbour to the north and the lower slopes of majestic Table Mountain (1,086m/3,562ft) to the south. The city has plenty of well preserved buildings and historic quarters that bear vivid testimony to its past. The refurbished Victoria & Alfred Waterfront is a great addition to the cityscape; once an unattractive harbour area, it is now a lively tourist and entertainment destination. The Bo-Kaap Malay quarter with its historic mosques, restored 18th-century houses and cobbled streets, stretches northwest of the city up the slopes of Signal Hill. South of Green Point the Atlantic stretch of coast has a string of attractive seaside suburbs from Sea Point to Hout Bay.

Stroll through the V&A Waterfront, named after Queen Victoria and her son Prince Alfred

Perfect Days in...

Cape Town & Around

Three Perfect Days

If you are not quite sure where to begin your travels, this itinerary recommends three practical and enjoyable days in Cape Town, taking in some of the best places to see. For more information see the main entries (➤ 50–59).

Day 1

Morning
Head into the ⭐**city centre** (below: an aerial view of Cape Town and Table Mountain; ➤ 50) for breakfast in a streetside café, stroll in **Company's Garden** (➤ 51) and visit the museums and browse the trendy boutiques, antiques and book shops along Long Street.

Lunch
Catch the bus to the ⑪**V&A Waterfront** (➤ 52), wander around the giant shopping mall, watch the harbour at work and grab a bite to eat.

Afternoon
Hop on the ⑬**Robben Island** (➤ 56) ferry for a thought-provoking two-and-a-half hour tour of the old island prison where Nelson Mandela was incarcerated during apartheid.

Evening
Look out for seals in the Waterfront's harbour from an outside restaurant deck and end the evening at a music venue: try **The Dubliner** (251 Long Street; tel: 021 423 0910).

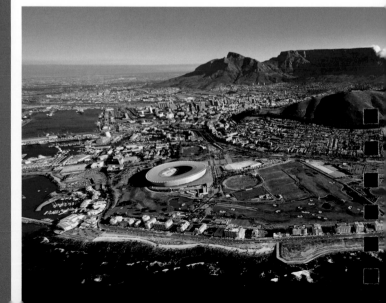

Day 2

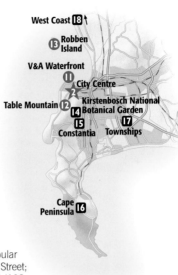

Morning
Walk up (approximately three hours) or ride the cable car (only three minutes) to the top of **12 Table Mountain** (➤ 53).

Lunch
Eat at the restaurant at the top cable car station, 1,067m (3,562ft) above Cape Town.

Afternoon
Sample fine wines around **15 Constantia** (➤ 57).

Evening
Dine at one of the city centre's popular restaurants: **Mama Africa** (178 Long Street; tel: 021 424 8634), the **Africa Café** (108 Shortmarket Street; tel: 021 422 0221) or **Marco's African Place** (15 Rose Lane; tel: 021 423 5412).

Day 3

Morning
Book a half day **17 township tour** (➤ 58) to learn the history of apartheid and meet the local communities. Most tours include a visit to the acclaimed **District Six Museum** (➤ 50).

Lunch
Be sure to book in advance for a sumptuous afternoon high tea of delicate sandwiches and wicked cakes on the shady terrace at the **Mount Nelson Hotel** (76 Orange Street; tel: 021 483 1000, www.mountnelson.co.za).

Afternoon
Stroll through the unique flora of the Cape in the **14 Kirstenbosch National Botanical Garden** (➤ 57).

Evening
Treat yourself to a seafood platter along the restaurant strip in Camps Bay: **The Codfather** (➤ 62), **Blues** (tel: 021 438 2040, www.blues.co.za) or **Paranga** (Victoria Road/Geneva Drive, Shop 1; tel: 021 438 0404; www.paranga.co.za).

Cape Town & Around

★ ² City Centre

Cape Town's city centre, known as the City Bowl, is bordered by Strand Street to the north, Orange Street to the south, and Buitengracht and Plein streets to the west and east. During the apartheid era Cape Town's residential areas were reserved for whites only; today visitors can enjoy the city's multicultural and cosmopolitan atmosphere. There are a number of interesting museums scattered around the city centre, dedicated to anything from apartheid to art, and many are housed in historic buildings. For a walking tour of the city's historic hub see ➤ 174.

District Six Museum
The superb District Six Museum tells the story of the forced removal of 60,000 residents from the city's District Six to Cape Flats from 1966. Once a diverse and mixed community, the apartheid planners razed the suburb. After the end of apartheid, some of the suburb's buildings were rebuilt and some of its residents returned. However, a large part of the site still remains empty and unused. The museum is staffed by displaced residents, who enhance the collection of historical material with their own moving stories.

The Slave Lodge
Built in 1679, the **Slave Lodge** provided very basic lodgings to slaves from Indonesia and India-Ceylon; up to 1,000 slaves were housed here in terrible conditions. There's a large copy of the "Slave Code" on the wall – they had to go barefoot, couldn't sing or whistle, and were beaten if they stopped to talk on the street.

Colourful homes in the Bo-Kaap district

In 1811 the building was converted into a post office and it later served as the seat of the Supreme Court. The museum documents the colonial period, including the brutal suppression of the local population, the Dutch settlement and the establishment of Cape Town. In the interior courtyard are replicas of the tombstones of the founder of the first colony in South Africa, Jan van Riebeeck and his wife, who are buried in Jakarta, Indonesia.

Historic Museums
The oldest surviving stone building in South Africa, the imposing **Castle of Good Hope** was built between 1666 and 1679 as the seat of the governors and to protect the first settlers. Today it houses a military museum, the William Fehr Collection (furniture from the 17th–19th century) and is the military headquarters of the provincial army. It's a pleasant

OTHER PLACES TO VISIT

South African National Gallery
✚ 206 B1 ✉ Government Avenue
☎ 021 481 3970; www.iziko.org.za
🕘 Daily 10–5 ✋R30

South African Museum and Planetarium
✚ 206 B1 ✉ Queen Victoria Street
☎ 021 481 3900; www.iziko.org.za
🕘 Daily 10–5 ✋R30
🕘 Planetarium show: daily 2pm ✋R40

South African Jewish Museum
✚ 206 B1 ✉ 88 Hatfield Street
☎ 021 465 1546; www.sajewishmuseum.co.za 🕘 Sun–Thu 10–5, Fri 10–2, ID required! ✋R50

place to stroll around with Table Mountain as a backdrop – look out for regular photographic exhibitions. **Martin Melck House** (the former Gold of Africa Museum) houses an exhibition on the life of Nelson Mandela. The building is one of the oldest in the Cape.

Bo-Kaap is an Islamic residential area of exceptionally photogenic, brightly painted single-storey houses packed tightly on cobbled streets; the **Bo-Kaap Museum** is furnished as a house depicting the lifestyle of a 19th-century Muslim family.

TAKING A BREAK
Have tea and scones on the lawns inside the **castle** at the **De Goewerneur Restaurant** (R).

District Six Museum
✚ 206 C2 ✉ 25 Buitenkant Street ☎ 021 466 7200; www.districtsix.co.za
🕘 Mon–Sat 9–4 ✋R30

Slave Lodge
✚ 206 C2 ✉ Adderley Street ☎ 021 467 7229; www.iziko.org.za
🕘 Mon–Sat 10–5 ✋R30

Castle of Good Hope
✚ 206 C2 ✉ Buitenkant Street ☎ 021 405 1540; www.castleofgoodhope.co.za
🕘 Daily 9–4 ✋R30

Martin Melck House
✚ 206 B3 ✉ 96 Strand Street ☎ 021 405 1540; www.capetown.travel/products/martin-melck-house 🕘 Mon–Sat 9:30–5 ✋R40

Bo-Kaap Museum
✚ 206 B2 ✉ 71 Wale Street ☎ 021 481 3938; www.iziko.org.za
🕘 Mon–Sat 10–5 ✋R20

INSIDER INFO

- Try to catch the **changing of the guard at the castle at noon**, and listen out for the midday cannon fired from Signal Hill.
- If you only go to one museum, make it **District Six** and allow two to three hours. A visit is usually included in a guided township tour, and should definitely be included in your sightseeing programme.
- The historic 🏛 **Company's Garden** (Queen Victoria Street, daily 7:30–6:30, 7–6 in winter) is a great place to spend a few hours unwinding and feeding nuts to the squirrels that have the run of the place. With a little luck you may spot the garden's famous albino squirrel, in which case you can then make a wish!

Ⅱ V&A Waterfront

The successful regeneration of this harbour area in Cape Town has transformed it into a lively tourist and entertainment destination that is now a real enhancement of the urban landscape.

Victoria Wharf is a giant shopping mall with cafés, restaurants, cinemas and the adjoining King's Warehouse and Red Shed Craft Market. In front of Victoria Wharf is the **Union Castle Building** housing the **Iziko Maritime Centre**, which showcases the maritime history of Table Bay. West from the Union Castle Building is the **Time Ball Tower** (1894) which ships' navigators used to set Cape Town time. Beyond, the **Two Oceans Aquarium** focuses on the rich marine environment off the Cape coast. On the opposite side of Alfred Basin and reached by a pedestrian swing bridge that periodically opens for boats to pass through, is the **Clock Tower Centre**, with more shops and restaurants, and the octagonal **Clock Tower**, built in 1882 to house the port captain.

Guests at a Waterfront restaurant with the silhouette of Table Mountain in the background

TAKING A BREAK
There are over 80 restaurants, cafés, fast food joints and bars so you'll be spoiled for choice (R–RRR).

🔲 206 C5
✉ Portswood Ridge ☎ 021 408 7600; www.waterfront.co.za ⊙ Daily 9–9

Iziko Maritime Centre
🔲 206 B4 ✉ Portswood Road ☎ 021 405 2880; www.iziko.org.za
⊙ Daily 10–5 🎫 R20

Two Oceans Aquarium
🔲 206 B4 ✉ Dock Road ☎ 021 418 3823; www.aquarium.co.za
⊙ Daily 9:30–6, predator feeding 3 🎫 R150 (online R135)

INSIDER INFO

- Look out for frequent and free **live performances** in the outdoor amphitheatre.
- Enjoy the spectacular scenery around Table Bay from **a boat or helicopter trip**, which depart from the Waterfront daily.
- **V&A Waterfront Information Centre** is in Dock Road (at Ferryman's Pub; tel: 021 408 7600; 9–5/6). In Victoria Wharf you'll find a **tourist information desk** (tel: 021 408 7791; 9–9).
- The 🚩 **Scratch Patch** (Dock Road, next to the Aquarium; tel: 021 419 8429, www.scratchpatch.co.za, daily 9–6) is a great place to take children. Purchase a small bag or container (R17–R95, depending on size) and the children can scratch and dig amongst the colourful gemstones collecting the ones they like the most.

⑫ Table Mountain

Brooding, sentinel and ruggedly handsome, Table Mountain offers spectacular views and defines Cape Town.

Table Mountain does not always look this serene: when the strong southeasterly wind – known as the Cape Doctor – blows, the summit is engulfed in clouds, creating the famous tablecloth

To the indigenous nomadic people of the Cape, the Khoi, it was *hoeri kwaggo* meaning "mountain in the sea". It is named after the first man to climb it in 1503, the Portuguese explorer António de Saldanha, who named it *Taboa do Cabo* (Table of the Cape). You need not climb the towering 1,086m (3,562ft) mountain yourself, as there is a comfortable cableway up to its lofty heights. There are also several hiking paths, of varying difficulty, leading from the lower cable car station up to the top.

TAKING A BREAK

At the upper cable car station there's a bistro restaurant and cheaper café (R).

➕ 204 B3

Aerial Cableway
✉ Table Mountain Road
☎ 021 424 8181; www.tablemountain.net (online booking available)
🕐 Daily, first car up 8am, last car down 6–9:30pm, depending on season
🎟 R255 (return)

INSIDER INFO

- The more adventurous can try a 112m (368ft) **abseil** from near the upper cable car station (tel: 021 424 4760; www.abseilafrica.co.za; about R1,000).
- In clear weather, pack a basket of food and take the cable car up the mountain – the children will already be entertained by the ride up – at the top there are benches conveniently placed for a 👪 **family picnic** with a view.

Insider Tip

Cape Town's Landmark

The iconic flat-topped mountain, built from massive layers of sandstone and slate, forms the northern end of the Cape Peninsula.

❶ Table Mountain: At the summit there is a café, a self-service restaurant with a panoramic terrace and a network of short walkways (5 to 45 minutes) leading to viewpoints offering fantastic views. On weekends, floodlights illuminate the mountain.

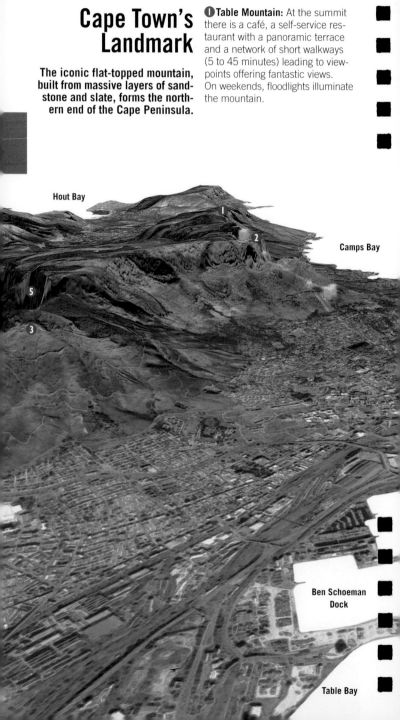

Hout Bay

Camps Bay

Ben Schoeman Dock

Table Bay

❷Cableway: The Aerial Cableway has been in operation on Table Mountain since 1929. It was upgraded in 1997 and the new Swiss-made cable cars rotate 360 degrees during the journey. The cableway carries up to 2,500 visitors every day. Alternatively, you can take one of the more than 300 hiking paths (of varying difficulty) up to the top. Depending on your starting point, the hike will take two to four hours.
❸Devil's Peak, ❹Lion's Head: Table Mountain is flanked by the 1,000m-high (3,000ft) Devil's Peak in the east – and separated by a wide valley – the 669m-high (2,200ft) Lion's Head in the west.

Table Mountain continues southwards as a wide plateau and descends steeply into Orange Kloof, which rises 200m (700ft) above sea level.
❺Kirstenbosch: Table Mountain's position between the Atlantic and False Bay brings rain to its slopes and the southeast slope, where Kirstenbosch National Botanical Garden lies, has the highest rainfall (1,400mm per annum), the perfect climate for an extraordinary variety of plants (more than 2,200 species) to flourish.
❻Signal Hill: The road winding up Signal Hill has the best views and is perfect for capturing shots of the city.

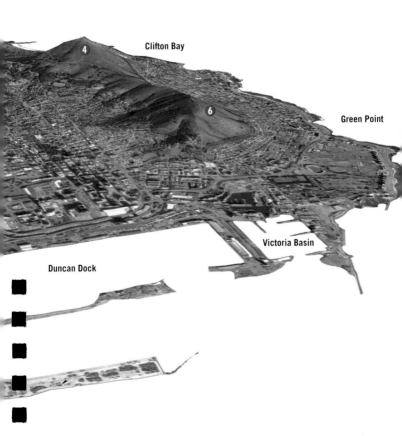

Clifton Bay

Green Point

Victoria Basin

Duncan Dock

Cape Town & Around

⓭ Robben Island

The island, 11km (7mi) north of Cape Town, has a history as a place of banishment. As far back as 1525 Portuguese sailors were believed to have abandoned a group of prisoners on the island and left them to die. Today the island is a UNESCO World Heritage Site, famed for the notorious B Section high security building, where Nelson Mandela was imprisoned until 1982.

Over 3,000 political prisoners were sent to the windswept isle during apartheid. Conditions were harsh, yet when Nelson Mandela was finally granted freedom, he rejected recrimination in favour of reconciliation. He made history as the first black president of South Africa and winner of the Nobel Peace Prize, and even after his death, he remains as *tata,* "the father of all South Africans", alive in the hearts of his countrymen. The island can be visited only on a guided tour. These depart from the Nelson Mandela Gateway at the V&A Waterfront and last three and a half hours, including the 30-minute boat ride to and from the island. The tour includes a bus ride around the island, a visit to the limestone quarry where Mandela was made to do hard labour and his prison cell.

In his autobiography Nelson Mandela described the beginning of his imprisonment on Robben Island: "We were met by a group of burly white warders shouting (in Afrikaans) 'This is the island. Here you will die!'"

TAKING A BREAK

Refreshments are available on the ferry and on the island.

🖙 204 A3 (Gateway); 194 C2 (Island)
✉ Clock Tower, V&A Waterfront ☎ 021 413 4202; www.robben-island.org.za
🕔 Daily 9–3; tours depart at 9, 11, 1, and 3 (in summer) 💷 R320

INSIDER INFO

- This is an enormously popular excursion and to avoid disappointment **pre-booking** online or by phone before your arrival is strongly advised.
- The ferry **doesn't run in bad weather** so phone ahead and check if the sea looks rough.
- **Animals** on the island include African penguins, ostriches and bontebok and there is the ever-present view of Table Mountain and Cape Town.

At Your Leisure

Groot Constantia, South Africa's oldest wine estate, outside Cape Town

🔟 Kirstenbosch National Botanical Garden

The botanical garden on the eastern slope of Table Mountain is one of the most beautiful in the world. Cecil Rhodes bequeathed the area to the state in 1902. About 9,000 of the 24,000 indigenous South African plant species are cultivated on 40ha (100 acres) of the 528ha (1,304-acres) garden. Of historical interest are some wild almonds planted by Jan van Riebeeck in 1660, and an avenue of camphor and sycamore trees planted by Cecil Rhodes in 1898. The main flowering season is from mid-August to mid-October. From January to March the red disa orchid, called the Pride of Table Mountain, blooms along the garden's streams and shady ravines while the proteas display their colourful splendour from May to October. Special attractions include the Fragrance and Useful Plants gardens as well as the Protea and the Sculpture gardens. *Insider Tip* Colonel Bird's Bath – a pond built by Colonel Bird in 1811 – lies within a collection of endangered southern African cycads. The restaurant has a lovely shady terrace and in summer people

like to picnic on the rolling lawns during the outdoor Sunday sunset concerts.

✚ 204 B3 ✉ 13km (8mi) southwest of the city centre off Rhodes Drive (M63)
☎ 021 799 8782; www.sanbi.org
🕐 Sep–Mar daily 8–7; Apr–Aug 8–6 💷 R60

🔟 Constantia

Nestled in the Constantia Valley is the oldest and most famous winery in South Africa, Groot Constantia. In 1685 the Dutch East India Company granted land to Governor Simon van der Stel, who built the gabled, whitewashed manor house and

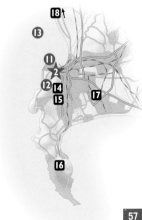

lived there from 1699 until his death in 1712. In 1791, as their wines became popular in Europe, the ground floor wine cellar was added and the vineyard was expanded. The manor house, with its valuable 18th and 19th century furniture, has been a museum since 1926. The estate offers wine tastings in the cellar; try to avoid weekends when Groot Constantia is very busy. The other prestigious estates on the Constantia Wine Route are also worth a visit – not only do they produce excellent wines, but they also have fine guesthouses and/or restaurants.

🔶 204 B3 ✉ The estates are off Constantia Main Road (M41), 20km (12mi) south of Cape Town ☎ www.constantiavalley.com

🕐 Mon–Fri 9–5, Sat 10–1 (Groot Constantia, Constantia Uitsig and Steenberg also open Sun)

Groot Constantia: ☎ 021 794 5128
Klein Constantia: ☎ 021 794 5188
Buitenverwachting: ☎ 021 794 5190
Constantia Uitsig: ☎ 021 794 6500
Steenberg: ☎ 021 713 2211

🔟 Cape Peninsula

Cape Town lies at the northern end of a narrow, mountainous peninsula that extends southward for 60km (36mi) and is dotted with pretty coastal villages. Since 1998, two-thirds of the peninsula, including the southerly Cape of Good Hope sector and the Boulders Beach penguin colony, has been protected within the discontinuous Table Mountain National Park. Well worth a leisurely day's drive (► 176), the peninsula offers a succession of scenic highlights, but none matches the windswept vistas from Cape Point Lighthouse at its southernmost tip. *Insider Tip*

Table Mountain National Park

🔶 204 B2 ☎ 021 712 2337; www.sanparks.org
Cape of Good Hope sector: 🕐 Oct–Mar 6–6; Apr–Sep 7–5 💲 R135
Boulders Beach: 🕐 Dec–Jan 7–7:30; Feb–Mar, Oct–Nov 8–6:30; Apr–Sep 8–5 💲 R70

🔟 Townships

Cape Town's townships are still home to the majority of Cape Town's

---

👪 FOR KIDS

At the **Clay Café** (4080 Main Road, Hout Bay; tel: 021 790 3318; www.claycafe.co.za; Tue–Sun 95) children can create their very own souvenir by painting on unfired crockery (purchased on site). Once the masterpiece has been fired they can take it home in their luggage. There is also a garden and playground to explore once they are finished. *Insider Tip*

Traditional fishermen on Fish Hoek beach, Cape Peninsula

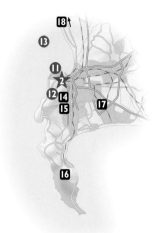

black residents. Visiting the townships is most safely done on a guided tour, as offered by the companies listed below. A typical tour will start off at Cape Town's **District Six Museum** (➤ 50) before heading along the N2 highway and on to the Cape Flats, where the townships spread east for approximately 30km (18mi) and house more than a million people.

➕ 204 B3

Cape Capers
☎ 021 448 3117; www.tourcapers.co.za
African Eagle
☎ 021 464 4266; www.daytours.co.za
Cape Rainbow
☎ 021 551 5465; www.caperainbow.com

⓲ West Coast

During September and October, it is well worth making the two-hour drive from Cape Town to see the thousands of indigenous flowers that carpet the valleys and nature reserves along the West Coast. For most of the year, the veld is dominated by a few perennial shrubs but in spring, more than 1,000 species of flowering plants emerge. The village of **Darling**, 72km (45mi) north of Cape Town, hosts an annual flower festival in September. Further north, 125km (77mi) from Cape Town, is the Langebaan Lagoon with four islets, which forms the **West Coast National Park.** The reserve covers and area of about 300km² (115mi²) and its unique and rich bird life makes it one of international importance. The vegetation is sparse, but in the spring, between August and October, the land is transformed into a spectacular sea of flowers.

➕ 204 A4

Darling Tourist Information
✉ Pastorie Street ☎ 022 492 3361; www.darlingtourism.co.za

West Coast National Park
☎ 022 772 2144; www.sanparks.org
🕐 Apr–Aug 7–6; Sep–Mar 7–7
💰 R75 (R150 in flower season)

Kitesurfers on the beach at Langebaan Lagoon, West Coast National Park

Where to...
Stay

The Backpack and Africa Travel Centre R
Cape Town's longest running up-market backpackers' hostel is spread over three pleasant adjoining 19th-century houses with great views of Table Mountain. It is a popular place, so to avoid disappointment make reservations well in advance.
➕ 206 A2 ✉ 74 New Church Street
☎ 021 423 4530; www.backpackers.co.za

Cape Grace RRR
This smart 5-star hotel is in a commanding position at the V&A Waterfront, with spacious luxurious rooms, modern African-theme décor, and superb dining at the One Waterfront restaurant. The Bascule Bar looks like a ship's galley and boasts the largest collection of whiskies in the southern hemisphere.
➕ 206 B4 ✉ V&A Waterfront, West Quay Road
☎ 021 410 7100; www.capegrace.com

Cape Heritage RR
In historic Heritage Square where wine bars and restaurants huddle in restored 18th-century buildings complete with a still-operating black-smith, this 4-star boutique hotel has 17 tasteful rooms and suites with historical features. Growing by the front door, and providing welcome shade in the courtyard, is reputedly the oldest vine in South Africa.
➕ 206 B3 ✉ 90 Bree Street
☎ 021 424 4646; www.capeheritage.co.za

Daddy Longlegs R
If you are looking for an art hotel, this one has 13 rooms up a steep wooden staircase in a 1903 restored building in the heart of Long Street. Each room was individually designed by Cape Town artists. *Insider Tip* They have minuscule bathrooms and not much furniture aside from a bed, but there's no denying their style.
➕ 206 B2 ✉ 263 Long Street
☎ 021 422 3074; www.daddylonglegs.co.za

Mount Nelson RRR
The Mount Nelson is Cape Town's famous Victorian colonial hotel built in 1899 and set in expansive grounds with a grand driveway lined with palms. The 198 rooms are in four individual accommodation wings, each with its own style of décor and private gardens. Facilities include a gym, two pools, tennis courts, two excellent restaurants and a 10-seater private kitchen where you can watch and talk to the chefs. You can visit for the sumptuous afternoon tea served on the terrace.
➕ 206 A1 ✉ 76 Orange Street, Gardens
☎ 021 483 1000; www.mountnelson.co.za

De Waterkant RR
Choose from over 40 self-catering flats and cottages sleeping between 2 and 6 people, or Charles House and De Waterkant House, two stylish and intimate guest houses. These are scattered around the historic 18th-century quarter of Waterkant. Many have roof decks for great views, splash pools or pretty courtyards, and each is individually decorated.
➕ 206 B3 ✉ 1 Loader Street
☎ 021 437 9706; www.dewaterkant.com

Where to…
Eat and Drink

Prices
Expect to pay for a two-course meal per person excluding drinks:
R under R150   **RR** R150–R300   **RRR** over R300

Baia RRR
This is the Waterfront's best spot for seafood with sweeping outdoor terraces and a sophisticated cocktail bar. The menu will tantalize your palate with fresh Mozambican shellfish, freshly caught Cape lobster, West Coast oysters or Norwegian salmon. For meat-lovers, there is a gourmet selection of grilled meat and poultry dishes. Linger at tables illuminated by the soft pink glow of hurricane lamps.
Insider Tip
➕ 206 C5
✉ Victoria Wharf, V&A Waterfront
☎ 021 421 0935;
www.baiarestaurant.co.za
🕐 Daily 12–3, 7–11

Beluga RRR
You will find Beluga in the Foundry, a 100-year-old red-brick building that used to be a metal works. It is a bistro-style restaurant that offers plenty of robust flavours, interesting ingredients and generous portions. Specialities include tender lamb shank, Belgian chocolate truffle cake and sushi. You can watch the chefs at work in the open kitchen. There's also a fashionable cocktail bar and a courtyard café where light meals are served.
➕ 206 B4
✉ Prestwich Street, Green Point
☎ 021 418 2948; www.beluga.co.za
🕐 Mon–Fri 11–11, Sat, Sun 4–11

Buena Vista Social Cafe RR
At Long Street, this cheery Cuban-inspired place has Latino music and a menu of hot and cold tapas, nachos and unusual mains such as slices of roast lamb and peppers in a Cuban rum and creamy spiced salsa sauce.
➕ 206 B4
✉ 230 Long Street
☎ 021 422 0469;
www.buenavista.co.za
🕐 Daily 11:30am–1am

Bukhara RRR
Elegant, fine-dining restaurant serving authentic North Indian dishes. The tandoori prawns and fluffy *naan* breads are delicious, and vegetarians will be in chick-pea heaven. In fine weather you can sit outside on the veranda. There's another branch in the Grand West Casino.
➕ 206 B2
✉ 33 Church Street
☎ 021 424 0000; www.bukhara.com
🕐 Mon–Sun 12–3, 6–11

Café Mozart R
Pop into Café Mozart, just off Long Street, for a delicious full farmhouse breakfast with wonderful freshly squeezed juices. It's housed in a tall, narrow building between antiques shops and art galleries, and there are tables on the pavement. There are daily lunchtime specials and some decadent desserts. Try the home-made soups such as spicy pumpkin and gooseberry broth with a garlic roll.
➕ 206 B2
✉ 37 Church Street
☎ 021 424 3774; www.themozart.co.za
🕐 Mon–Fri 8–3:30, Sat 9–3

Cape Town & Around

Chef Pon's Asian Kitchen RR
Chef Pon runs a buzzy, lively place with a long menu of affordable Chinese and Thai cuisine. Dishes that stand out include the hot-and-sour prawn soup, *tom yum kung*, crispy duck and Szechuan prawns. The food is simple, fragrant, generously portioned and is quickly delivered to your table. Make a reservation as it's a hugely popular choice.
🞢 206 B1
✉ 12 Mill Street, Gardens
☎ 021 465 5846; www.chefpons.co.za
🕐 Mon–Sat 5–10

The Codfather RRR
Treat yourself in this fine seafood restaurant where there are no menus and you choose a platter of fish, mussels, prawns, langoustine, crayfish and Portuguese sardines to be cooked to your liking and accompanied by stir-fried vegetables and a variety of sauces. Try the Namibian oysters or freshly made sushi topped with caviar – if you can't decide, the friendly waiting staff can recommend something.
🞢 204 B3
✉ 37 The Drive, Camps Bay
☎ 021 438 0782; www.codfather.co.za
🕐 Daily noon–late

Giovanni's R
Insider Tip
The city's best deli, Giovanni's has a vast choice of Italian hams, cheeses and home-made pasta imported from Italy, while the shelves are filled with olive oils, balsamic vinegars, pickles, dried fruit and nuts, foie gras, truffles, fresh breads and pastries. There is a vast counter with freshly cooked ready meals and sandwiches sold by weight to eat in at the coffee bar or take away.
🞢 Off map at 206 A4
✉ 103 Main Road, Green Point
☎ 021 434 6893
🕐 Daily 7:30am–8:30pm

Gold Restaurant RRR
Housed in a large warehouse with exposed brick walls, this dinner-only venue serves a different multiple-course pan-African set menu every night, accompanied by traditional drumming and Malian masked dancers.
🞢 206 B4
✉ 15 Bennett Street
☎ 021 421 4653;
www.goldrestaurant.co.za
🕐 Daily 10–11

Millers Thumb RR
Run by chef Solly who cooks up a storm in the kitchen and his wife Jane who reels off the menu in such a way it has you salivating, this Cape Town old favourite is set in a delightful house with three inter-leading rooms. Order Cajun and Creole dishes and look out for specials like seared tuna. The house speciality is Yaki Soba, a divine mix of chicken, prawns, stir-fried vegetables and fresh ginger in oyster and soy sauce.
🞢 206 A1
✉ 10b Kloofnek Road, Tamboerskloof
☎ 021 424 3838;
www.millersthumb.co.za
🕐 Tue–Fri 12:30–2:30, Mon–Sat 6:30–10:30

Newport Market and Deli R
With a counter and stools overlooking the ocean at Mouille Point near the lighthouse, this deli is great for lunches and light snacks. It offers coffees, smoothies, excellent sandwiches, salads and some hot dishes. The smoked salmon and cream cheese bagel is a firm favourite, or try the Cajun chicken wrap or lentil and barley soup.
🞢 Off map at 206 A5
✉ 125 Beach Road, Mouille Point
☎ 021 439 1538;
www.newportdeli.co.za
🕐 Daily 6:30am–7pm

Where to…
Shop

SHOPS

The enormous malls sell a wide range of items, with branches of the South African chain stores, as well as individual shops, restaurants, coffee shops and cinemas.

With its unique position, harbour atmosphere and well-kept historical buildings, the **V&A Waterfront** (Portswood Ridge; tel: 021 408 7600; www.waterfront.co.za) remains the most popular, and sells clothes, jewellery, African curios, gifts, books and market-style crafts at the Red Shed and Blue Shed.

The impressive **Canal Walk** on the N1 highway near Milnerton about 10km (6mi) north of the city (tel: 021 529 9600; www.canalwalk.co.za) and part of the **Century City** complex, one of the largest shopping malls in the southern hemisphere. It houses more than 400 shops, restaurants, fast-food courts and cinemas. Next door is **Ratanga Junction theme park**, which has a dozen or so rides.

Cavendish Square (Main Road, Claremont; tel: 021 657 5620; www.cavendish.co.za) is a smaller mall with fashionable shops geared towards the affluent middle-class residents of the southern suburbs. It's particularly good for clothing and has some great boutiques.

In the city centre **Adderley Street** has a full complement of chain stores and the **Golden Acre Centre** (goldenacre.mobi), while the red-bricked **St George's Mall**, the pedestrian zone between Castle and Adderley streets, has branches of the leading clothing chain stores and is peppered with informal stalls offering African artworks and curios.

Running parallel with St George's Mall is Cape Town's most eclectic shopping thoroughfare, **Long Street**, which gets quirkier and more bohemian as it leads closer towards Table Mountain. It has antiques shops (including the treasure trove of **Long Street Antiques Arcade**; www.theantiquearcade.co.za, 127 Long Street); new and used book shops; fashionable boutiques such as **Mali South** (96 Long Street; tel: 021 426 1519), selling clothing made from West African fabrics; craft shops, including the superlative **Tribal Trends** (72–4 Long Street; tel: 021 423 8008); and the unique **African Music Store** (234 Long Street; tel: 021 426 0857; www.facebook.com/TheAfricanMusicStore), selling CDs from the Cape to Cairo and most places in between.

Elsewhere on the peninsula **Kalk Bay** and **Simon's Town** are well known for their antiques and bric-a-brac shops.

MARKETS

There is an outdoor market in **Greenmarket Square** (between St George's Mall and Long Street; Mon–Sat, 9–4) selling African curios, jewellery and clothes.

The three-storey **Pan African Market** (76 Long Street; tel: 021 426 4478; www.panafricanmarket.com; Mon–Fri 9–5, Sat 9–3) sells items from all over the continent: here you can also get your hair braided African-style or pick up an African snack.

Green Point Flea Market on Sundays, however, is the best place to pick up souvenirs *Insider Tip* (tel: 021 439 4805; 8:30–5). Hundreds of stands are set up in front of the stadium in Green Point selling woodcarvings, ethnic jewellery and cloth, and a good selection of South African crafts.

One lane is food, so you can grab a snack as you browse.

Elsewhere on the peninsula there's a Sunday craft market (www.bayharbour.co.za; Fri 5pm–9pm, Sat, Sun 9:30–4) at **Hout Bay** which sells a decent selection of African curios, jewellery and clothes.

Where to...
Go Out

CINEMA

Cinema complexes are found in the shopping malls. The city's most atmospheric cinema is the four-screen **Labia** (68 Orange Street, Gardens; tel: 021 424 5927; www.labia.co.za). It tends to show the more arty, independent movies, with some foreign-language films.

THEATRE AND CONCERTS

The Cape Town Philharmonic Orchestra, opera and ballet troupes and imported musicals perform at **Artscape** (DF Malan Street, Foreshore; tel: 021 410 9800; www.artscape.co.za) or the **Baxter Theatre** (Main Road, Rondebosch; tel: 021 685 7880; www.baxter.co.za): both have several theatres for plays.

Comedy and cabaret can be seen at **Theatre on the Bay** (1a Link Street, Camps Bay; tel: 021 438 3301; www.pietertoerien.co.za).

The Fugard (corner of Harrington and Caledon streets, District Six; tel: 021 461 4554; www.thefugard.com), named after the renowned contemporary political playwright Athol Fugard, hosts a varied selection of locally written productions.

There are sunset concerts at **Kirstenbosch National Botanical Garden** on Sunday evenings in summer. To find out what's on and get tickets, go to one of the Computicket offices in the shopping malls or visit www.computicket.co.za.

NIGHTLIFE

The trendy strip along Victoria Road in Camps Bay offers cocktails and sundowners in a sophisticated setting and is the place to see and be seen. People-watch at **Blues** (Shop 9, The Promenade; tel: 021 438 2040; www.blues.co.za; noon–11) or at **Café Caprice** (37 Victoria Road; tel: 021 438 8315; www.cafecaprice.co.za; 9:30am–2am).

Mercury Live & Lounge (43 De Villiers Street, tel. 021 465 2106; www.mercuryl.co.za) is one of Cape Town's best spots for live entertainment and it is always crowded.

The top end of Somerset Road in Green Point offers a number of gay bars, and there are several trendy nightclubs here and in the Long Street area.

Right on Somerset Road is **Beaulah** (28 Somerset Road; tel: 021 418 5244, www.facebook.com/Beaulahbar; Tue–Sat 5pm–2/4am), a mainly-lesbian bar and dance venue that welcomes everyone.

There is a great vibe and live music (jazz, funk, soul and blues) at **The Piano Bar** (47 Napier Street; tel: 021 418 1096; www.thepianobar.co.za; daily from 12:30pm-midnight), which also serves delicious tapas.

Jazz fans should head over to the small and intimate **Crypt Jazz Restaurant** (1 Wale Street; tel: 079 683 4658, www.thecryptjazz.com; Tue–Sat 7pm–midnight) a popular live jazz venue where booking is advisable.

Out of the city is **GrandWest Casino** (1 Vanguard Drive, Goodwood; tel: 021 505 7777; www.suninternational.com) with several nightlife venues and a vast gaming floor.

Southern Coast

 Little Treats

Walk the Wine Bars

Early evening is an ideal time to taste some of the wines on offer in the wine bars and cafés around **Stellenbosch's** historic Dorp Street (➤ 73).

River Ride

Get the adrenalin flowing and explore the Tsitsikamma National Park's spectacular **Storms River Gorge** (➤ 70) in an inflatable tube.

Panoramic View

In Port Elizabeth (➤ 77) climb the 204 steps of the landmark **Campanile** (52m/170ft) for a magnificent view of the harbour and surrounds.

Getting Your Bearings

After Cape Town the dramatic southern coast of South Africa, which runs the entire length of the Western and Eastern Cape provinces, is the most visited region of South Africa. It has a wide variety of landscapes from indigenous forests and swathes of wide beach, to pretty winelands and pretty country towns.

The region is linked from west to east by the N2 highway and the alternative Route 62 (▶ 179). The tourist infrastructure is well developed and there are countless attractions and activities. The first port of call should be the impossibly scenic winelands that occupy the valleys from Stellenbosch to the Breede River. Southeast of Cape Town is the self-proclaimed Whale Coast from where humpback and southern right whales can be seen in the Atlantic in season. Then the celebrated Garden Route stretches to Port Elizabeth with its nature reserves and lush coastal forests. Worth visiting is the Addo Elephant National Park and, northeast of East London, the rural and ruggedly beautiful Wild Coast with its deserted beaches and isolated seaside resorts.

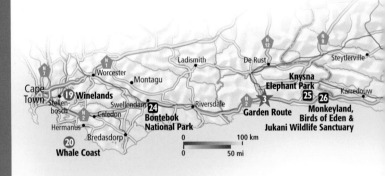

Vineyards near Stellenbosch, at the heart of the Cape Winelands

Southern Coast

Seven Perfect Days

If you are not quite sure where to begin your travels, this itinerary recommends seven practical and enjoyable days on South Africa's southern coast, taking in some of the best places to see. For more information see the main entries (►70–83).

Day 1

From Cape Town, drive to Franschhoek and lunch at one of the superb restaurants along the main street. Then spend the afternoon exploring the **⑲ Winelands** (►73). Spend the night in a country manor house and eat at **Eight Restaurant** (►85) on the Spier wine estate.

Day 2

Follow the **⑳ Whale Coast** (►75) to Hermanus, stopping en route to see the penguins in Betty's Bay. Spend the afternoon and evening in Hermanus.

Hogsback & Amatola Mountains ㉘

Grahamstown ㉗

Knysna Elephant Park

Addo Elephant National Park ㉒

Wild Coast ㉓

㉕ ㉖

㉑ Port Elizabeth

⑲ Winelands   Garden ⌂
㉔   ③
Bontebok   Route
National Park

Monkeyland, Birds of Eden & Jukani Wildlife Sanctuary

⑳ Whale Coast

If you come between July and November, look out for breeching and blowing whales from Hermanus's cliff tops. In the evening head to **Bientang's Cave** (►86) to enjoy a delicious seafood dinner on a platform overlooking the ocean.

Day 3

Follow the N2 to the ★ **Garden Route** (►70), stopping in Swellendam along the way for lunch at the atmospheric **Old Gaol Coffee Shop** (8a Voortrek Street; tel: 028 514 3847; www.oldgaolrestaurant.co.za). Head to the seaside resort of **Mossel Bay** in the afternoon to visit the Bartolomeu Dias Museum. Stay overnight in Mossel Bay, either at the **African Oceans Manor** (►84) or at the cheaper **Point Hotel** (►84).

Day 4

In the morning, romp on the beach or take a hike in the **Wilderness Section of Garden Route National Park** (right – twilight on the coast near Storms

River Mouth; ► 70). Then head to **Knysna** (► 71) and spend the afternoon cruising on the lagoon or cross the causeway to visit Thesen Island. Stay in Knysna for the evening, heading to one of the fine restaurants in the Knysna Quays for something to eat.

Day 5

In the morning, visit the **25 Knysna Elephant Park** (► 82) or go on the tour at **26 Monkeyland** (► 83). Then after lunch, head to Tsitsikamma National Park to see dolphins riding the waves or try the highest bungee jump in the world at Bloukrans River Bridge. In the evening, either stay and eat at Hacklewood Hill Country House (► 85) in **21 Port Elizabeth** (► 77) or push on to the **22 Addo Elephant National Park** (► 78).

Day 6

Make an early start to go on a game drive in Addo to see the herds of elephant. Then, follow the N2 to **27 Grahamstown** (► 83), visit the museums and historic buildings and lunch or stay at the Cock House (10 Market Street; tel: 046 636 1287; www.cockhouse.co.za), an 1820s National Monument, or push on to **Cintsa** (► 80), the first town on the Wild Coast. The **Barefoot Café** (www.barefootcafe.co.za) in Cintsa is known for its laid-back atmosphere, good breakfasts and tasty burgers and pizzas.

Day 7

Follow the N2 across the **23 Wild Coast's** (► 80) rolling pastures dotted with colourful *kraals* to one of the several resorts on the coast at Haga-Haga, Morgan's Bay, Qolora Mouth, Qora Mouth, Coffee Bay or Port St Johns. Spend a peaceful afternoon exploring the empty beaches, coastal forests, craggy cliffs, caves and shipwrecks. Eat a seafood dinner directly by the beach at one of the Wild Coast resorts.

⭐ Garden Route

The Garden Route is a stretch of rugged coast with beautiful white sandy beaches, backed by a lush green hinterland. Its spectacular natural beauty has made it one of the most important tourist attractions in the country – a must-see destination.

The Garden Route (*Tuinroete* in Afrikaans) takes in a 220km (135mi) stretch of the N2 (2,200km/1,400mi), which follows the Indian Ocean coast from Cape Town to Swaziland. The Garden Route section between **Mossel Bay** in the west and and the mouth of the **Storms River** in the east is probably the most famous route in the country and it is particularly popular in December and January. Where possible you should leave the N2, a section of the road is tolled, to explore some of the hidden places off the beaten track.

Mossel Bay to George
Mossel Bay is an attractive seaside resort and highlights include the **Bartolomeu Dias Museum**, which is actually a collection of museums – the Shell Museum, Maritime Museum and Aquarium. The Post Office Tree in the grounds was once used by early sailors to leave messages and you can still post a letter here today which gets a special frank. Although not on the coast, **George** has some interesting churches and an old slave tree where a lock and chain are

Insider Tip

FOR KIDS
Children love the **Cango Ostrich Show Farm** (14km/8.5mi on the road to the Cango Caves, Oudtshoorn; tel: 044 272 4623; www.cangoostrich.co.za, daily 8–4:30; R100), where they can see ostrich eggs hatching, feed the young birds, stand on an egg and even ride an ostrich.

embedded in the trunk. North of George and through the dramatic Outeniqua Pass is **Oudtshoorn,** known for its many **ostrich farms**, where you can learn all about the giant birds and even ride one, and the intriguing **Cango Caves** with their beautiful caverns of stalagmites and stalactites.

Victoria Bay to Knysna

The bridge over the mouth of Storms River in the Tsitsikamma Section of Garden Route National Park

South of George are the picturesque village of **Victoria Bay**, in a quaint cove, with a single row of houses and safe swimming beach. The adjacent **Wilderness Section** of **Garden Route National Park** encompasses a network of rivers, lagoons and coastal forest, which is ideal for hiking or bird watching. Next is **Knysna**, the unofficial capital of the Garden Route, which surrounds the Knysna Lagoon, and is sheltered from the ocean by the Knysna Heads, a pair of rocky outcrops that form part of the **Featherbed Nature Reserve**. There is plenty to do here, with a slick waterfront of shops and restaurants, boat rides, indigenous forests to explore, or oysters to slurp on **Thesen Island**, just a short drive across a causeway from Knysna's waterfront.

Plettenberg to Storms River

Further along the coast, the seaside resort of **Plettenberg Bay** slopes downhill from a rocky peninsula overlooking great beaches – a good place for whale-watching. **Robberg Peninsula Nature Reserve** (R40) offers good cliff-top hiking on a rocky peninsula 6km (4mi) south of Plettenburg Bay, while you can take a cruise or paddle a canoe on the **Keurbooms River**. Worth a detour off the N2 is the sleepy village of **Nature's Valley** in an idyllic setting on the beach and next to a calm lagoon; it is surrounded by forests, where you may spot vervet monkeys. Back on the N2, stop as it crosses the **Bloukrans River Bridge**, and if you dare, try the highest commercial bungee jump in the world at 216m (708ft). A little further on at **Storms River Bridge** look down into the river gorge, and then spend some time hiking and enjoying the tremendous coastal and forest scenery in the **Tsitsikamma Section** of **Garden Route National Park**. There's a wooden swing bridge across the rocks from where you may spot dolphins or the Cape clawless otter, or you can float down the Storms River on an inner-tube.

Insider Tip

Insider Tip

Southern Coast

INSIDER INFO

- For full details of the Garden Route visit www.gardenroute.co.za.
- From Cape Town it's just less than 400km (248mi) to Mossel Bay on the N2. An ideal stop roughly halfway is the historic town of **Swellendam**, one of the oldest settlements in the country.
- **Stormsriver Adventures** (Storms River Village; tel: 042 281 1836; www.stormsriver. com) organizes a number of activities in the Tsitsikamma region, including guided hikes, mountain biking, abseiling, black water tubing, snorkelling, scuba diving and a canopy tour – you glide through the forest along steel ropes between platforms in the trees.
- The five-day **Otter Trail**, South Africa's most famous hiking route, runs westward through the Tsitsikamma Section of Garden Route National Park. It's usually booked solid months in advance, but casual visitors can cover the trail's spectacular first leg as a round day hike from Storms River Mouth Restcamp, with a good chance of seeing otters, small antelope and local birds such as the dazzling Knysna loerie. If you are interested in undertaking the whole trail tel: 012 426 5111 or visit www. sanparks.org for booking details (R1,150).

TAKING A BREAK

There's no shortage of quality restaurants and cafés along the Garden Route. A Knysna must-do is to savour a dozen oysters with a glass of champagne at **Quay Four** (formerly the renowned Knysna Oyster Co). The restaurant cultivates oysters in the lagoon and has a terrific view of the Knysna Heads (Thesen Island; tel: 044 382 4202; www.quay4 knysna.co.za; open daily 8–late; RR).

Mossel Bay Tourism
197 D1 ✉ Corner of Market and Church streets ☎ 044 691 2202; www.visitmosselbay.co.za
🕐 Mon–Fri 8–6, Sat 9–4, Sun 9–2

Bartolomeu Dias Museum
197 D1 ✉ Market Street, Mossel Bay ☎ 044 691 1067; www.diasmuseum.co.za
🕐 Mon–Fri 9–4:45, Sat, Sun 9–3:45
💷 R20

Cango Caves
197 D2 ✉ R328 near Oudtshoorn ☎ 044 272 7410; www.cango-caves. co.za 🕐 Tours daily 9–4 every hour
💷 R100/R150 (depending on tour)

Garden Route National Park (Wilderness Section)
197 D2
☎ 044 877 1197; www.sanparks.org
🕐 Daily 7–6 💷 R120

Knysna Tourism
197 D1 ✉ 40 Main Street
☎ 044 382 5510; visitknysna.co.za
🕐 Mon–Fri 8–5, Sat 8:30–1

Plettenberg Bay Tourism
197 E1 ✉ Main Street
☎ 044 533 4065;
www.plett-tourism.co.za
🕐 Mon–Fri 9–5, Sat 9–1

Bloukrans Bungee Jump
197 E1 ✉ 40km (25mi) east of Plettenberg Bay on the N2
☎ 042 281 1458;
www.faceadrenalin.com 🕐 Daily 9–5
💷 R900 online, R950 on site

Garden Route National Park (Tsitsikamma Section)
197 E2 ✉ 20km (12mi) northeast of Plettenberg Bay on the N2
☎ 042 281 1607; www.sanparks.org
🕐 Daily 6–9:30 💷 R196

⑲ Winelands

The scenic Cape Wineland region has all the ingredients for producing excellent quality wines: well-drained, rather poor soil, warm, dry summers and cool winters. As far as the eye can see there are lush vineyards dotted with whitewashed, gabled Cape Dutch homesteads set against a backdrop of craggy mountains. The wine estates on the hillsides and in the valleys have names such as La Dauphine or La Provence, reflecting the French heritage of the settlers who, along with the Dutch, brought viticulture to the Cape.

More than a dozen well-signposted wine routes link those estates that are open to the public: pick up maps at the tourist offices. Most of the estates lie in idyllic countryside and wine-tasting takes place in superb whitewashed manor houses or atmospheric cool wine cellars next to the vines. At some, port, brandy and cheese are also on offer. Also stop in the regional towns where you will see splendidly restored Cape Dutch, Georgian and Victorian buildings, and you can browse in the many arts and craft shops and galleries.

The fertile Zorgvliet Estate in the picturesque Banhoek Valley near Stellenbosch

Regional Centres

Established in 1679, **Stellenbosch** is the oldest town in South Africa after Cape Town, and Dorp Street has a number of historic buildings. Some can be visited and have been restored and furnished in the style of their particular period.

Southern Coast

Paarl (Afrikaans for "pearl") is named after the huge granite dome that overshadows the town and appears shiny like a pearl after rain. The town was established in 1720 and there are several historic buildings on the famous 11km-long (7mi) Main Street. The beautiful wine estate of Laborie is today home to the KWV cellar complex, which at 22ha (54 acres) is the largest wine cellar in the world. **Franschhoek** was founded in 1688 on land granted to the Huguenots and today is frequently dubbed the "Gastronomic capital of South Africa" with several superb restaurants to choose from. The Franschhoek Valley is where some of the Cape's most beautiful homesteads are found.

Ntsiki Biyela, the winemaker at Stellenkaya, was also named Woman Winemaker of the Year

TAKING A BREAK

Most of the estates have superb restaurants and some offer **picnic baskets** to eat among the vines (R–RRR).

✚ 204 C3

Stellenbosch Tourist Office
✉ 36 Market Street
☎ 021 883 3584; www.stellenboschtourism.co.za
🕐 Mon–Fri 8–6, Sat 9–5, Sun 10–4

Paarl Tourist Office
✉ 216 Main Road
☎ 021 872 4842; www.paarlonline.com
🕐 Mon–Fri 8:30–5, Sat, Sun 10–1

Franschhoek Tourist Office
✉ 62 Huguenot Road
☎ 021 876 2861; www.franschhoek.org.za
🕐 Mon–Fri 8–5, Sat 9–5, Sun 9–4

INSIDER INFO

■ A popular way of visiting the wine estates is on an **organized guided day trip** from Cape Town. This option is safer than driving your own car. Most estates are open Mon–Sat 9–5, and an increasing number now also open on Sundays.

■ In addition to wine tastings, **Spier** wine estate (on the R310 south of Stellenbosch; tel: 021 809 1100; www.spier.co.za) offers a bird of prey centre, summer concerts, a golf course, hotel, a deli and a farm-to-table restaurant, Eight Restaurant (▶ 85).

■ **Fairview Winery** (Suid Agter Paarl Road; tel: 021 863 2450; www.fairview.co.za) also has goat's cheese to taste and you can see the resident goats who live in a unique goat tower. It produces wine labels that are a delightful dig at French wine – "Goats do Roam" and "Bored Doe".

■ The 🏠 **Drakenstein Lion Park** (Old Paarl Road, Paarl; tel: 021 863 3290; www.lion rescue.org.za, 9:30–4:30; R60, combined ticket with Chimp Haven: R90) is a sanctuary for captive bred lions that cannot be rehabilitated to the wild. Watching the lions at feeding time (Mon, Wed and Fri 4pm) is especially exciting for children. Next door is Chimp Haven, a sanctuary for chimpanzees who were displaced after the closure of a zoo.

⑳ Whale Coast

From July to November whales visit the shores of South Africa on their migration route from Antarctica. They can be seen between False Bay and Cape Agulhas, and the town of Hermanus is one of the best places in the world for shore-based whale-watching.

Mussels straight from the sea to the table at Fishermans Cottage, Hermanus

From Cape Town follow the N2 to Somerset West and then follow the R44, and then the R43 around the rocky coast. From this route, there are some spectacular mountain and ocean views; on the way stop in **Gordon's Bay** for its fine swathe of beach and at **Betty's Bay** to see the colony of African penguins at Stoney Point.

Hermanus
The attractive town of **Hermanus** lines the sheltered Walker Bay, and these warm waters attract the female southern right whale to calve and nurse their young. Mothers with calves can often be spotted from the cliff-top paths. The town's harbour has some restored fisherman's cottages and fishing boats, and to the south of town are some good beaches.

Insider Tip

Stanford to Cape Agulhas
Further around the coast is **Stanford**, a Victorian village set on the picturesque Klein River, and the busy fishing harbour of **Gansbaai**. Off the coast are

WHALE FACTS
Southern right whales (*Eubalaena australis*), which can grow up to 18m (60ft), come in to Walker Bay to mate and to calve from June to the end of November and their 6m (19ft) calves are born in the shallow, sheltered bay during August and September. The horny calluses on their heads and V-shaped blowholes readily distinguish them. In Walker Bay and along the West Coast you can also see **Bryde's whales** (*Balaenoptera edeni*), which can be up to 14m (46ft) long and weigh up to 20 tonnes, from the **rorqual** family, the largest group of **baleen whales** (*Mysticeti*). Another baleen is the almost 15m (49ft) **humpback whale** (*Megaptera novaeangliae*), with its long distinctive white flippers. The **pygmy right whale** (*Caperea marginata*), which can grow up to 6m (19ft) and is only found in the southern hemisphere, can also be seen along South African coasts. Baleen whales filter their food from the water through their baleen plates. The second suborder, the **toothed whales** (*Odontoceti*) are also represented along South African coasts. Among them are the strap-toothed whale, the humpback dolphin, the True's beaked whale, the dusky dolphin, the Heaviside's dolphin, the short-beaked common dolphin and the common bottlenose dolphin. The most spectacular toothed whale is the **orca** (*Orcinus orca*), which also attacks other whales and, due to its hunting technique, has earned the name killer whale.

Southern Coast

Dyer Island, a breeding spot for African penguins, and **Geyser Rock** where there's a Cape fur seal colony. The penguins and seals are both prized morsels for hungry sharks, and great white sharks patrol the stretch of ocean between the rock and the island, known as Shark Alley. There are seasonal whale-watching trips around Dyer Island. Further east at the end of the R319 is the **Agulhas National Park**, in which **Cape Agulhas** is the southernmost point of Africa.

TAKING A BREAK

If whales are in Walker Bay than grab a table on the rocks next to the ocean at **Bientang's Cave** (➤ 86). You won't get a closer view unless you are actually on a boat. *Insider Tip*

There is always a lot to see on the Whale Coast

➕ 197 D1

The cliffs at Hermanus drop steeply into the ocean, where the whales in the waters below feel close enough to touch

Hermanus Tourist Office
➕ 205 D2 ✉ Old Station building, Mitchell Street
☎ 028 312 2629; www.hermanustourism.info ⊕ Mon–Fri 8–6, Sat, Sun 9–3

Dyer Island Cruises
➕ 205 D1 ✉ Kleinbaai Harbour ☎ 082 801 8014;
www.dyer-island-cruises.co.za 💰 R800 (R1,000 in whale season)

INSIDER INFO

- Hermanus's **Whale Festival** is in September with performances, craft markets and children's events (http://hermanuswhalefestival.co.za).
- Hermanus has its own **Whale Crier** in season, who keeps watch from the cliff top and yells out sightings through his horn.
- **Look out for blowing** – the spout of water from a whale's blowhole as air is expelled from the lungs; breaching – when the whale leaps from the water in an effortless arch; lobtailing – slapping its tail against the water; and spyhopping – lifting its head out of the water, which gives the whale a 360-degree view of the sea.

Insider Tip

- It is hard to imagine anything more exciting than **Shark Cage Diving** (Gaansbaai; tel: 082 559 6858; www.sharkcagediving.co.za; R1,750). On the 🚢 boat trip the family (children over 12) can go down in a cage and come face to face with these fearsome creatures.

㉑ Port Elizabeth

Port Elizabeth, dubbed PE by its residents, is the largest coastal town between Cape Town and Durban. It is the Eastern Cape Province's industrial and trade centre and forms part of the Nelson Mandela Bay Metropolitan Municipality, along with Uitenhage, Despatch and Coega.

Nicknamed the "Detroit of South Africa", the automotive industry is the city's main economic sector. Culturally, PE is on par with the other large cities in the country; there is a thriving student scene with plenty of lively pubs and bars. Its long beaches also make it a popular holiday destination.

TAKING A BREAK

Enjoy calamari on the beach at **Die Walskipper** (►86) in Jeffrey's Bay.

✚ 197 F2

The Port Elizabeth City Hall | **Nelson Mandela Bay Tourism**
✉ Donkin Lighthouse, Belmont Terrace ☎ 041 585 8884; www.nmbt.co.za
🕐 Mon–Fri 8–4:30, Sat, Sun 9:30–3:30

INSIDER INFO

- Watch some of the **world's best surfers** compete in Jeffrey's Bay (for events see www.surfingsouthafrica.co.za).
- **Climb the Cape St Francis lighthouse**, at 27m (89ft) the tallest lighthouse in South Africa (tel: 042 294 0076; www.stfrancistourism.co.za).
- The 🔂 **Holmeleigh Farmyard** (Colleen Glen; tel: 041 379 2901; www.holmeleigh farmyard.co.za; Tue–Sun 9–4:30; R25, children under 12: free) is geared for children and has a petting zoo (lots of cute animals), a jumping castle, playground, tractor rides and activities such as cow milking.

㉒ Addo Elephant National Park

When the third largest South African national park was established in the Sunday River region of the Eastern Cape in 1931, there were only eleven elephants living there. Today the 1,800km² (695mi²) site, which is to be expanded with a 1,200km² (463mi²) maritime protection area, is home to more than 600 elephants, 400 buffaloes and many other animals.

The park is proud to be the only one in the world where visitors can see the Big Seven, which includes the Big Five on the mainland, and the great white shark and southern right whale (*Eubalaena australis*) in the sea off the coast. The main interest of most visitors remains the original elephant section where flat bush, waterholes and a 75km (46mi) network of roads ensure superb sightings of the elephants. You can visit the elephant section for the day or stay overnight in basic but attractive chalets, which overlook a well-trodden path to the waterhole in front of the main reception building. Seeing herds over 100-strong is a magnificent experience.

Insider Tip

Private Reserves

From Port Elizabeth you can also visit a few other private wildlife reserves located in the vicinity of the Addo Elephant National Park. **Shamwari Game Reserve** is one of the Eastern

Addo Elephant National Park

INSIDER INFO

- Look out for the highly localized **dung beetle** *Circellium bacchus*. These beetles roll up dung into small balls to eat and, as an elephant produces 60kg (130lbs) of dung every day, they have quite a job to do.
- The best time to go is **January and February** when the females give birth.
- **No citrus fruits** can be taken into Addo as the elephants have developed a craving for them.

Cape's success stories where 250km² (62,000 acres) of bush has been repopulated with animals not seen in this region since the 19th century. These include black rhino, elephant, buffalo, lion, wild dog and antelope of all sizes. You can stay in one of the seven luxurious lodges. The **Amakhala Game Reserve** now has black rhino, giraffe, Cape buffalo, wildebeest and zebra and, again, there are eleven luxury lodges. Alternatively, you can visit for the day, go on game drives or take a cruise on the Sundays River. The **Kwandwe Game Reserve**, whose 250km² (54,400 acres) border Addo, also protects the Big Five and is studded with four exclusive lodges. **Lalibela Game Reserve** is home to the Big Five, plus wild dog, hippo and giraffe, and there are five game lodges. It is geared toward families, with special game drives for children.

Elephants at a waterhole in Addo Elephant National Park, a one-hour drive northeast of Port Elizabeth

TAKING A BREAK

You can eat at Addo's basic restaurant or cook your own food on your patio **barbecue** while watching elephants pass by.

Addo Elephant National Park
197 F2 ✉ Off the R335, 72km (45mi) northeast of Port Elizabeth
☎ 042 233 8600; www.sanparks.org 🕐 7–7 R248

Shamwari Game Reserve
197 F2 ✉ 72km (45mi) east of Port Elizabeth
☎ 042 203 1111; www.shamwari.com
ℹ No day visitors to the reserve

Amakhala Game Reserve
✉ 63km (39mi) east of Port Elizabeth
☎ 041 502 9400; www.amakhala.co.za
🕐 May–Aug 11–6; Sep–Apr noon–6 R950

Kwandwe Game Reserve
198 B2 ✉ 160km (96mi) northeast from Port Elizabeth on the R67
☎ 046 603 3400; www.kwandwe.com
ℹ No day visitors to the reserve

Lalibela Game Reserve
197 F2 ✉ 64km (40mi) east of Port Elizabeth
☎ 041 581 8170; www.lalibela.net
ℹ No day visitors to the reserve

㉓ Wild Coast

Formerly known as the Transkei, the homeland of the Xhosa people, the dramatic coastline that stretches 280km (174mi) from East London to Port Edward in KwaZulu-Natal easily befits its name of the Wild Coast. This is a region of isolated shipwreck-strewn beaches, rocky cliffs and rural green pastures. Waterfalls tumble directly into the sea, dolphins play in the waves and people live traditional lives in colourful _kraals_.

Though it has some good surfing beaches, don't dwell in the largely industrial and drab city of **East London** for long, but head northeast along the N2 to the coastal resorts. A short distance beyond East London you can go on a guided game drive to see elephant, giraffe, zebra, rhino and antelope in the **Inkwenkwezi Game Reserve**. The resort of **Cintsa** overlooks forested dunes and lagoons, while the isolated hotels in the beautiful bays at **Haga-Haga, Morgan's Bay, Kei Mouth, Qolora Mouth, Nxaxo Mouth, Mazeppa Bay** and **Qora Mouth** offer fishing, shell

Insider Tip collecting, hiking along the cliff tops and endless near-deserted beaches.

At **Coffee Bay**, named after a ship that ran aground

Insider Tip with a cargo of coffee beans in the 1860s, visit the **Hole in the Wall** – huge waves crash through a hole in the cliff eroded by the sea.

Port St Johns further north lies in lush, hilly, steamy forest where a couple of nature reserves are home to small mammals.

Nelson Mandela Museum

Inland and back on the N2, stop in **Umtata (Mthatha)**, former capital of the defunct Transkei homeland, to visit the **Nelson Mandela Museum**, which focuses on the life of the formidable man. The museum is in two sections: the main section is housed in Mthatha's former parliamentary building and documents Nelson _Mandela's Long Walk to_

The peaceful beach at Cintsa: the Wild Coast remains unspoiled and rural

INSIDER INFO

■ Get right off the beaten track: African Heartland Journeys in Cintsa (www.ahj.co.za), Active Escapes (www.active-escapes.co.za) and Wild Coast Hikes (www.wild-coasthikes.com) offer multi-day **tours of the Wild Coast** on foot, bike, horseback or canoe.

■ For some action-packed fun head to the 🎡 **Wild Waves Water Park** (Main Bizana Road, 5km/3mi from Port Edward at the Wild Coast Sun Resort, tel: 039 305 4800; 9–5; R160), which offers and exciting selection of water activities.

Bontebok (*Damaliscus pygargus*) are among the animals that live in the Inkwenkwezi Game Reserve

Freedom (the title of his autobiography) and the staggering number of gifts he has received from around the world. The other section is his primary school at **Qunu** 32km (20mi) west of Mthatha where Mandela grew up, and you can also spend the night here.

TAKING A BREAK

On Sundays, don't miss the buffet lunch at the thatched restaurant in the **Inkwenkwezi Game Reserve** (noon–4; RR).

Insider Tip

🞜 198 C2–199 D3

Inkwenkwezi Game Reserve
✉ 33km (20mi) northeast from East London ☎ 043 734 3234; http://eastlondon-info.co.za 🥾 Hiking tours: R250; safaris: R800

Nelson Mandela Museum
🞜 198 C3 ✉ Nelson Mandela Drive and Owen Street, Mthatha
☎ 047 532 5110; www.nelsonmandelamuseum.org.za 🕐 Daily 9–4 🎫 Free

At Your Leisure

The unspoiled Amatola Mountains are an excellent destination for hikers

24 Bontebok National Park

The original habitat of the bonte-bok antelope (▶81) was the 56km (35mi) wide plain between Bot River in the west and Mossel Bay in the east. Up until the end of the 18th century, large herds grazed there but they were hunted to near extinc-tion and by the 19th century their numbers had dwindled to 17. This small park (37km²/14mi²) was es-tablished in order to protect these remaining animals. Lang Elsie's Kraal – once a camp of the indige-nous Khoi – is an excellent place to watch them. The park is also home to grey rhebok, Cape mountain zebra, and duikers, as well as more than 200 bird species. The area is covered in rare fynbos and in the spring over 470 plant species put on a lovely floral display. You can see the fascinating wildlife as you drive through the park but there are also three short hiking trails.

Insider Tip

🞣 196 C1   ✉ Off the N2, 6km (4mi) southeast of Swellendam
☎ 028 514 2735; www.sanparks.org
🕒 Oct–Apr 7–7; May–Sep 7–6   💵 R100

25 🛉🛉 Knysna Elephant Park

To get up close and personal with an elephant is a marvellous ex-perience, especially for children. Knysna Elephant Park has 12 tame elephants in the small park and offers one-hour tours to meet, touch, feed and interact with them. Guides give out plenty of interesting elephant-related information. You can also walk with them or ride on top at elephant-pace through the bush. The park has a six-bedroom lodge overlooking the elephants' night *boma* (enclosure) so you can fall asleep to the sounds of them communicating.

Insider Tip

Insider Tip

🞣 197 E1   ✉ On the N2 20km (12mi) east of Knysna ☎ 044 532 7732;

www.knysnaelephantpark.co.za ⏰ 8:30–4:30; tours every hour on the half hour 🎟 R275

26 Monkeyland & Birds of Eden & Jukani Wildlife Sanctuary

Monkeyland harbours primates from all over the world, most of which are rescued pets. You can go on a guided walk through a wonderfully lush tract of tropical forest to spot the creatures swinging through the trees. A 118m (387ft) rope bridge spans a deep valley and allows views into the upper reaches of the forest canopy where some of the animals spend their lives.

Next door, the **Birds of Eden**, a free-flight aviary housed in a 2.3ha (5.7-acre) mesh dome, spans more of the forest with a network of board-walks; periodically a clever irrigation system sets off a mock thunderstorm with lifelike sounds. There are ma-caws, parrots, hornbills, sunbirds and cockatoos to name but a few.

Just 10km (6mi) west is **Jukani Wildlife Sanctuary**, home to all kinds of big cats, not just those from Africa.

✚ 197 E2 ✉ Off the N2 16km (10mi) east of Plettenberg Bay ☎ 044 534 8906; www.monkeyland.co.za ⏰ Daily 8–5 🎟 R210–R260 per attraction; combined ticket: R430–R520 depending on season

27 Grahamstown

Dominated by Rhodes University, one of the country's most prestig-ious seats of learning, Grahamstown has some wonderful historical archi-tecture dating back to the 1830s when the town was established by British settlers. There are some fine buildings along the High Street and around Church Square. Leisurely wander around the impressive museums, churches, monuments and libraries in streets that retain a distinctively English air.

Grahamstown is also the location of the annual National Arts Festival, South Africa's most prominent fes-tival, which attracts over 50,000 people to the city every July.

Grahamstown and surrounding areas form part of the Makana Municipality.

✚ 198 B2
ℹ 63 High Street
☎ 046 622 3241; www.grahamstown.co.za
⏰ Mon–Fri 8:30–5, Sat 9–noon

28 Hogsback & Amatola Mountains

A one-hour drive north of Grahamstown in the heart of the Amatola Mountains is the delight-ful village of Hogsback. Named after one of the mountains that supposedly resembles the back of a hog, this beautiful region has excellent hiking through rolling hills, hardwood forests and misty waterfalls. Hogsback itself is a laid-back little place with tea gardens and craft shops strung out along the main road lined with giant oak trees; cottages have English-style gardens full of blooms, and black-berry and gooseberry bushes. The local people sell country fare such as jam and hearty soups, and you can pick up booklets detailing hikes in the region.

✚ 198 B2

Hogsback Tourism
✉ Main Road
☎ 045 962 1245; www.hogsback.com
⏰ Mon–Sat 10–4, Sun 9–3

Southern Coast

Where to...
Stay

Prices

Expect to pay per double room, per night

R under R1,500   **RR** R1,500–R2,500   **RRR** over R2,500

WINELANDS

Grande Roche RRR

This is one of the Winelands' most atmospheric hotels, set in a Cape Dutch manor house surrounded by vines. The rooms are lavishly decorated, with pretty terraces and vast double showers. Facilities include a heated palm-fringed pool, tennis courts, beauty spa, the excellent formal Bosman's restaurant and a more contemporary bistro with modern art.

✚ 204 C3

✉ Plantasie Street, Paarl

☎ 021 863 5100; http://granderoche.com

D'Ouwe Werf RR

On oak-lined Church Street in the historic heart of Stellenbosch, D'Ouwe Werf was established in 1802 and is South Africa's oldest hostelry. It retains a gracious old-world atmosphere, enhanced by period furnishings. Run by the same family for decades, the hotel has just 38 rooms and a welcoming atmosphere. The courtyard coffee garden and 1802 Restaurant serve traditional Cape cuisine at reasonable prices.

✚ 204 C3

✉ 30 Church Street, Stellenbosch

☎ 021 887 4608; www.oudewerfhotel.co.za

WHALE COAST

The Marine RRR

This luxury hotel has an outstanding position overlooking Walker Bay. Furnishings are lavish with marble bathrooms and chandeliers.

Facilities include a spacious garden with a heated pool, two restaurants and a spa. *In front is Hermanus's tidal pool where you can swim just 100m (330ft) from a whale, if you're lucky.* **Insider Tip**

✚ 205 D2

✉ Marine Drive, Hermanus

☎ 028 313 1000; www.marine-hermanus.co.za

GARDEN ROUTE

African Ocean Manor RR–RRR

This stylish guest house on the beachfront offers its guests a fantastic view of the ocean. There are only nine rooms and suites, the facilities include a swimming pool and a *braai* area and the breakfast is excellent.

✚ 197 D1

✉ Bouwer Crescent, Mossel Bay

☎ 044 695 1846; africanoceans.co.za

The Point Hotel R

The Point Hotel has a prime position perched on the rocks with an unbeatable view of the ocean and you may spot whales in season. There are 48 modern rooms with full facilities. The Lighthouse Restaurant is just below St Blaize lighthouse.

✚ 197 D1

✉ Point Road, Mossel Bay

☎ 044 691 3512; www.pointhotel.co.za

Moontide Guest Lodge R

This is an intimate guest house on the edge of Wilderness National Park. Rooms are in thatched cottages lovingly decorated with

African art. If you fancy something different, you can sleep in a converted boathouse or a unique tree house. Hike in the park or take a canoe out on the lagoon.
🔗 197 D2 ✉ Southside Lane, Wilderness
☎ 044 877 0361; www.moontide.co.za

Phantom Forest Eco-Reserve RRR
Set high up in the forest, the Reserve comprises a delightful collection of elevated wooden tree suites with outdoor showers, giant double-ended baths and Moroccan-inspired furnishings. A pool and Jacuzzi are on a wooden deck, and dining tables are set among the trees. One of Africa's leading green hotels.
🔗 197 D1 ✉ 7km (4mi) west of Knysna
☎ 044 386 0046; www.phantomforest.com

PORT ELIZABETH

Hacklewood Hill Country House RRR
In a Victorian manor in the suburb of Walmer, Hacklewood Hill is decorated with antiques and paintings, and has beautiful English-style gardens. It is a romantic, intimate place to stay, with just eight immaculate rooms. There's a fine cordon bleu restaurant with an impressive collection of vintage wines.
🔗 197 F2
✉ 152 Prospect Road, Port Elizabeth
☎ 041 581 1300; www.hacklewood.co.za

WILD COAST

Buccaneers Backpackers R
Overlooking the beach, this rural backpacker hostel has a rustic feel with wooden-decked bar and a restaurant surrounded by a forest full of birds. There are cosy dorms, doubles, self-catering cottages, or you can camp on platforms beneath the trees. The hostel can organize tours throughout the Wild Coast and sports equipment is available for rental.
🔗 198 C2 ✉ Cintsa
☎ 043 734 3012; www.cintsa.com

Where to...
Eat and Drink

Prices
Expect to pay for a two-course meal per person excluding drinks:
R under R150 **RR** R150–R300 **RRR** over R300

WINELANDS

Eight Restaurant RR
This award-winning restaurant on the Spier wine estate is housed in a renovated farm barn with an interior that features contemporary décor made from recycled materials. The menu offers gourmet dishes made with seasonal ingredients sourced from the farm or locally. Guests can also enjoy a pre-booked picnic basket (order online at picnics.spier.co.za) from the restaurant's deli, Eight to Go.
🔗 204 B3
✉ Spier Estate, R310 south of Stellenbosch
☎ 021 809 1188;
www.spier.co.za/food/eight-restaurant
🕐 Tue–Sun noon–4:30, Thu–Sat 6pm–10pm

Reuben's RRR
Food lovers from Cape Town make the 45-minute trip to Franschhoek for lunch here at the weekends. The natural-stone-coloured building

is warmed by log fires in winter, while tables spill on to the street in summer. Dishes are refreshingly simple and really delicious.

➕ 194 C2 ✉ 19 Huguenot Street, Franschhoek
☎ 021 876 3772; www.reubens.co.za
🕐 Daily 9–3, 7–9

WHALE COAST

Bientang's Cave RR
Down a steep staircase from Hermanus's cliff top, this restaurant is partially concealed in a cave and the stone platform is on the ocean's edge; it is the perfect vantage point for whale-watching in season.

➕ 205 D2 ✉ Below Marine Drive, Hermanus
☎ 028 312 3454; www.bientangscave.com
🕐 Daily 11:30–8 (weather permitting); reservations recommended

Mogg's Country Cookhouse RR
In the beautiful Hemel-en-Aarde (Heaven and Earth) Valley, just a short drive from Hermanus, this welcoming family restaurant serves a hearty but imaginative selection of country food. The menu varies daily but expect a selection of tasty casseroles, venison dishes and roasts. Reservations are advised.

➕ 205 D2
✉ Hemel-en-Aarde Road, Hermanus
☎ 076 314 0671; www.moggscookhouse.com
🕐 Wed–Sun noon–2:30pm, dinner by arrangement only

GARDEN ROUTE

34° South RR
This is a very casual, laid-back spot with a wooden deck overlooking Knysna Lagoon. You make up a meal from the treats in the packed fridges in the deli or choose from the long menu of mezes and platters. Look for specials such as seafood paella, Cajun ostrich or seared tuna. Cookbooks and wine are sold in the shop.

➕ 197 D1 ✉ Knysna Quays, Knysna
☎ 044 382 7331; www.34south.biz
🕐 Daily 8:30am–11:30pm

Café Gannet RRR
The Protea Hotel's modern Café Gannet is an excellent seafood restaurant with a terrace that has a lovely view over the bay and the Outeniqua mountain range. It is right next to the Bartolomeu Dias Museum, and the staff is welcoming and friendly. The waiters will list the daily specials that are not printed on the menu; ask for the catch of the day or try their famous seafood casserole. The menu also features oysters, sushi and a few meat dishes, including ostrich.

➕ 197 D1
✉ Old Post Tree Square, Mossel Bay
☎ 044 691 3738; www.oldposttree.co.za
🕐 Daily noon–3, 7–10

PORT ELIZABETH & AROUND

Die Walskipper RR
With a simple corrugated-iron roof, shade cloth, and enamel tin plates and cups, this casual restaurant on the beach is a great place to kick your shoes off in the sand and enjoy the ocean views. The simple, tasty food includes sensibly priced seafood and meat, such as lamb shanks, crocodile, and ostrich.

➕ 197 F1
✉ Marina Martinique, Jeffrey's Bay
☎ 042 292 0005; www.walskipper.co.za
🕐 Tue–Sat noon–8, Sun until 3

EAST LONDON

Grazia RR
Its elevated position overlooking the Esplanade means that the tables on the terrace fill up quickly in the evening. This is not only due to the sea view but also because the spacious, tiled interior is rather noisy. However, the food is excellent. The cuisine is Italian with an eclectic mix of other influences – from game to seafood there is something for everyone.

➕ 198 C2 ✉ Upper Esplanade
☎ 043 722 2009; www.graziafinefood.co.za
🕐 Daily 11:30–3, 6:30–10:30

Where to…
Shop

WINELANDS

The most interesting shop in Stellenbosch is **Oom Samie se Winkel** or Uncle Samie's Shop (84 Dorp Street; tel: 021 887 0797), an old-fashioned general store, barely altered since it opened 150 years ago.

Most of Stellenbosch's other shops are centrally situated between Merriman Avenue, Bird and Dorp streets and only 15 minutes away is the region's largest shopping centre, **Somerset Mall** (tel: 021 852 7114/5; www.somerset-mall.co.za) on the N2 in Somerset West.

A must-stop is the gorgeous **Eight to Go Deli** on the Spier wine estate south of Stellenbosch (➤ 73), which is full to the brim of African products, often locally made.

In Franschhoek visit **Huguenot Fine Chocolates** (62 Huguenot Street; tel: 021 876 4096; www. huguenotchocolates.com). The staff are trained in chocolate making, and the shop produces a delicious range of hand-crafted chocolates.

The village centre boasts an array of art shops and galleries, including the **Moór Gallery** (4 Bordeaux Street, www.moorgalleryfranschhoek.co.za), which showcases local and international artists.

Also worth a visit is **Franschhoek Live Craft Centre** (Huguenot Road; tel: 021 876 4092), where you watch the resident potter and other craftsmen produce their items and also buy their handicraft.

For serious wine enthusiasts there is **La Cotte Inn** (Main Road; tel: 021 876 3775; www.lacotte.co.za), with a mind-boggling collection of Cape wines complemented by a vast array of local and imported cheeses.

Meander down Main Street in Paarl where there are soft furnishing, antiques and gift shops.

WHALE COAST

Hermanus has an interesting variety of shops and art galleries tucked away in unexpected places and the **Fisherman's Village Craft Market** (8:30–3) is held every weekend at Lemm's Corner. Enjoy the market hustle and bustle as you browse the crafts, curios and antiques, you'll be sure to find the perfect souvenir.

The biggest mall is **Gateway Centre** with the usual chain stores.

GARDEN ROUTE

The towns along the Garden Route have a wide selection of shops selling anything from beachwear to African trinkets. **The Garden Route Mall** (tel: 044 887 0044; www.gardenroutemall.co.za) is the biggest in the region, and is conveniently located on the N2 at the turn-off to George. It has in excess of 125 shops and restaurants.

Knysna is well known for its artists and craftsmen and there are galleries throughout the town and many shops around the waterfront development; roadside stalls sell carved wooden figures and drums. The **Knysna African Arts & Craft Market** is on the corner of George Rex Street and Vigilance Drive.

Knysna is also famous for its furniture made from indigenous timber, and **Timber Village** (tel: 044 382 5649; www.timbervillage.co.za), in the Welbedacht Valley 3km (2mi) from Knysna, is home to a community of wood craftsmen.

In Plettenberg Bay, the main mall is **Melville's Corner**, and be sure to visit the **Old Nick Village** on the N2 (tel: 044 533 1395; www.oldnickvillage.co.za) for the galleries, studios, a weaving museum and a restaurant in lush gardens.

PORT ELIZABETH & AROUND

Jeffrey's Bay, as South Africa's surfing capital, has factory outlets for the international surf brands **Billabong** (2a Da Gama Road; tel: 042 200 2640) and **Quiksilver** (10 St Croix Street; tel: 042 293 4116; www.quiksilver.co.za).

Port Elizabeth is a large city and has several giant shopping malls with the **Boardwalk Casino and Entertainment World** (www. suninternational.com) on the beachfront in Summerstrand being one of the most popular.

WILD COAST

Hemingways Mall (www.heming waysmall.co.za) in East London has over 200 stores, while the Wild Coast town of Mthatha has the **Eastern Cape Arts and Crafts Hub** (51 Vlunindlela Heights; tel: 047 531 3682) selling items produced in the region. It also includes a fashion design centre that combines traditional designs with modern influences.

Where to...
Go Out

MUSIC, THEATRE & FESTIVALS

Stellenbosch's **AmaZink Township Theatre** (118A Masithandane Street/ Khayamandi; tel: 083 758 1457; www.facebook.com/amazinklive) offers an authentic township theatre experience while the **Stellenbosch International Chamber Music Festival** (tel: 021 889 9158; www.sicmf.co.za) in September concentrates on art exhibitions and chamber music.

In Hermanus, the **Whale Festival** (tel: 071 606 3261;http://hermanus whalefestival.co.za) in September draws theatre, and musical and dancing groups, many of which perform on the street.

The **Barns Theatre** in Mossel Bay (tel: 044 698 1022; www.thebarns. co.za) is in an actual barnyard on a farm 3km (2mi) from town.

See cabaret, theatre and music in Knysna during July's 10-day **Oyster Festival** (www.oysterfestival. co.za) and at the 5-day gay **Pink Loerie Mardi Gras** (www.pinkloerie. co.za), held end April/early May.

There are several live performance venues in Port Elizabeth and festivals include a **Shakespearean Festival** (tel: 044 382 0386; www. facebook.com/PEShakespeare) in February and the four-day **Nelson Mandela Bay Splash Festival** (tel: 041 393 4844; www.splashfestival. com) over the Easter weekend.

South Africa's not-to-be-missed festival is the 10-day **National Arts Festival** (www.nationalartsfestival. co.za) held in Grahamstown (June/ July).

NIGHTLIFE

Nightlife is limited in the rural areas but the towns have a few nightspots. Stellenbosch is a student town so nightclubs come and go.

Aandklas (43 Bird Street; tel: 021 883 3545; twitter.com/aand klas) gets packed with students who come for the grungy bands and cheap beer on tap.

Mossel Bay is home to the **Garden Route Casino** (www.garden routecasino.co.za), and Knysna has thriving nightlife with more than 50 pubs and restaurants including the perennially popular **Zanzibar Cocktail Lounge** (Main Road; tel: 044 382 0386; www. zanzibarknysna.com).

Port Elizabeth's nightlife is based in the **Boardwalk Casino and Entertainment World** (tel: 041 507 7777; www.suninternational. com; daily 24 hours).

KwaZulu-Natal

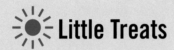 Little Treats

Spicy Street Food

For the most delicious bunny chow (a half loaf filled with curry) head to the little shops around **Durban's** (➤ 100) Victoria Street Market.

From Yesteryear

En route to the Sani Pass is the **Himeville Museum** (➤ 97), one of the country's top rural museums, with a wide range of exhibits and knowledgeable, enthusiastic staff.

High Point

Take a guided one-day tour up the spectacular **Sani Pass** (➤ 97) for some expansive views of the Drakensberg Mountains.

Getting Your Bearings

With a tropical climate, long sandy beaches, pristine wilderness areas and beautiful mountains, the highlight of KwaZulu-Natal is the diversity of its landscapes. It is also home to more game reserves than any other province in South Africa. The area's abundant natural water supply also contributed to its development, with 21 per cent of the population living here – the majority being Zulu. The original Zulu Kingdom was extended and consolidated with the creation of the province. The Durban metropolitan area is the province's largest city and its economic and administrative centre. It is also the centre of South Africa's Indian population with about 80 per cent living here.

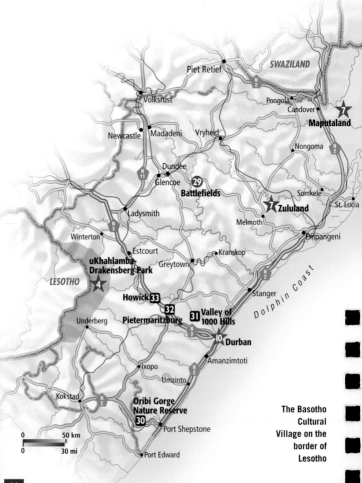

The Basotho Cultural Village on the border of Lesotho

The largest (almost 10.7 million) ethnic group in South Africa is the Zulu, and in the early 19th century, King Shaka led them in violent warfare, conquering and controlling large parts of southern Africa. The Zulu's oldest political rivals are the Xhosa. In 1994, animosities between the two groups went so far that their leader, Mangosuthu Buthelezi, risked a civil war to prevent a Xhosa-dominated ANC. It was only after Nelson Mandela succeeded in including Buthelezi in the government, that the unrest came to an end. Today, the majority of Zulu are members of the Inkatha Freedom Party (IFP), an opposition party that is open to other ethnic groups. The party recently won 2.4% of the votes in the 2014 elections and ten seats in the South African parliament.

Durban and the southern coast are heavily populated with a string of holiday resorts. The north coast, by contrast, is relatively untouched with much of it protected in parks and reserves. The most important of which is the iSimangaliso Wetland Park (formerly the Greater St Lucia Wetland Park), today a UNESCO World Heritage Site listed for its exceptional biodiversity.

Inland the N3 highway heads north from Durban to Johannesburg through the pretty farmlands of the Natal Midlands, which have the charm of a bygone era. To the southwest and encircling Lesotho, the mountains in the uKhahlamba-Drakensberg Park soar to over 3,000m (9,800ft). To the northeast the now peaceful rolling green pastures and historic towns of the Battlefields region testify to the bloody 19th-century wars between the Zulus, the British and the Boers. The Boers (*boere* is Afrikaans for farmer) are the descendants of the 17th-century Dutch settlers of the Cape. This group still represent an important part of South Africa's white minority, and retain their customs, language (Afrikaans) and the traditions of the Dutch Reformed Church.

MOÇAMBIQUE

TOP 10

Don't Miss

At Your Leisure

Seven Perfect Days

If you are not quite sure where to begin your travels, this itinerary recommends seven practical and enjoyable days in KwaZulu-Natal, taking in some of the best places to see. For more information see the main entries (➤ 94–107).

Day 1

Begin the day by taking a stroll along the beachfront in ⭐**Durban** (➤ 100) to watch the beach babes and surf rats, or take a ride on a brightly coloured rickshaw. Then in the afternoon, head out to Durban North to visit the **Umgeni River Bird Park** (➤ 101) to watch the birds perform in the free-flight show or, alternatively, take a tour of the **31 Valley of 1,000 Hills** (➤ 106). Spend the evening in Durban. Grab an authentic Indian curry and relax in one of the stylish bars in Morningside or Berea.

Day 2

Head north up the coast through the sugar plantations to ⭐**Zululand** (➤ 98) and stop at **Shakaland** (➤ 98) for something to eat and a glimpse of the Zulu way of life. After lunch, head into the **Hluhluwe-iMfolozi National Park** (➤ 98) for a late afternoon game drive. Spend the night in the reserve and enjoy the sweeping views from the veranda and bar at Hluhluwe's Hilltop Camp.

Day 3

Go out on an early morning game drive on the hunt for rhino and other interesting species. In the afternoon, drive to **St Lucia** (➤ 93) and visit the idyllic coast at Cape Vidal for a few hours or take a cruise on Lake St Lucia.

Spend the night in a peaceful lodge near the village of Hluhluwe or on the western shores of Lake St Lucia.

Day 4

Continue north to one of the province's lesser-known parks: Mkhuze or one of the remote parks in northern ★**Maputaland** (➤98). In Mkhuze arrange to go on a two-hour escorted game walk or settle in at a hide overlooking a waterhole. Spend the night at the beachside lodges and go looking for turtles by moonlight.

Day 5

Head east into the Natal Midlands and the **㉙Battlefields** (➤104) region around Dundee. Take a tour of **Isandlwana** (➤104) and the other battlefield sites and visit the museums. Then spend the night in a lodge or hotel which has a resident guide to get an insightful low-down on the battlefield stories.

Day 6

Drive to the Royal Natal National Park in the ★**uKhahlamba-Drakensberg Park** (left; ➤95) in the morning and gawp at the Amphitheatre rock formation. Stay in one of the luxury mountain resorts or move on to Didima Camp at Cathedral Peak in the afternoon. Enjoy dinner overlooking spectacular mountain scenery and, if your room has one, cosy up to the fireplace.

Day 7

Visit the **San Rock Art Centre** (➤96) at Didima Camp in the morning, then make your way to the resorts in the southern Berg or join the N3 and drive back to Durban in the afternoon. Break your journey by visiting the falls at **㉝Howick** (➤107) or the attractive city of **㉜Pietermaritzburg** (➤107). Head back to the coast for a buffet dinner and Durban harbour cruise with **La Vue** (Wilson's Wharf, departure: Wed–Sat at 7pm, www.la-vue.co.za).

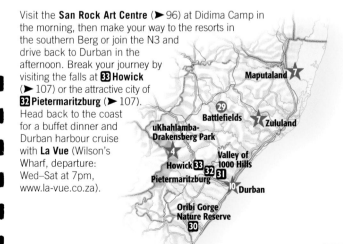

★4 uKhahlamba-Drakensberg Park

The Drakensberg traverses over 1,000km (620mi) inland from the South African Highlands down to the eastern coast. Its northern part, the Transvaal Drakensberg, includes the Blyde River Canyon Nature Reserve while the its southern part, the Natal Drakensberg, has dramatic craggy mountains, that soar more than 3,000m (10,000ft) and clear, secluded lakes. The area was proclaimed a UNESCO World Heritage Site in 2000 for its natural beauty.

The name, meaning "dragon mountains" in Afrikaans, was coined when an early farmer reported seeing a dragon flying above the misty peaks. The area is divided into three sections: the Northern Berg with the Royal Natal National Park, the Central Berg (Champagne Castle, Cathedral Peak, Giants Castle) and the Southern Berg (Loteni Nature Reserve, Kamberg Nature Reserve, Mzimkulwana Nature Reserve). The uKhahlamba-Drakensberg Park encompasses 12 nature reserves and covers an area of 2,500km² (965mi²). The Zulu name *uKhahlamba* means "fortress wall of spears", an appropriate description of the towering mountains and their near vertical cliffs and buttresses. Each park has its own scenic attractions and accommodation in the way of a camp managed by **KZN Wildlife**, but you can also opt to stay over in the other more exclusive country hotels nearby. Access depends on which direction you're coming from, but most people approach from the N3 highway that links Johannesburg and Durban from where there are many roads heading west into the mountains.

PEAK CONDITION
Cathedral Peak
3,004m (9,850ft)
Champagne Castle
3,377m (11,075ft)
Cathkin Peak
3,149m (10,330ft)
Giant's Castle
3,314m (10,870ft)
Mont-aux-Sources
3,282m (10,765ft)

Rural village life in the Drakensberg, about 40km/25mi west of Winterton

The Devil's Tooth rock formation, part of the Amphitheatre, in the Northern Berg

Northern Berg

One of the best parks in the Northern Berg is the **Royal Natal National Park**, which is dominated by the view to the famous **Amphitheatre**; a 5km (3mi) sheer cliff rising 1,000m (3,280ft) between two brooding mountains. The impressive **Tugela Falls**, the world's second highest water-fall, plunges 947m (3,110ft) down the rock wall and there's a spectacularly beautiful hike to the top of the Amphitheatre, which starts at the Mahai Camp parking area. It takes about five hours to do the return trip, and the trail, which includes a scramble up two chain ladders, takes you to the top of the **Tugela Falls**. This is by far the easiest day hike to the top of the Drakensberg escarpment.

Insider Tip

ROCK ART

The San (▶ 32), also known as the Bushmen, were hunters and gatherers that roamed the uKhahlamba-Drakensberg Mountains for thousands of years before the Boer and Zulu people arrived in the 19th century. Today all that remains of the San culture in South Africa is the unique legacy of their rock art (paintings, engravings and carvings). Some of the uKhahlamba-Drakensberg Park rock art was done in the last 300 years, but overlays pigments dating back 4,000 years. The works are found in sites connected to ritual use and were made using pigment mixed from antelope blood and other organic materials such as plant sap, clay and burnt wood. Some of the art relates to the San spirit realm and the most frequently depicted animal, the eland (*Taurotragus oryx*), reflects its great mythological significance. There are over 35,000 documented rock paintings scattered around the park.

Central Berg

South of Royal Natal in the Central Berg, **Mlambonja Wilderness Area** is accessed from Winterton. The peaks offer challenging hikes and this is one of the best places to learn about the San rock paintings in the uKhahlamba-Drakensberg Park. At the **San Rock Art Centre** at Didima Camp a reconstructed cave shows reproductions of some of the paintings.

Further south, the road to the **Mdedelelo Wilderness Area** and **Monk's Cowl** is dotted with luxury resorts and is dubbed Champagne Valley. It's where the **Central Drakensberg Information Centre** is located, and is home to the exclusive boarding school of the world-renowned **Drakensberg Boys' Choir**, who perform for visitors once a week during term time.

Nottingham Road is the access town to the **Mkhomazi Wilderness Area** where the tallest mountain in southern Africa, **Thabana-Ntlenyana** (3,482m/11,420ft) over the border in Lesotho, is clearly visible. Trout fishing is popular in the foothills of the **Kamberg Nature Reserve** where there is another **San Rock Art Centre** from where you can take a guided walk to see some paintings.

San rock art often depicts animals and human figures

Southern Berg

Underberg and **Himeville**, with one of the finest rural museums in South Africa, are the gateway to the Southern Berg region. Here the rugged **Sani Pass** (the only eastern road into Lesotho) winds up an increasingly narrow V-shaped valley flanked by towering buttresses. You can go on an organized four-wheel drive day excursion over into Lesotho or walk up. At the top is a village where you can meet the friendly Basotho people.

A crystal-clear waterfall in the wooded foothills of the Drakensberg Mountains

TAKING A BREAK

Sip a glass of tea and take in the views from the **Sani Mountain Lodge** (tel: 078 634 7496; www.sanimountain. co.za; RR–RRR) at the top of Sani Pass.

➕ 203 D1

KZN Wildlife
☎ 033 845 1000; www.kznwildlife.com

Didima San Rock Art Centre
✉ Didima Camp ☎ 036 488 8025; www.didima.info 🕐 Daily 8–6 💲 R60

Central Drakensberg Information Centre
✉ Thokozisa Centre, R600 ☎ 036 488 1207; www.cdic.co.za 🕐 Daily 9–5

Drakensberg Boys' Choir
✉ R600 ☎ 036 468 1012; http://dbchoir.com/web/
🕐 Concerts 3:30 Wednesdays during term time 💲 R120

Himeville Museum
✉ Arbuckle Street ☎ 033 702 1184 🕐 Tue–Sat 9–3, Sun 9–12:30 💲 Free

Kamberg San Rock Art Interpretive Centre
✉ Kamberg Nature Reserve ☎ 033 267 7251
🕐 Daily tours 8:30, 11 and 1:30 💲 R40

INSIDER INFO

- There are hundreds of **hikes** through the mountains. Most people stay at KZN Wildlife camps and hike for the day but you can go on overnight trails and stay in huts and caves.
- You must carry your **passport** with you when hiking close to the Lesotho border or to complete the ascent of Sani Pass whether by road or on foot.
- Keen birdwatchers should book the **Lammergeyer Hide** at Giant's Castle through KZN Wildlife (tel: 036 353 37 18; R1,100). Lammergeyers are one of the world's rarest vultures and they live in isolated high mountain crags.

Insider Tip

Insider Tip

KwaZulu-Natal

⭐ Zululand & Maputaland

The holiday resorts on the north KwaZulu-Natal coast taper out to wetlands, lagoons, forests and isolated beaches where turtles, dolphins, sharks and even crocodiles frolic.

Game is harboured in several protected areas, and this is also the traditional stronghold of the Zulu people.

Eshowe, about 150km (95mi) north of Durban, is the gateway to Zululand. About 15km (9mi) further north of Eshowe is **Shakaland**, a popular Zulu theme park, named after King Shaka, founder of the 19th-century empire for which the region is named. Here you can tour a traditional village and eat local specialities. Further north, the **Hluhluwe-iMfolozi National Park** was instrumental in saving the white rhino from extinction. Today it is home to an estimated population of 1,600 white and 400 black rhino along with the Big Five and many other animals.

The **iSimangaliso Wetland Park**, a UNESCO World Heritage Site, protects a mosaic of forest, savannah, dune, mangrove, freshwater and marine habitats centred on a series of coastal wetlands running north from the St Lucia Estuary – one of the few places on earth where hippos, crocodiles and bull sharks share the same water. Set at the estuary mouth, **St Lucia** village is a useful springboard for hiking around the lake, exploring by boat, or driving the 40km (24mi) to the stunning beach and rock pools at Cape Vidal, with a chance of spotting reedbuck, kudu or zebra en route. For more reliable game viewing, **Mkhuze Game Reserve** harbours rhino, elephant and a renowned diversity of birds in what amounts to a western extension of the wetland park.

Above: A close encounter in the iSimangaliso Wetland Park

Below: Fishing from the shore in St Lucia

Set in an area known as **Maputaland**, the remote north of the iSimangaliso Wetland Park consists of a narrow strip of coastland running for 100km (62mi) from the estuary's northern tip to the Mozambique border. The best-known site here is Sodwana Bay, where Africa's southernmost coral reefs attract whales, sharks and turtles. Further north still, the idyllic Kosi Bay features mangrove swamps, dunes, wetlands and a variety of birds and animals including hippos and crocodiles.

West of Kosi Bay, the **Lubombo Transfrontier Conservation Area** is a cross-border reserve linking South Africa's Ndumo

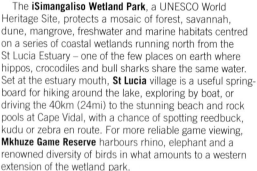

Game Reserve and Tembe Elephant Park to Mozambique's Maputo Special Reserve via the Futi Corridor. Home to one of South Africa's last free-ranging elephant populations, Tembe has been subject to an extensive programme of reintroductions and is now home to the Big Five. Many local enthusiasts rate the birdwatching opportunities to be the best in the country.

TAKING A BREAK

The restaurant in St Lucia's **Elephant Lake Hotel** (tel: 035 590 1001; www.elephantlakestlucia.co.za; RR) is a great spot for a meal or drink in view of the estuary and within earshot of its grunting hippos.

➕ 203 E2 (Zululand); 203 F2 (Maputaland)
ℹ️ Information for all parks: www.kznwildlife.com
🕐 Oct–Mar daily 5am–7pm; Apr–Sep 6–6

Shakaland
➕ 203 E1 (Eshowe) ✉️ R66 near Eshowe
☎️ 035 460 0912; http://aha.co.za/shakaland
🕐 Daily 11–2 💰 R560, lunch included

Hluhluwe-iMfolozi National Park
➕ 203 F2 ✉️ 280km (174mi) north of Durban
☎️ 035 562 0848; www.kznwildlife.com
🕐 Nov–Feb daily 5am–7pm; Mar–Oct 6–6 💰 R210

iSimangaliso Wetland Park
➕ 203 F2 ✉️ 245km (152mi) north of Durban
☎️ 035 590 1633; http://isimangaliso.com
🕐 Times vary at different locations within the park 💰 R45

Mkhuze Game Reserve
➕ 203 F2 ✉️ 335km (208mi) north of Durban
☎️ 033 845 1000; www.kznwildlife.com
🕐 Oct–Mar daily 5am–7pm; Apr–Sep 6–6 💰 R45

Lubombo Transfrontier Conservation Area
➕ 203 F2 ✉️ Turn off the N2 at Jozini and follow road signs
☎️ 035 572 1560; www.peaceparks.org
🕐 Oct–Mar daily 5am–7pm; Apr–Sep 6–6 💰 R40

INSIDER INFO

- Zululand is **ideal for self-driving** but visits to locations north of Sodwana Bay and east of N2 are best organized by the lodges in the region.
- Consider staying in good value self-catering accommodation in the parks.
- With its pristine sandy beaches and forested dunes 🏨 **Sodwana Bay** in the iSimangaliso Wetland Park is ideal for a family outing. Remember to take your snorkel and fins – the coral reefs are legendary – and you may be lucky enough to spot a turtle.

⭐10 Durban

Durban is South Africa's third largest city (after Johannesburg and Cape Town), a modern, vibrant and colourful metropolis with an unmistakeably African and Asian feel to it. It boasts a subtropical climate, stylish cafés, chic restaurants and bars and some good shopping opportunities in its upmarket suburbs – and wide golden beaches that stretch endlessly along the warm Indian Ocean.

In December 1497 Vasco da Gama sailed along the coast and, as he saw the bay on Christmas Day, he named it Port Natal. It was not until 1823, when a few British traders set up a settlement, that the area developed into a port and trading centre for ivory. In 1835 the British renamed the settlement Durban in honour of Sir Benjamin D'Urban, governor of the Cape Colony. Durban grew quickly in the 1860s when the British brought in thousands of Indian indentured labourers to work the region's sugar plantations. Today part of the greater eThekweni municipality, Durban has the largest Indian community in Africa, and original shopping arcades of Indian traders thrive around Victoria, Queen and Grey streets. The **Juma Masjid Mosque** is the largest mosque in the southern hemisphere, and **Victoria Street Market** sells Indian spices and snacks. The old neo-baroque City Hall is now home to the **Natural Science Museum** and to **Durban Art Gallery**, with a fine collection of European-style paintings and a wide range of African art.

The ornate 19th-century Da Gama Clock on Victoria Embankment

    West of the centre is **KwaMuhle Museum** in what was the notorious Department of Native Affairs during apartheid; exhibits show the oppressive administration of the black population of Durban during the 20th century. On the port side of the city on Victoria Embankment is the Victorian **Da Gama Clock**, erected to commemorate the 400th anniversary of the Portuguese seafarer sighting the bay. Further down the embankment is the shopping mall at **Wilson's**

Durban is known as Surf City

Modern skyscrapers tower above colonial buildings in Durban's centre

Wharf and the **Yacht Mole** where you can watch the comings and goings of a huge variety of craft, see the harbour at work and buy fresh fish from the fish shop.

The Golden Mile: Durban's beachfront

The Golden Mile extends along Marine Parade (between Snell Parade and Erskine Parade) and the beachfront is lined with hotels, high-rise apartments, restaurants and bars. Look out for the rickshaw pullers with their giant hats and vibrant costumes: you can bargain with them for a short ride (about R40 per person for a 5-minute ride; photographs cost extra). The beach is wide and sandy and there are demarcated areas for swimming, sunbathing and surfing, and it's punctuated with a number of piers that are popular with anglers. The paved promenade has various attractions strung along it from waterslides and saltwater paddling pools to snake parks and fairground rides.

The **uShaka Marine World** has aquariums, a dolphinarium and seal tank, and on Battery Beach, the **Suncoast Casino and Entertainment World** has restaurants, a multi-screen cinema, a boardwalk and Waterworld with a variety of slides.

Outlying Attractions

On the Umgeni River in Durban North, the **Umgeni River Bird Park** has a spectacular collection of more than 800 exotic and indigenous birds to view from a network of paths. The highlight is the free-flight show when the larger raptors, cranes, storks and owls hop on to a stage and fly over the audience as a presenter introduces them.

In Berea the **Durban Botanic Gardens** have subtropical plants, orchids and a collection of cycads. There is a fine tea-room, pleasant picnic spots and the Japanese Gardens have an enchanting atmosphere with ponds and oriental designs.

Further north, **Umhlanga Rocks** has a couple of worth-while diversions. Lose yourself for a few hours in **Gateway** (▶ 111), the largest shopping mall in the southern hemisphere. Alternatively, visit the **KwaZulu-Natal Sharks Board**,

KwaZulu-Natal

a one-of-its-kind institution that looks after more than 400 shark nets along 50 beaches on the KwaZulu-Natal coast. You can visit the information centre to learn about **Insider Tip** sharks and arrange to go out on a boat with the staff to service the nets.

South of Durban

Resorts, holiday apartments and caravan (camper) parks follow the beaches south from Durban. The **Aliwal Shoal** and the wreck of the steamer Nebo that sank in 1884 lie 5km (3mi) off the coast of Umkomaas and are popular with scuba divers; ragged tooth sharks are often spotted. Further south the ribbon of development continues between **Scottburgh** and **Port Edward**, broken by banana and eucalyptus plantations. On offer here you will find diving, surfing or jet-skiing in the ocean and endless hours on the sandy beaches. **Margate**, one of the more upmarket resorts, is a popular holiday spot for people from Jo'burg. **Port Edward** with its palm-fringed beach marks the border with the Wild Coast in the Eastern Cape Province; crossing into the rural former homeland from the commercialized south coast of KwaZulu-Natal is quite a contrast.

The Royal Natal Yacht Club affords beautiful views of Durban's modern urban skyline at night

▪ TAKING A BREAK

Relax at the **BAT (Bartle Arts Trust) Centre's** café on Victoria Embankment for the fine harbour views, live music and craft shops (tel: 031 332 0451; www.batcentre.co.za; R).

✚ 203 E3

Tourist Junction
✉ 90 Florida Road ☎ 031 322 6164; www.durbanexperience.co.za
🕐 Mon–Fri 8–4:30, Sat, Sun 9–1

Natural Science Museum
✉ City Hall, 234 Anton Lembede Street ☎ 031 311 2256
🕐 Mon–Sat 8:30–4, Sun 11–4 👆 Free

Durban Art Gallery
✉ City Hall, 234 Anton Lembede Street ☎ 031 311 2264
🕐 Mon–Sat 8:30–4, Sun 11–4 👆 Free

KwaMuhle Museum
✉ 130 Bram Fischer Road ☎ 031 311 2237; http://durbanhistorymuseums.
org.za 🕐 Mon–Fri 8:30–4, Sat 8.30–12:30 👆 Free

uShaka Marine World
✉ Beachfront ☎ 031 328 8000; www.ushakamarineworld.co.za 🕐 9–5 👆 R209

Suncoast Casino and Entertainment World
✉ Marine Parade ☎ 031 328 3000; www.tsogosun.com

Umgeni River Bird Park
✉ 490 Riverside Road, Durban North ☎ 031 579 4600;
www.umgeniriverbirdpark.co.za 🕐 9–5, free-flight show 11 and 2 👆 R52

Durban Botanic Gardens
✉ Sydenham Road, Berea ☎ 031 309 9240; www.durbanbotanicgardens.org.za
🕐 Daily 7:30–5:15 👆 Free

KwaZulu-Natal Sharks Board
✉ Herrwood Drive ☎ 031 566 0400; www.shark.co.za 🕐 Mon–Fri 8–4 👆 R45

INSIDER INFO

- ▪ The **tourist office** organizes a range of guided walks through the city – make reservations a day in advance.
- ▪ Look out for the Durban speciality, **bunny chow** – half a loaf of bread with the middle scooped out and filled with curry.
- ▪ Surfers should use the **Baz Bus** (▶ 38) that runs the entire length of the south coast and drops off at hostels where surfboards are available to rent.
- ▪ At the 🎯 **Giba Gorge Mountain Bike Park** (110 Stockville Road, Westmead, on the N3 towards Pietermaritzburg; tel: 031 769 1527; www.gibagorge.co.za, 7–5; R60) the whole family can enjoy bike trails that cater for all abilities. The more adventurous can test out the BMX track. Bicycles are available to rent and there is also a campground.

Insider Tip

Insider Tip

㉙ Battlefields

In the Midlands, between the Drakensberg and the Natal coast on the Indian Ocean, lies Dundee. Once a coal mining town, it is now a good base for exploring the battlefield sites. The rolling hills witnessed numerous brutal, blood-soaked conflicts during the Zulu-Boer War (1838), the Anglo-Zulu War (1879) and the Anglo-Boer War (1899–1902).

The violent military clashes continued for over 70 years and there are more than 50 battlefield sites. There are 14 historic towns, including **Ladysmith** and **Dundee**, some informative museums. The area is best explored by self-driving or as part of a tour.

Blood River
The Battle of Blood River was one of the biggest battles during the Zulu-Boer War, when 460 Boers defeated 15,000 Zulus. The **Blood River Monument**, built in 1971 to commemorate the Boer victory, consists of 64 bronze Voortrekker wagons arranged as they were on the day of the famous battle. Also on display are replicas of the three cannons that proved so decisive in halting repeated Zulu charges. On the opposite side of the river, the **Ncome Museum**, built in 1998, explores the conflict from a Zulu perspective.

THE GREAT TREK
Voortrekkers (Afrikaans for "pioneers") is the name of the group of approximately 10,000 Boers who, dissatisfied with the banning of slavery, left the British Cape Colony from 1835 and migrated northwards into the interior. This move was known as the Great Trek and led to the founding of the Boer republics of Natalia, Oranje-Freistaat and Transvaal. As strong Calvinists they believed that they were predestined to salvation, something that was used to justify their land seizure and the subjugation of the indigenous people. The Boers moved into territories north of the Orange River and into an area held by the Zulu, which resulted in many bloody battles.

Isandlwana
The British were badly defeated at Isandlwana in 1879 during the Anglo-Zulu War, and at the foot of the isolated hill are the white-painted cairns marking the spot where British soldiers were buried. There's also a trail around the various memorials including the Zulu one, which is fashioned as a bronze Zulu victory necklace.

INSIDER INFO

- Blood River, Isandlwana, Rorke's Drift and Talana Hill, the principal battlefield sites, are all accessed off the R68 between Dundee and Ulundi.
- If you would like an **in-depth tour** of the battlefields, Endumeni Tourism (Victoria Street, Dundee; tel: 034 212 2121; www.tourdundee.co.za) can organize informative personal tour guides to come with you in your own car. Alternatively they can recommend a lodge with a resident historian.

Reminders of a turbulent past: one of four cannons outside the Siege Museum in Ladysmith

Rorke's Drift

At Rorke's Drift the tiny museum displaying pictures of the battle and war memorabilia is housed in the mission station where 4,000 Zulus attacked a small garrison of British soldiers in 1879.

Talana Hill

In 1899, during the Anglo-Boer War, the British were attacked at Talana Hill near Dundee after which they retreated to Ladysmith where they were held under siege by the Boers for 118 days. Today you can visit the **Talana Hill Museum**, which is set in an 8ha (20-acre) park and has 17 buildings (so allow for half a day). The main museum covers the history of the battlefields while smaller buildings have displays on glass, beads and early coal mining in the region. The **Siege Museum** in Ladysmith has a varied collection of war memorabilia and a bookshop.

TAKING A BREAK

Sit down for a cuppa in the **Miners' Rest** restaurant, housed in a 1914 corrugated iron miner's home at Talana Hill Museum.

Ncome Museum
➕ 203 D1 ✉ 48km (30mi) from Dundee toward Vryheid ☎ 034 271 8121; www.ncomemuseum.co.za
🕐 Daily 8–4:30 ✋ Free

Isandlwana
➕ 203 E2 ✉ 80km (50mi) southeast of Dundee ☎ 034 271 8165
🕐 Mon–Fri 8–4, Sat, Sun 9–4
✋ R35

Rorke's Drift Museum
➕ 203 E2 ✉ 42km (26mi) southeast from Dundee, a road connects it to

Isandlwana 15km (9mi) away to the east ☎ 034 642 1687
🕐 Daily 9–4 ✋ R35

Talana Hill Museum
➕ 203 D2 ✉ R33, Dundee
☎ 034 212 2654; www.talana.co.za
🕐 Mon–Fri 8–4:30, Sat, Sun 9–4
✋ R30.20

Siege Museum
➕ 203 D2
✉ Murchison Street, Ladysmith
☎ 036 637 2992
🕐 Mon–Fri 9–4, Sat 9–1 ✋ R11

At Your Leisure

The undulating landscape of the Valley of 1,000 Hills

30 Oribi Gorge Nature Reserve

Formed by the Umzimkulwana River, the 400m-deep (1,312ft) Oribi Gorge has magnificent red-orange sandstone cliffs, which tower over a valley lined with trees, flowers and ferns. Several waterfalls gush into the river, which has rapids, pools and sandbanks. There are some well-marked hiking and mountain-bike trails, picnic spots, and horseback rides and white-water rafting are other options. If you are adventure-minded, you can try the 120m (400ft) zip line, go abseiling, or try the gorge swing that takes you on a 100m (330ft) arc into the gorge and past Lehr's Falls.

Insider Tip

🕂 199 D3
✉ Off the N2, 21km (13mi) from Port Shepstone
☎ 039 679 1644; www.kznwildlife.com
🕓 Daily 6:30am–7:30pm 💷 R30

Wild 5 Adventures (Wild Swing, Bungee)
☎ 082 566 74 24; www.wild5adventures.co.za

31 Valley of 1,000 Hills

The Valley of 1,000 Hills is a region along the R103 about 35km (22mi) from the northern outskirts of Durban where hundreds of low hills spill down to the Umgeni River and its tributaries. The highlights here are the undulating scenery of hillsides dotted with settlements and the opportunity to learn about Zulu culture. You can follow signs for the 1,000 Hills Experience to enjoy the views and stop at the many gift shops and tea gardens. At the **PheZulu Safari Park** is a reconstruction of a Zulu village with beehive huts; a guide will explain Zulu beliefs and rituals before a show of dancing. There's also an animal and reptile park, restaurant and curio shop.

🕂 199 E4

PheZulu Safari Park
✉ 5 Old Main Road, Botha's Hill
☎ 031 777 1000; www.phezulusafaripark.co.za
🕓 8:30–4:30; shows at 10, 11:30, 2 and 3:30
💷 dance shows R110, combined ticket R150; game drive R225

BEST BEACHES
KwaZulu-Natal boasts the highest number of Blue Flag beaches in South Africa.
- Addington Beach, Durban
- Bay of Plenty Beach, Durban
- Lucien Beach, south coast
- Ramsgate Main Beach, south coast
- San Lameer Beach, south coast
- South Beach, Durban
- Umhlanga Rocks Main Beach, Durban

The dramatic 95m (312ft) Howick Falls

🎏 FOR KIDS

Take a ride on a classic steam train with **Umgeni Steam Railway**. On the last Sunday of each month trains depart from Kloof Station to Inchanga return, and the three-hour ride through the picturesque landscape is an impressive experience for adults and children alike (tel: 082 353 6003; www.umgenisteamrailway.com; R220; children R150).

🔟 Pietermaritzburg

With its beautiful Victorian brick buildings and tree-lined streets, Pietermaritzburg – once the administrative capital of the Colony of Natal – today still has an old-fashioned British town feel, were it not for its lively African street life. But with its large, vibrant Indian community, Asia also seems to be close at hand. Of interest are the Parliament Buildings built in 1887 with soaring columns and copper domes, and the City Hall built in 1900 entirely of red bricks and boasting some fine stained-glass windows. On Church Street is a statue of Gandhi, who travelled to South Africa in April 1893 to settle a legal dispute. He was forced to leave the train at Pietermaritzburg

after he was expelled from the whites only First Class (for which he had a valid ticket). This incident sparked off his idea of passive resistance. The **Voortrekker/Msunduzi Museum**, set in a 1905 former girls' school, houses an interesting local history section.

🗺 199 D4   🏠 177 Chief Albert Luthuli Street
☎ 033 345 1348; www.pmbtourism.co.za
🕐 Mon–Fri 8–5, Sat 8–1

Voortrekker/Msunduzi Museum
✉ 351 Langalibalele Street   ☎ 033 394 6834;
www.msunduzimuseum.org.za
🕐 Mon–Fri 9–4, Sat 9–1   💳 R10

🔟 Howick

The small unassuming rural town of Howick, 18km (11mi) north of Pietermaritzburg, is famous for two things – the attractive Howick Falls, and the place just out of town on a quiet country road where Nelson Mandela was arrested in 1962. The world's most famous political prisoner was disguised as a driver when he was stopped by police, who were working on a tip-off. It was these disguises that often led to him being described as the Black Pimpernel. Today a monument marks the spot. The Howick Falls dominate the centre of town where the Umgeni River spills dramatically 95m (312ft) into a gorge.

Insider Tip

🗺 199 D4   ✉ Follow the signposts from Main Road to the Howick Falls Viewpoint
☎ 033 330 5305   🕐 Daily 9:30–4

Midlands Meander Association
☎ 033 330 8195; www.midlandsmeander.co.za

KwaZulu-Natal

Where to…
Stay

Prices
Expect to pay per double room, per night
R under R1,500   **RR** R1,500–R2,500   **RRR** over R2,500

DURBAN

Concierge Hotel RR
This boutique hotel is a little tucked
away from the hustle and bustle.
It has twelve contemporary rooms,
some with verandas. Its small
garden courtyard makes it an oasis
of peace in the middle of the busy
metropolis; the adjoining Freedom
Café serves a selection of salads
and burgers. The quirky hotel's
designer credentials make it one
of the coolest places in town.
✚ 203 E1 ✉ 37–43 St Mary's Ave, Morningside
☎ 031 309 44 53; www.the-concierge.co.za

Quarters RR
A stylish boutique hotel in Durban's
stately Morningside suburb, Quarters
is housed in four restored Victorian
homes with lattice wrap-around
verandas, shady courtyards and
gardens full of tropical palms.
Each of the 25 rooms has been
individually decorated in unfussy
modern designs. There's a brasse-
rie that serves tasty, traditional
cuisine throughout the day and it's
in an excellent location right in the
middle of the restaurant district.
✚ 203 E1 ✉ 101 Florida Road, Morningside
☎ 031 303 5246; www.quarters.co.za

ZULULAND & MAPUTALAND

Ghost Mountain Inn R–RR
An informal and affordable 4-star
country inn in Mkuze village, just
20 minutes' drive from the only gate
to Mkhuze Game Reserve, Ghost
Mountain also makes a good springboard for overnight stays deeper in
Maputaland. The smartly decorated
rooms are scattered around the
garden. There's a pool, two pubs,
a restaurant and beauty spa.
✚ 203 F2 ✉ Mkhuze, off the N2
☎ 035 573 1025; www.ghostmountaininn.co.za

Hilltop Camp R–RR
This is the largest of camps run by
KZN Wildlife at Hluhluwe-iMfolozi
National Park, set in a stunning
location with fabulous views over the
bush. Accommodation is in simple
but comfortable self-catering chalets. Facilities include a central restaurant, bar and pool.
✚ 203 F2 ✉ In the northern Hluhluwe section of
the park ☎ 033 845 1000; www.kznwildlife.com

Kosi Forest Lodge RRR
Easily one of the most gorgeous
places to stay in KwaZulu-Natal,
this lodge is set in the shady sand
forest overlooking Lake Shengeza.
The 8 luxurious suites, scattered
among trees, are under wood and
canvas with open-air bathrooms
and lit by twinkling lanterns.
Activities include canoeing, fishing
and snorkelling.
✚ 203 F2 ✉ Kosi Bay Nature Reserve
☎ 035 474 1473; www.kosiforestlodge.co.za

Makakatana Bay Lodge RRR
Enjoy super luxury at one of the
few privately run lodges in the
iSimangaliso Wetland Park, set in
an idyllic dune forest. The six suites
are linked by elevated boardwalks
with private wooden decks and
outside showers.
✚ 203 F2 ✉ Off the Charters Creek road
☎ 035 550 4198; www.makakatana.co.za

BATTLEFIELDS

Isandlwana Lodge RR
This double-storey stone and thatch lodge is built on the rock where the Zulu commander stood when he started the Battle of Isandlwana. The lodge's 12 rooms have balconies and facilities include a well-appointed pool, restaurant and bar.
➕ 203 E2 ✉ 80km (50mi) southeast of Dundee
☎ 034 271 8301; www.isandlwana.co.za

MIDLANDS & UKHAHLAMBA-DRAKENSBERG

The Cavern RR
Adjacent to the Royal Natal National Park, the comfortable thatched cottages are scattered through mature gardens with mountain views. Rates represent excellent value as they include three meals a day.
➕ 203 D2
✉ Off the R74
☎ 036 438 6270 or 083 701 5724; www.cavern.co.za

Fordoun RRR
Fordoun lies between the central uKhahlamba-Drakensberg and Howick. The luxury rooms are in restored farm buildings. There's an intimate and lovingly decorated restaurant and the spa has all sorts of treats.
➕ 203 D1
✉ Nottingham Road
☎ 033 266 6217; http://fordoun.com

Where to...
Eat and Drink

Prices
Expect to pay for a two-course meal per person excluding drinks:
R under R150   **RR** R150–R300   **RRR** over R300

DURBAN

Mali's Indian Restaurant RR
Durban is famous for its authentic Indian food. At this restaurant set in a converted house you'll find a mix of north and south Indian dishes; some say it's the best Indian restaurant in town.
➕ 203 E1
✉ Smiso Nkwanyana Rd, Morningside
☎ 031 312 8535; www.facebook.com/malisindian
🕓 Tue–Sun 12:30–3:30, 5:30–10

Green Mango RR–RRR
This small, intimate restaurant in the Avonmore Centre serves excellent Japanese (very good sushi) and Thai cuisine. Try a Thai-styled grilled kebab or a spicy fish curry.
➕ 203 E1
✉ 9th Avenue, Avonmore Centre, Morningside
☎ 031 312 7054; www.thegreenmango.co.za
🕓 Daily noon–2:30, 6–9:30

Kashmir RR
An elegant restaurant (formal table settings, a rose on each table) with a veranda overlooking the sea. Serving mainly North Indian cuisine – the curries are considered the best Durban – and the bread is freshly baked (order the delicious garlic *naan*). Top-notch quality and excellent presentation.
➕ 203 E1
✉ 11 McCausland Crescent, Umhlanga Rock ☎ 031 561 7486; www.kashmir-restaurant.co.za
🕓 Daily noon–2:30, 6–10

KwaZulu-Natal

Ile Maurice RR–RRR
Positioned to take advantage of the sea views, and featuring island-style décor, this restaurant focuses mainly on freshly caught line fish and seafood dishes. The cuisine is a unique blend of South African and Mauritian recipes. There is also a selection of meat dishes and remember to save room for the tempting desserts; reservations essential.

🟥 203 E1
✉ 9 McCausland Cresent, Umhlanga Rocks
☎ 031 561 76 09 50 62;
http://ilemauricerestaurant.co.za
🕐 Tue–Sun noon–2:30, 6–9:30

Roma Revolving Restaurant RR
The décor is a little dated, but you can't beat the view over Durban Harbour 32 floors below. **[Insider Tip]** Delightfully old-fashioned set menus include the likes of prawn cocktail or pâté followed by steak, or pasta and something decadent from the dessert trolley. The à la carte menu offers more adventurous dishes. The restaurant takes an hour to complete its 360-degree circuit.

🟥 203 E1 ✉ Victoria Embankment
☎ 031 337 6707; www.roma.co.za
🕐 Mon–Sat 6–10 and Fri, Sat noon–2:30

MIDLANDS & UKHAHLAMBA-DRAKENSBERG

Bingelela Contemporary Classic Restaurant RR
Probably the best eatery in the Northern Berg, Bingelela is tucked away in a shady copse between Royal Natal National Park and the small town of Bergville. In an immense thatched construction complete with swimming pool, it has an imaginative menu dominated by the steak and trout, as well as a selection of excellent pizzas, cooked in a wood-fired pizza oven.

🟥 203 D1
✉ R74 about 4km (3mi) north of Bergville
☎ 036 448 1336; www.bingelela.co.za
🕐 Mon–Sat 7am–10pm, Sun 7–3

Moorcroft Manor RR
Set beside a tranquil dam and with great mountain views, this is a relaxed and shady terrace restaurant. Start your day with a buffet breakfast, enjoy lunch of salmon and Camembert salad or ploughman's platter, and for dinner choose grilled sole, crispy duck or fresh trout.

🟥 203 D1
✉ Sani Road, Himeville
☎ 033 702 1967; www.moorcroft.co.za
🕐 Daily 7:30–8:30

Rosehurst R
This lovely little café, housed in a red-brick Victorian building, is surrounded by a wonderful, aromatic garden full of rose bushes. You can sit in the sun on the terrace for breakfasts of light scrambled eggs, delicious home-made breads, scones and jams, and frothy cappuccinos, or come for the light lunch menu with a Mediterranean feel: roasted vegetables, quiches and salads.

🟥 203 D1
✉ 239 Boom Street, Pietermaritzburg
☎ 033 394 3833
🕐 Mon–Fri 8:30–4:30, Sat 8:30–1:30

Yellowwood Café R
Set in an attractive 1870s farmhouse with polished wooden floors, fireplaces, crooked windows and a pretty garden with views of Howick Falls, this child-friendly café and pub serves up an ever-changing menu of hearty, country-style cuisine. Full meals include tender lamb shanks and melt-in-the-mouth oxtail, while the pub menu has lighter meals, and tea and cake is served in the afternoons.

🟥 198 C3
✉ Shafton Road, Howick
☎ 033 330 2461; http://yellowwood.co.za
🕐 Tue–Sat 9:30–10, Sun 9:30–4:30

Where to...
Shop

DURBAN

The **Gateway** mall (M12, Umhlanga Rocks; tel: 031 514 0500; www.gatewayworld.co.za) is one of the largest malls in the southern hemisphere with more than 300 shops, 60 places to eat and many other recreational facilities. Most international brands are represented here, as well as the local chain stores.

The **Pavilion** (N3, Westville; tel: 031 275 9800; www.thepav.co.za) is popular, particularly with Indian families and has giant hypermarkets selling just about everything, while the **Musgrave Centre** (115 Musgrave Road, Berea; tel: 031 201 5129; www.musgrave centre.co.za) has upmarket boutiques and holds a craft-and-curio market in the parking area on Sundays.

In the city centre, the **Workshop** (99 Samora Machel Street; tel: 031 304 9894; www.thework shopcentre.co.za) is housed in a restored 1860 industrial building that used to serve as the railway station's workshop and is now home to dozens of cheap shops and counters where you can buy Indian snacks. Like most of the larger shopping centres, there is also a multi-screen cinema with the latest international film releases.

Out of town, the **Valley of 1,000 Hills** is dotted with craft and cottage furniture shops.

There are several markets in Durban and the central **Victoria Street Market** (155 Victoria Street; tel: 031 306 4021; www.indian market.co.za) is a bustling Indian market, where the scents of incense mingle with curries, spices and the odours of the fish market

next door; colourful saris, brassware and trinkets are on display.

At the **Warwick Triangle** adjoining the Victoria Street Market is the **Muti Market**. Not for the fainthearted, it should be visited with a guide to help avoid petty crime. Traditional healers sell pungent mixtures of indigenous herbs, plants, bark, snake skins, bird wings, crocodile teeth, dolphin skulls and monkey paws.

Insider Tip

For African crafts and curios go to the **Amphitheatre flea market** held on Sunday mornings on the beachfront (corner Old Fort Road/Snell Parade; tel: 031 301 3200; 9am–4pm).

The **Essenwood Craft Market** in Berea (Essenwood Road; tel: 081 370 7577; Sat 9–2) is popular with families and offers plenty of craft stalls along with farmers selling fresh produce. The children's 🛝 playground is conveniently situated so parents can easily keep an eye on them.

West of Durban's centre is **Shongweni Farmer's & Craft Market** (Mr551 Road, Outer West Durban; tel: 083 777 4686; www.shongweni market.co.za; Sat 6am–11:30am) an authentic farmer's market with stalls of farm fresh food, delicious cakes, bread, jams and much more.

For contemporary African art, pay a visit to the artists' studios in the **BAT Centre** (Victoria Embankment; tel: 031 332 0451; www.batcentre.co.za) and look out for Zulu beadwork and jewellery, woven baskets, wooden carvings, drums and soapstone figures from Zimbabwe.

MIDLANDS & UKHAHLAMBA-DRAKENSBERG

Many towns in the Drakensberg and Battlefields region have their own arts and crafts routes. The **Midlands Meander** (tel: 033 330 8195; www.midlandsmeander.co.za), which extends some 80km (50mi)

KwaZulu-Natal

along the country lanes between Pietermaritzburg and Mooi River, is perhaps one of the most popular routes in the country. There are shops and galleries for a whole range of artists, potters, leather workers, furniture makers, blacksmiths, cheese makers and brewers. As well as a good range of restaurants and places to stay along the way.

In the Central Berg visit the **Thokozisa Village** on the R600, 13km (8mi) west of Winterton, (tel: 036 488 1207; www.cdic.co.za/thokozisa.htm), a one-stop complex gathering together craft shops, art galleries, a deli, restaurant and nursery.

Also worth a visit is the **Rorke's Drift Arts and Crafts Centre** (tel: 034 642 1627; www.centre-rorkesdrift.com) next to the museum at the Rorke's Drift battle site, 42km (26mi) southeast from Dundee, which specializes in beautiful hand-woven tapestries, pottery and silkscreen fabrics.

Where to...
Go Out

CINEMA & THEATRE

Large cinema complexes can be found in the shopping malls, and Durban's **Gateway** mall has 18 screens alone, along with an indoor climbing wall, skate park, a man-made surfing wave and the **Barnyard Theatre** (tel: 031 566 3045; www.barnyardtheatres.co.za).

Durban's premier theatre is the **Playhouse**, which also offers backstage tours (231 Smith Street; tel: 031 369 9555; www.playhousecompany.com).

The **Elizabeth Sneddon Theatre** (Mazisi Kunene Road, Glenwood; www.sneddontheatre.co.za) is part of the university's drama department and stages a wide variety of shows and music reviews.

Other theatres include the **BAT Centre** (Victoria Embankment; tel: 031 332 0451; www.batcentre.co.za) and the **Catalina Theatre** (Wilson's Wharf, Victoria Embankment; tel: 031 309 7945; www.facebook.com/CatalinaTheatre).

The **Rhumbelow Theatre** (Cunningham Avenue, Umbilo; tel: 031 205 7602; www.rhumbelow.za.net) is a venue for revues; there's a bar and you can take a picnic.

NIGHTLIFE

Durban's casinos are large glitzy affairs. The **Sibaya Casino** (1 Sibaya Road, Umhlanga; tel: 031 580 5000; www.sibaya.co.za) has a theatre and a show bar, while the **Suncoast Casino** (Marine Parade; tel: 031 328 3000; www.suncoast-casino.co.za) has a beach, boardwalk, cinema, water-slide park and several restaurants and bars.

Florida Road in Morningside or Musgrave Road in Berea have a good choice of venues.

Jazzy Rainbow (93 Smiso Nkwanyana, Morningside; tel: 031 303 8398) is a chic jazz venue, featuring live bands.

Its namesake, the **Rainbow Restaurant** (23 Stanfield Lane; tel: 031 702 9161; www.therainbow.co.za) is an institution of the local jazz scene.

Also a popular choice, **Billy the Bums** (504 Lilian Ngoyi Road, Morningside; tel: 031 303 1988; www.billythebums.co.za) serves up cocktails and the latest dance music.

For a more relaxed drink to a musical backdrop of reggae and other Caribbean sounds, head to **Cool Runnings** (49 Milne Road; tel: 084 701 6912).

In Pietermaritzburg, **La Casa** (5 Quarry Road; tel: 082 873 7372) presents live music every Tuesday and Friday night.

Johannesburg & Gauteng

 **Little Treats**

Urban Culture

Stroll through Johannesburg's (➤ 124) revamped **Newtown** district and enjoy its art galleries and exhibitions.

Soweto Route

For a safe and efficient trip to **Soweto** (➤ 122) hop aboard one of the Rea Vaya public transport buses.

City Break

Join the locals as they enjoy their lunch break on the steps of the monument on Church Square in **Pretoria** (➤ 119).

Getting Your Bearings

Johannesburg is the capital of Gauteng, the smallest province in the country but due to its legacy of gold, also the richest. Until a few years ago the city centre was plagued by crime and much of the action moved to the suburbs. The area has since experienced an urban renewal and, now that it is cleaner and safer, businesses are returning.

The Greater Johannesburg Metropolitan Area covers more than 500 suburbs sprawled over 1,300km² (500mi²), which makes it the largest city in Africa in size, though not in population, which is about 3.2 million. A ribbon of development, the N1 highway and the Gautrain rail link, join Johannesburg to the country's capital Pretoria, 50km (30mi) to the north.

Johannesburg's city centre is dense with high-rises, further out is the township of Soweto, which played a crucial part in the struggle against apartheid. The attractive leafy northern suburbs are where most hotels can be found, as well as superb restaurants, vast shopping malls, glitzy casino resorts, lovely parks and the Johannesburg Zoo.

TOP 10

Don't Miss

At Your Leisure

The Johannesburg skyline in the distance with the FNB Stadium in foreground

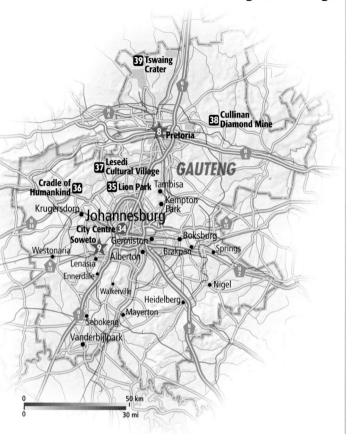

39 Tswaing Crater

38 Cullinan Diamond Mine

8 Pretoria

GAUTENG

37 Lesedi Cultural Village

35 Lion Park

Tambisa

Kempton Park

Cradle of Humankind 36

Krugersdorp

Johannesburg

City Centre 34

Soweto 9

Germiston

Boksburg

Westonaria

Brakpan

Springs

Lenasia

Alberton

Ennerdale

Nigel

Walkerville

Heidelberg

Mayerton

Sebokeng

Vanderbijlpark

0   50 km

0   30 mi

Perfect Days in...

Three Perfect Days

If you are not quite sure where to begin your travels, this itinerary recommends three practical and enjoyable days in Johannesburg & Gauteng, taking in some of the best places to see. For more information see the main entries (► 118–129).

Day 1

Morning

Take a half-day organized tour of Johannesburg's **34** **city centre** (► 124) and visit Newtown, Mary Fitzgerald Square, MuseuMAfricA and the Museum of Man and Science. Don't miss the sweeping views of the city from the viewing platform at the top of the Carlton Centre.

Lunch

Eat at **Niki's Oasis** (► 132), a jazz club in **Newtown**, where you can try traditional dishes such *potjiekos* with *mieliepap* (stew with maize porridge).

Afternoon

Explore **Gold Reef City** (► 125). See gold being poured into bars, drop down a mine shaft and ride the roller coasters.

Evening

Eat at **Moyo** (► 132) in Melrose Arch: Johannesburg's most extravagant restaurant spread over five themed floors, with fine African food and entertainment.

Day 2

Morning

Spend a few hours learning more about South Africa's 20th-century history in the critically acclaimed **Apartheid Museum** (► 126), which documents the creation of apartheid and the rise of black consciousness and opposition. It is one of the best and most thought-provoking museums in the world, so allow plenty of time to do it justice.

Lunch
Reflect on what you've seen in the museum's **Truth Café** and pick up further reading in the shop.

Afternoon
With an informative guide, take a half-day tour of the country's most famous township, ★**Soweto** (right; ➤ 122). Visit Mandela House, Walter Sisulu Square and the Hector Pieterson Museum and Memorial.

Evening
Eat dinner at one of the over-the-top **casinos** and gaze at the extravagant décor and architecture. Party animals should head to **Melville** and its streets of late-night bars.

Day 3

Morning
Spend the morning exploring the historical sites in ★**Pretoria** (➤ 118) and learn about the other periods of South Africa's history at the Voortrekker Monument.

Lunch
On your way back towards Johannesburg, go for a gut-busting lunch at **Carnivore** (69 Drift Boulevard, Muldersdrift, off the N1; tel: 011 950 6000; www.carnivore.co.za) where meat (from kudu to crocodile) is piled on to your plate.

Afternoon
Around 10km (6mi) from Carnivore, visit **35 Lion Park** (➤ 128) and drive around the spacious enclosures to see prides of lion and many other species. Don't miss the chance to play with a lion cub or feed a giraffe at Cub World by the entrance.

Evening
Dine alfresco and people-watch in one of the restaurants lining the atmospheric **Nelson Mandela Square** in Sandton City.

⑧⭐Pretoria

With attractive jacaranda-lined streets and imposing government and historical buildings, Pretoria is South Africa's capital and is steeped in history from the Voortrekker period. It's joined to Johannesburg 50km (30mi) to the south by a ribbon of development and green-belt towns along the N1, and it's estimated in another decade or so the area will be one big mega-city.

Between 1835 and 1852, the descendants of the early Dutch settlers (collectively known over the centuries as Voortrekkers, Boers and Afrikaners) left the British colony in the Cape with their ox wagons and sought new land in the interior. Many put down their roots in the region that is now Pretoria (Tshwane), and the first church was built in 1854, streets were laid out and Pretoria was declared the official capital of the independent Voortrekker republic of Transvaal in 1860.

CHANGING FACE
Pretoria was named after Voortrekker leader, Andries Pretorius (1798–1853), but while the city itself has retained this old name, the greater municipality it falls within is now called **Tshwane**, meaning "we are the same".

After the Anglo-Boer War, Pretoria was named the capital of the new British colony when the Union of South Africa was created in 1910. Soon after, the imposing **Union Buildings** were built in Arcadia to the east of the centre by renowned architect Herbert Baker. Today, the magnificent sandstone complex, in a commanding position on top of a hill, still serves as the seat of South Africa's government. Nelson Mandela made his 1994 inaugural presidential speech in

The imposing sandstone Union Buildings, the seat of the South African government

Now a museum, the house where President Paul Kruger lived from 1883 to 1900 is decorated with original Victorian furnishings

front of it. The buildings are not open to the public so the best reason to come here is to stroll through the manicured gardens, where there are statues of South Africa's famous generals and an outstanding view of the city.

Insider Tip

Also in Arcadia, the **Pretoria Art Museum** is in a light and airy building with an adjoining sculpture park and displays a fine collection of traditional and modern South African art by artists such as Pierneef, Frans Oerder and Anton van Wouw, as well as a collection of old Dutch and Flemish paintings. The nearby 80ha (198-acre) **National Zoological Gardens of South Africa** has spacious enclosures that are home to over 2,500 animals. There's a cableway across the two attractions, you can rent golf buggies to get around and there are 6km (4mi) of trails with picnic sites.

Insider Tip

The city's main thoroughfare is the 26km-long (16mi) Church Street, which is intercepted by **Church Square** – the city's first market place and churchyard. Historic buildings surround the square, in the north is the **Palace of Justice** and the **South African Reserve Bank** building (designed by Herbert Baker), in the south is the old **Raadsaal** (council chamber) of the 1891 neo-Renaissance-style Zuid-Afrikaansche Republiek. Pretty **Café Riche** (6–6), housed in a national monument, is a very pleasant place to take a break. The **Kruger Museum** on Church Street served as the residence for President Paul Kruger.

The **National Museum of Natural History** (formerly the Transvaal Museum) opposite Pretoria City Hall (Paul Kruger Street) documents the county's natural heritage with exhibits of mammals, reptiles and fossils as well as geological and archaeological finds, including the skull fragment known as Mrs Ples (*Australopithecus africanus*) found at the Sterkfontein Caves, now a UNESCO World Heritage Site (▶ 128). Overlooking Burgers Park is **Melrose House**, which is where the Treaty of Vereeniging was signed in 1902 to end the Anglo-Boer War (1899–1902). The house was headquarters for the British forces during the war and is today an elegant building with Victorian and Edwardian architectural styles and interiors. The pretty grounds are used for occasional craft fairs and classical concerts.

South of the city there are two imposing buildings. The first is the unmissable enormous concrete monstrosity of UNISA, South Africa's largest university and one of the

world's biggest correspondence universities. The second is the looming granite **Voortrekker Monument** on Monument Hill, which was built in 1949 to celebrate the Great Trek and associated wars fought by the Boers in the early to mid-19th century. It's an impressive, solid, windowless, 40m² (431ft²) cube. The bas-relief frieze on the inside has 27 panels depicting the story of the Great Trek. The cenotaph has an opening through which the sun shines at noon on 16 December each year and illuminates the Afrikaans phrase meaning "We for thee, South Africa". It was on 16 December, 1838 that the Boers defeated the Zulus in the Battle of Blood River, and under the apartheid government the date was taken as a public holiday, called the Day of the Covenant in reference to the Afrikaner belief that victory was achieved as a result of a vow with God. Today, 16 December is still a public holiday but has been renamed Day of Reconciliation, with different reasons for celebration.

Historic Melrose House, overlooking Burgers Park

TAKING A BREAK

The stables at Melrose House have been converted into a delightful **tea garden** with wrought-iron furniture serving light meals, cakes, tea, coffee and wine.

✚ 202 C3

Tshwane Tourist Information Centre
✉ Church Street, Old Nederlandsche Bank Building
☎ 012 358 1430; www.gopretoria.co.za, www.tshwane.gov.za
🕓 Mon–Fri 9–5, Sat until 1pm

Pretoria Art Museum
✉ Arcadia Park ☎ 012 358 6750; www.pretoriaartmuseum.co.za
🕓 Tue–Sun 10–5 💰 R22

National Zoological Gardens of South Africa
✉ 232 Boom Street ☎ 012 339 2700; www.nzg.ac.za
🕓 Daily 8:30–5:30 💰 R110

JACARANDA CITY

An early resident imported jacaranda trees to Pretoria in 1888 from Rio de Janeiro. They flourished, and today the city has aptly been dubbed the Jacaranda City, with about 50,000 jacarandas lining its streets. These look incredible when the bright purple flowers burst open from late September to mid-November.

A street of jacaranda trees in full bloom

Kruger Museum
✉ 60 Church Street ☎ 012 000 0010; www.ditsong.org.za
🕓 Tue–Sat 8:30–4:30, Sun 9–4:30 💰 R60

National Museum of Natural History
✉ 423 Paul Kruger Street ☎ 012 322 7632; www.ditsong.org.za 🕓 8–4 💰 R30

Melrose House
✉ 275 Jeff Masemola Street (entrance: 280 Scheiding Street)
☎ 012 322 2805 🕓 Tue–Sun 10–5 💰 22

Whale skeleton at the entrance to the National Museum of Natural History

Voortrekker Monument
✉ Eeufees Road (M7, Groenkloof) ☎ 012 326 6770; www.vtm.org.za
🕓 May–Aug 8–5; Sep–Apr 8–6 💰 R70

INSIDER INFO

- If you are travelling to the national parks in the rest of the country, call in at South African National Parks (SANParks) head office while you're in Pretoria to make reservations (643 Leyds Street, Muckleneuk; tel: 012 428 9111; www.sanparks.org; Mon–Fri 7:30–3:45).

- Go full steam ahead on the 🔟 **Diamond Express** (152 Miechaelson St, Hermanstad, Pretoria, tel: 012 767 7913; www.friendsoftherail.com; R250 return) a vintage steam train that departs from Hermanstad station several times a month to the diamond mining town Cullinan 50km (30mi) away. The village has numerous historical buildings.

Insider Tip

★ Soweto

Soweto – short for South Western Township – lies 15km (9mi) south-west of Johannesburg city centre. It gained the world's attention during the 1976 Soweto Uprising when school children, protesting against the introduction of Afrikaans as the language of instruction, sparked a nationwide wave of resistance. The police opened fire on the children and the famous photo of the lifeless body of 13-year-old Hector Pietersen went all around the world.

Today, with an estimated 1.3 to 2 million inhabitants (almost exclusively black and coloured) Soweto is the largest township in South Africa. A seemingly endless sea of small (a few rooms, kitchen and bath) boxy houses, with the less privileged living in crudely built corrugated iron shacks. The residents of Soweto belong to all of the indigenous groups found in the country, although Zulus predominate (almost 33 per cent). Nowadays signs of change are evident: well-maintained streets, attractive houses and a golf course. But, while hundreds of kindergartens and schools have been built, there are still not enough, and the only hospital is the massive Chris Hani Baragwaneth Hospital (with 429 buildings, 6,750 staff members and 3,200 beds it is the third largest in the world). Mirroring much of the country, the social gulf between white and black has shifted to a gulf between the rich and the poor; the vast majority of people here live in impoverished conditions. Only a few have a steady income and, as there are hardly any jobs in Soweto, most have to commute to Johannesburg for work. Most areas of Soweto have electricity and there are some tarred roads but the lack of infrastructure (drinking water and sanitation) remains striking.

Soweto has grown from about 50 small settlements into a huge suburb

Face to Face
Soweto's struggle against, and the triumph over, apartheid have made it a tourist attraction, which also generates in-

1976 SOWETO UPRISING

Hector Pieterson was a 13-year-old school-boy who was one of many who were shot dead by police in the 1976 Soweto Uprising. Students had been peacefully demonstrating against Afrikaans being used as the predominant language in schools when the police opened fire. A photograph of his lifeless body being carried away with his wailing 17-year-old sister running alongside, was flashed across the globe. It showed the world that the government was capable of killing defenceless children. This event sparked worldwide condemnation and heightened the struggle against apartheid to new levels.

Mahatma Gandhi said: "If we want to achieve true peace in the world, we must begin with the children" and this is still relevant in today's Soweto

come and creates jobs for its residents. More than 1,000 people visit daily on well-organized township bus tours. Jimmy Ntintili was the township tour pioneer; he started Jimmy's Face to Face tours back in 1985. A tour itinerary usually includes a visit to **Mandela House** (in the same street where the Anglican Archbishop and Nobel Peace Prize winner Desmond Tutu lives), **Chris Hani Baragwanath Hospital**, the excellent **Hector Pieterson Museum and Memorial** and the **Regina Mundi Catholic Church**. If you want to get to know Soweto better, you can stay over in one of the welcoming guest houses or in private lodging, which range from simple B&Bs to five-star accommodation with swimming pool and sauna. It is best not to drive alone in Soweto as the lack of street names and landmarks makes it hard to navigate. There are surprisingly few criminal incidents involving tourists but it is advisable to remain vigilant.

TAKING A BREAK

Choose a tour that includes lunch at famous **Wandie's Place**, which serves up hearty township cuisine (618 Makhalamele Street, Dube; tel: 081 420 6051; R). Insider Tip

➕ 202 C3

Soweto Tourism
✉ Walter Sisulu Square, Kliptown ☎ 011 342 4316 🕐 Mon–Fri 8–5

Mandela House
✉ Ngakane Street, Orlando ☎ 011 936 7754; www.mandelahouse.com
🕐 Mon–Sun 9–5 💲 R60

Hector Pieterson Museum and Memorial
✉ 8287 Khumalo Street, Orlando, West Soweto ☎ 011 536 0611
🕐 Mon–Sat 10–5, Sun 10–4 💲 R30

㉞ City Centre

Johannesburg – known locally as Jo'burg by the whites and as eGoli by the blacks – is one of the largest cities in Africa. On the Highveld (the high centre section of the South Africa inland plateau) the Greater Johannesburg metropolitan area, with Pretoria in the north and the industrial areas of Vanderbijlpark and Vereeniging in the south, is growing into one endless urban sprawl. Together they form the province of Gauteng, which accounts for only two per cent of the South African state but is home to 22 per cent of the population. Despite its problems – which continue even through apartheid is over – Johannesburg remains the best place to experience the true buzz of an African city in South Africa.

The city centre – a cluch of skyscrapers hemmed in by the M1 and M2 motorway, and concentrated around Commissioner and Market streets – is comparatively small and its grid layout and high-rise buildings give it an American feel. There are old colonial façades side by side with glass skyscrapers, quiet a few of which stand empty. However, the city's vibrant **Newtown** district, east of the M1 and around the central **Mary Fitzgerald Square**, has recently been revamped and its streets are filled with cafés, galleries, flea markets and music clubs.

At Lilian Ngoyi (formerly Bree), what was once the city's fruit and vegetable market, **MuseuMAfricA** tells the history of Johannesburg since the gold mining days. Next door the **Market Theatre Complex** has three performance stages and a craft market outside. On the opposite side of the square, at Jeppe Street in **Newtown Park** is the **Workers' Museum** where exhibits are dedicated to the migrant labour that came to the city from other parts of Africa to work in the mines.

East of the park is the **World of Beer** run by South African Breweries, which tells you the history of beer and takes you through the brewing process in the greenhouse. There's also a mock-up of a township *shebeen* (pub).

Nearby on Diagonal Street the **Museum of Man and Science** is actually a shop selling paraphernalia for *sangomas* (traditional healers) and stocks all kinds of ingredients, from plants and herbs to animal parts. It's a compelling sight – though the smells may send your senses reeling.

North of Newtown the impressive 284m (931ft) **Nelson Mandela Bridge** links the city centre with Braamfontein and spans 42 railway lines. The steel cable suspension bridge is 42m (138ft) high at its north pylon and 27m (89ft) high at the south pylon and has become an iconic symbol of reconciliation after the end of apartheid.

In the suburb of **Braamfontein**, **Constitutional Hill** is on the site of the notorious **Old Fort Prison** complex, also known as Number Four, and was where blacks were kept in harsh conditions in overcrowded and dirty cells and were given

Panoramic view from the Carlton Centre

SAFETY FIRST

Johannesburg has a reputation when it comes to crime, but if you take some sensible precautions your visit should be without incident. Don't carry valuables, large quantities of cash or passports on the street. Keep your car doors locked and your wits about you when stopped at traffic lights after dark and avoid quiet side streets. Seek advice from locals about the areas to avoid and stay away from Hillbrow and Yeoville unless you are with a guide.

meagre food. Meanwhile the white prisoners had two-bunk cells and proper meals. It has now been converted into a fascinating museum and you can hear stories about some of its most famous inmates such as Nelson Mandela and Mahatma Gandhi. Next door is the highest court in South Africa, the **Constitutional Court**. To the south, at the top of Rissik Street, look out for the **Miners' Monument**, depicting three giant miners in hard hats holding a drill. To the east of the city is the 223m-high (730ft), 50-floor

Carlton Centre where you can ride a rapid lift up to the viewing floor, called the **Top of Africa**, and take in the fabulous views of the busy skyline.

Southwest of the city centre is **Gold Reef City** and – as the name suggests – is dedicated to Johannesburg's history of gold. It's based at the top of Johannesburg's 3,293m-deep (10,800ft) Shaft Number 14, which opened in 1897 and closed in 1971, during which time it produced 1.4 million kilograms (3.08 million pounds) of gold. You can go 220m (722ft) down into the shaft where it's easy to imagine how tough working conditions were for the early miners in the hot, airless tunnels. Above ground is a reconstruction of an early Victorian mining town where the staff wear period dress, you can watch gold being poured, be entertained by street performers, and have fun on the 30 rides in the adjoining theme park. Not to be missed is the outstanding **Apartheid Museum**. At the entrance to the museum are pillars

Insider Tip

Insider Tip

Johannesburg & Gauteng

representing the seven fundamental principles of South Africa's post-apartheid constitution: democracy, equality, reconciliation, diversity, responsibility, respect and freedom.

TAKING A BREAK

Head to the **café** at the top of the **Carlton Centre** (R), sit back and enjoy the views.

➕ 202 C3

Johannesburg Tourism
✉ Park City Transit Centre, Jo'burg Station (corner Rissik/Wolmarans Street), 1st Floor ☎ 011 338 5051; www.joburgtourism.com ⏰ Mon–Fri 8–5

MuseuMAfricA
✉ 121 Lilian Ngoyi Street ☎ 011 833 5624 ⏰ Tue–Sun 9–5 ✋ Free

Workers' Museum
✉ 52 Rahima Moosa Street ☎ 011 492 0600 ⏰ Thu–Sat 9–4:30 ✋ Free

World of Beer
✉ 15 Helen Joseph Street, Newtown ☎ 011 836 4900; www.worldofbeer.co.za ⏰ 10–6, tours start hourly on the hour ✋ R115

KwaZulu Muti – Museum of Man and Science
✉ 14 Diagonal Street ☎ 011 836 4470 ⏰ Mon–Fri 7:30–5, Sat 7:30–1 ✋ Free

Constitutional Hill
✉ 1 Kotze Street ☎ 011 381 3100; www.constitutionhill.org.za ⏰ 9–5 ✋ R65

Top of Africa
✉ Carlton Centre, 150 Commissioner Street ☎ 011 308 1331 ⏰ Mon–Fri 9–6, Sat 9–5, Sun 9–2 ✋ R15

Gold Reef City
✉ Northern Parkway, Ormonde ☎ 011 248 6800; www.goldreefcity.co.za ⏰ Tue–Sun 9:30–6 ✋ R190

Apartheid Museum
✉ Northern Parkway, Ormonde ☎ 011 309 4700; www.apartheidmuseum.org ⏰ Tue–Sun 10–5 ✋ R80

The Nelson Mandela Bridge is the largest cable-stayed bridge in South Africa

INSIDER INFO

- **Past Experiences** (tel: 011 782 5250, 083 701 3046; www.pastexperiences.co.za) offer inner city walking tours that focus on the Jo'burg art scene and local culture.
- If you only visit one museum in Johannesburg make it the **Apartheid Museum** and allow at least three to four hours. **Ernest Cole's (1940–90) photographs** of the townships in the 1960s are vivid and moving.
- At the 🌟 **Johannesburg Planetarium** (Yale Road, Braamfontein; tel: 011 717 1390; www.planetarium.co.za, Thu–Sat 2–3 shows daily; R50, children R35) children can view the glittering night sky without having to staying up past their bedtime.

At Your Leisure

35 Lion Park

A popular day trip destination, the Lion Park is 23km (14mi) north of Johannesburg on the R55. There are two restaurants, shopping facilities and a supervised playground. You can drive through yourself, go on a guided safari from the parking area, or arrange a visit from Johannesburg with one of the tour operators.

➕ 202 C3 ✉ M34, near Lanseria Airport
☎ 087 150 0100; www.lion-park.com
🕐 Daily 8:30am–9pm 💲 R165

36 Cradle of Humankind

A UNESCO World Heritage Site, the Cradle of Humankind covers almost 500km² (195mi²) about 40km (25mi) to the west of Johannesburg, and is the location of dozens of palaeontological sites that have yielded more human fossils than anywhere else in the world. These sites include the caves of Sterkfontein, Swartkrans, Kromdraai and the surrounding area. In 1947 the skull of an *Australopithecus africanus* was discovered, the first bipedal human ancestor, who populated southern Africa and the Great Rift Valley more than 3 million years ago. The age of the skull is estimated to be 2.6 million years old. Scientists nicknamed it Mrs. Ples but it is now believed to have been a male, roughly 150cm (4.9ft) tall, weighing 35–60kg (77–130lbs) and about 22 years old. In 1997 palaeontologists found the near complete skeleton of another prehistoric man (Little Foot), who lived 3.5 million years ago. Discoveries like these confirm Charles Darwin's theory that the transition from apes to humans took place here in Africa (www.cradleofhumankind.co.za).

Maropeng is a fabulous interactive exhibition, 10km (6mi) from Sterkfontein, which begins with a boat ride through icebergs, volcanoes and mists demonstrating how the earth and its continents were formed by gases. It then takes visitors on a journey through the story of mankind to the present time. It covers the emergence of man, globalization, population and the effects humans have had on

Sterkfontein Caves, part of the Cradle of Humankind UNESCO World Heritage Site

the world and its resources. Each of the exhibits is interactive; you can pick up a phone and listen to the voice of an extinct animal or build up DNA blocks, for example.

➕ 202 C3 ✉ Maropeng is on the D400 about 50km (30mi) west of Johannesburg; Sterkfontein is 10km (6mi) away off the R563 ☎ 014 577 9000; www.maropeng.co.za ⏱ 9–5 🎟 Combination tickets for both sites: R190

⒊⒎ Lesedi Cultural Village

Head here if you want to witness some of southern Africa's tribal customs. There are fully working Zulu, Xhosa, Basotho, Pedi and Sotho mock-up villages that demonstrate traditional tribal living. The programme begins with a presentation on the history and origins of South Africa's rainbow nation. Lunch or dinner is included depending on the tour and both are accompanied by singing and dancing. You can stay overnight in comfortable traditional homesteads, which are grouped in villages (Zulu, Xhosa, Nguni, Basotho, Pedi and Ndebele) hosted by local families.

➕ 202 C3 ✉ R512 toward Hartbeespoort ☎ 012 205 1394; www.lesedi.com ⏱ 7am–8:30pm; guided tours at 11:30 and 4:30 🎟 R310 (R500 including lunch)

⒊⒏ Cullinan Diamond Mine

Founded in 1903 by Sir Thomas Cullinan, this mine was the source of the Star of Africa, the largest gem diamond ever unearthed, which was presented to King Edward VII for his 66th birthday. The 3,106-carat sparkler was cut into nine major pieces – the largest of which is set as the main stone in the Sceptre of the British monarchy's Crown Jewels – and 96 smaller ones. Cullinan is also the world's main source for blue diamonds, and the mine – which is still operational – can be visited on a 90-minute tour that includes a viewpoint over the immense hole formed by the original diggings. Four-hour underground tours to the modern mine are also available.

Insider Tip

➕ 202 C3 ✉ 30km (18mi) east of Pretoria along the R513 ☎ 012 734 2626; www.cullinandiamonds.co.za 🛈 Surface tours can be booked at: Premier Diamond Tours ☎ 012 734 0081; www. diamondtourscullinan.co.za, and Cullinan Tours ☎ 012 734 0260; www.cullinan-tours.co.za Cullinan Tourism and History helps booking underground tours ☎ 012 734 2170; www.cullinantourismandhistory.co.za 🎟 Surface tours (1–2½hrs): R150. Underground tours (4–4½hrs): about R500

⒊⒐ Tswaing Crater

The most impressive scenic attraction in Gauteng, this 1.4km-wide (1mi) and 200m-deep (700ft) crater was created about 220,000 years ago when a meteorite crashed to earth. The Setswana name Tswaing (meaning "Place of Salt") refers to a saline lake on the crater floor. Protected in a small nature reserve, the crater can be circled on foot in around two hours.

➕ 202 C4 ✉ Approximately 35km (21mi) north of Pretoria on the M35 ☎ 076 9455 911; www.ditsong.org.za ⏱ Daily 7:30–4 🎟 R25

👫 FOR KIDS

Children will enjoy getting lost and found at **Honeydew Mazes** (82 Boland Street, Honeydew, 25km/16mi north-west of Johannesburg centre; tel: 073 795 2174; www.honeydewmazes.co. za; Sat, Sun 10–5; R150, children R120). They will need at least an hour and a half to navigate the main maze, which is made of maize in summer and of reeds in winter.

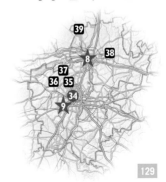

Johannesburg & Gauteng

Where to...
Stay

Prices
Expect to pay per double room, per night
R under R1,500   **RR** R1,500–R2,500   **RRR** over R2,500

JOHANNESBURG

54 on Bath Rosebank RRR
If you are looking for a luxury hotel in a central location then look no further. Formerly known as The Grace in Rosebank, this hotel is close to the Rosebank Mall and has 73 exclusive rooms and 3 suites. All the rooms have marble bathrooms, and the ones near the top of the nine-storey building have great city views. There's a gym and library, and on the roof a delightful English-style garden with a stunning long pool.
✚ 202 C3 ✉ 54 Bath Avenue, Rosebank
☎ 011 344 8500; www.tsogosun.com

A Room with a View R
With wonderful views over Melville (as the name would suggest), this affordable guest house is in the style of an Italian villa, with arched windows, gargoyles, soaring ceilings, bare brick walls and black slate bathrooms. The rooms are bright and cheery, some have balconies and fireplaces, and there's a lovely indoor heated pool. Melville's restaurants are within walking distance.
✚ 202 C3 ✉ 1 Tolip Street, Melville
☎ 011 482 5435; www.aroomwithaview.co.za

Backpacker's Ritz R
This is the best of Johannesburg's backpacker hostels, with roomy dorms, neat doubles and a pool in the gardens. The useful travel centre can organize all activities, tours and transport, there's a kitchen for residents and Hyde Park Corner mall is within walking distance. They also run their own affordable day tours using guides from Soweto.
✚ 202 C3 ✉ 1A North Road, Dunkeld West
☎ 011 325 7125; www.backpackers-ritz.com

De Kuilen Country House R
This 5-star guest house has four delightful cottages in Cape Dutch style and one unique tree house in 1ha (3 acres) of peaceful gardens. The French-trained chef presents delicious four-course dinners served on silver, crystal and white linen; there's an extensive wine collection. Beauty treatments are on offer.
✚ 202 C3 ✉ 30 Glenluce Drive, Sandton
☎ 011 462 4670; www.dekuilen.co.za

Maropeng Boutique Hotel R
Attached to the Maropeng Visitor Centre, this isolated 24-room hotel provides a peaceful, scenic alternative to staying in central Johannesburg, offering spacious accommodation with fine views to the Witwatersrand and Magaliesberg ranges. It is especially convenient for extended exploration of the Cradle of Humankind.
✚ 202 C3 ✉ On the D400 about 50km (30mi) west of Johannesburg
☎ 014 577 9100; www.maropeng.co.za

African Pride Melrose Arch Hotel RR–RRR
This ultra-stylish modern hotel is in the Melrose Arch business, residential and shopping development. Rooms have designer furniture, flat-screen TVs, DVDs and great bathrooms (complete with rubber ducks and candles). Facilities include a panelled 24-hour library,

130

bar and an excellent restaurant with outside tables that sit in the pool.

➕ 202 C3 ✉ 1 Melrose Square, Melrose Arch ☎ 011 214 6666; http://protea.marriott.com

Michelangelo Towers RRR

This 5-star hotel in a wonderful location overlooking Nelson Mandela Square. The spacious rooms are elegantly decorated and there's a luxurious turndown service when the room is scattered with rose petals. There is also a heated indoor pool and spa.

➕ 202 C3 ✉ 8 Maude Street, Sandton ☎ 011 245 4000; www.legacyhotels.co.za

The Saxon RRR

Tucked away in the leafy northern suburbs and set in a 2.5ha (6-acre) estate with manicured lawns and a vast infinity pool, this boutique hotel was where Nelson Mandela stayed to edit his autobiography when he was released from prison. The luxurious furnishings feature African art and antiques.

➕ 202 C3 ✉ 36 Saxon Road, Sandhurst ☎ 011 292 6000; www.saxon.co.za

Ten Bompas RRR

With just 10 suites this is a peaceful boutique hotel within walking distance of Hyde Park Corner mall. The modern interior design uses an appealing collection of African art, and each room is individually decorated. The restaurant is superb and there are lots of special touches such as cookies and hot drinks delivered to the rooms.

➕ 192 B2 ✉ 10 Bompas Road, Dunkeld West ☎ 011 325 2442; www.tenbompas.com

PRETORIA

Cricklewood Manor RRR

The 5-star hotel, set in the sleepy, shady suburb of Waterkloof, only five minutes' drive from central Pretoria, combines luxurious, modern all-suite accommodation with elegant architecture and lovely green grounds. There is also an excellent restaurant and on-site spa.

➕ 202 C3 ✉ 193 Albert Street, Waterkloof, ☎ 012 460 8225; www.cricklewood.co.za

Where to...
Eat and Drink

Prices

Expect to pay for a two-course meal per person excluding drinks:

R under R150   **RR** R150–R300   **RRR** over R300

JOHANNESBURG

Browns of Rivonia RR

Exclusive spot for fine dining with a staggering 33,000 bottles of wine in its cellar and a cheese room where you can choose your own platter. The menu is extensive and there are some wicked desserts.

➕ 202 C3 ✉ 21 Wessels Road, Rivonia ☎ 011 803 7533; www.browns.co.za 🕐 Sun–Fri noon–2:30, Mon–Sat 6pm–10pm

Bukhara RRR

Within the Michelangelo Hotel in Nelson Mandela Square, this is one of the country's top Indian restaurants. The cuisine is authentic and each dish is made from scratch. There's a full range of tikka masala, murg and tandoori dishes.

➕ 202 C3
✉ Nelson Mandela Square, Sandton ☎ 011 883 5555; www.bukhara.com 🕐 Mon–Sat noon–3, 6–11, Sun 6pm–10pm

Johannesburg & Gauteng

The Butcher Shop and Grill RR–RRR

For a tender South African steak, head to this celebrated steak restaurant. Steaks are cut and cooked to order and served with a variety of sauces and vegetables. Lamb, pork and seafood are also on the menu, but there's not much choice for vegetarians.

➕ 202 C3 ✉ Nelson Mandela Square, Sandton
☎ 011 784 8676; www.thebutchershop.co.za
🕐 Daily noon–11

Fourno's Bakery R

This is the northern suburbs' most popular pavement-side spot for breakfast – try the bacon bagels or poached egg and salmon. The in-house bakery turns out fresh bread, cakes, quiches, pies and sausage rolls; the extensive deli counter offers takeaway meals.

➕ 202 C3
✉ Dunkeld West Centre, Jan Smuts Avenue
☎ 011 325 2110; www.fournos.co.za
🕐 Mon–Fri 7–6, Sat 6–6, Sun 7–3

Moyo Melrose Arch RRR

A flamboyant chain of restaurants that offer a combination of fine food from across the African continent and an excellent range of wines and entertainment. Musicians wander among the tables, ladies wash your hands or give you henna tattoos, the staff are dressed in beautiful African fabrics, and there's always something going on, from Zulu dancing to tap dancing. The food ranges from Moroccan tajines and Tunisian meze, to Mozambique curries and South African seafood. The shop too, sells some wonderful hand-crafted art. Dining here would be a highlight to any trip to Johannesburg and it is hugely popular so make reservations.

➕ 202 C3 ✉ Melrose Square
☎ 011 684 1477; www.moyo.co.za
🕐 Daily 11–11
Also at: ✉ Zoo Lake ☎ 011 646 0058
🕐 Daily 8:30–10

Niki's Oasis RR

Niki Sondlo was the first to rediscover the inner city and invest in it. Her jazz club and restaurant is a success story, a Newtown institution that attracts top local and international jazz musicians, and Niki is always on hand to chat about the pictures of cultural icons that line the walls. There is live music on Friday nights and before the music kicks off you can enjoy some traditional food and sandwiches, barbecue chicken, T-bone steaks or burgers. The club attracts the art scene crowd and the hip Jo'burg youth.

➕ 202 C3 ✉ 138 Lilian Ngoyi Street, Newtown
☎ 011 838 9733 🕐 Daily noon–midnight

Nuno's Portuguese Restaurant R–RR

In the heart of lively Melville, a Johannesburg suburb renowned for its relaxed bars and casual eateries, this long-established Portuguese restaurant serves seafood and other dishes associated with neighbouring Mozambique, as well as a selection of Italian main courses. Specialities include fiery chicken *piri-piri*, grilled prawns (shrimp) and classic Portuguese beef *trinchado* (marinated beef in a spicy sauce)

➕ 202 C3 ✉ 7th Street, Melville
☎ 011 482 6990
🕐 Daily 8–midnight

PRETORIA

O'Galito RR

It's best known for its affordable seafood including sardines, crab, lobster and skewers of queen prawns. Try the oysters with a sauce of shrimps, mushrooms, sherry and parmesan; meat eaters can go for the rabbit in red wine or oxtail with butter beans.

➕ 202 C3
✉ 30A Woodlands Boulevard, Pretoria East
☎ 012 997 4164; www.ogalito.com
🕐 Daily noon–2:30, 6–10

Where to...
Shop

SHOPS

In Johannesburg's northern sub-urbs is the glitzy **Sandton City** mall (Rivonia Road, Sandton; tel: 011 217 6000; www.sandtoncity.com) and its adjacent piazza-style **Nelson Mandela Square**, lined with restaurants and with a wonderful atmosphere.

Rosebank Mall (Cradock Road; tel: 011 788 5530; www.themall ofrosebank.co.za) has a good selection of shops, spacious out-door areas and alfresco cafés.

Of particular interest is also the **Rosebank Art & Craft Market** sell-ing a wide selection of jewellery, traditional clothing and crafts. The mall has more than 160 tenants including **Maple Galleries** (antiques and gifts), a **post office** and a **Computicket** where you can make bookings for theatre performances or other events.

Other malls include the vast **Cresta Mall** (Beyers Naude Drive, Northcliff; tel: 011 678 5306; www. crestashoppingcentre.co.za), **Hyde Park Corner** (Jan Smuts Avenue, Hyde Park; tel: 011 325 4340; www. hydeparkshopping.co.za), which features designer clothing and jewellery stores, and **Brightwater Commons** (Republic Road, Randburg; tel: 011 886 0663; www.brightwatercommons.co.za) where the shops are set amongst attractive lawns and waterfalls.

For a more serious selection of South African art, visit the **Everard Read Gallery** (6 Jellicoe Avenue, Rosebank; tel: 011 788 4805; www.everard-read.co.za), the **Kim Sacks Gallery** (153 Jan Smuts Avenue, Parkwood; tel: 011 447 5804; www.kimsacksgallery.com)

and the nearby **Goodman Gallery** (163 Jan Smuts Ave; tel: 011 788 1113; www.goodman-gallery.com).

For antiques, collectables and home-wares head to the shops along Parkhurst's **Fourth Avenue**. For books, try **Exclusive Books** (www.exclusivebooks.co.za), with branches in all the malls.

Thrupps (Thrupps Shopping Centre, Oxford Road, Ilovo; tel: 011 268 0298; www.thrupps.co.za), Johannesburg's original grocery shop back in the mining camp days, sells a variety of top-class produce such as French champagne, Italian cheeses, caviar and quails' eggs.

MARKETS

The **African Craft Market** (Norwood Mall; corner African Street/Sarie Marais Road, Norwood; Sun 9–4) is the best place to shop for African crafts.

Clothing, handicrafts and every-thing else imaginable (often made in China) can be found at the **Bruma Lake Flea Market** (corner Ernest Oppenheimer and Marcia avenues, Bruma; tel: 011 622 9648; Tue–Sun 9:30–5). There is also live entertainment and a wide range of food stalls.

Michael Mount Organic Village Market (Bryanston Road, Bryanston; www.bryanstonorganicmarket. co.za) offers organic produce and crafts on Thursdays and Saturdays.

The residents of the hip Maboneng Precinct have set up a community street market with **Market on Main** (corner Sivewright Avenue and Fox Street, http:// marketonmain.co.za, 10–3) it takes place every Sunday and offers a vibrant atmosphere and lots of tasty food.

Rosebank Sunday Market (Rosebank Mall, Cradock Road, www.rosebanksundaymarket. co.za; Sun 9–5) is a flea market held on the Rosebank Mall rooftop where you'll find clothing, crafts,

Insider Tip

collectibles, food stalls and live entertainment.

The **Oriental Plaza** (38–60 Lilian Ngoyi Street, Fordsburg; www. orientalplaza.co.za; Mon–Fri 9–5, Sat 6–3) is where the Indian traders sell clothing, spices and Indian snacks; it is also open Monday to Saturday.

Where to...
Go out

NIGHTLIFE

Montecasino (William Nicol Drive, Fourways; tel: 011 510 7995; www. montecasino.co.za) has a casino, and also a flea market at the weekends, a theatre, several restaurants and bars (such as Cantare or the Cobblestone Pub), and the **Montecasino Bird Garden** (tel: 011 511 1864), a unique bird park which has an excellent free-flight show.

Insider Tip

Emperor's Palace (64 Jones Street, Kempton Park; tel: 011 928 1000; www.emperorspalace.com) has a casino, theatre, show bar (with stars like Johnny Clegg), restaurants and fashionable nightclubs.

Another popular club, the **Moon Light Lounge** of the **Back o' the Moon** is at the **Gold Reef City Casino** (Northern Parkway Drive, Ormonde; tel: 011 496 1423; www. goldreefcity.co.za), which often features live jazz.

Another excellent jazz venue **Bassline** (10 Henry Nxumalo Street, Newtown; tel: 011 838 9145; www.basslinejazzclub.co.za), also specializes in kwaito (South African rap) and hip-hop artists.

Katzy's (corner Oxford Road and Bierman Avenue at The Firs/Hyatt Shopping Centre; tel: 011 880 3945, www.katzys.co.za) is one of Johannesburg's best jazz clubs

and also offers over one hundred varieties of whiskies, some excellent cocktails and a plush leather-and-wood interior.

The best spot for the party scene is around 7th Avenue in Melville where new bars pop up all the time.

Nightclubs tend to come and go, but popular venues include **ESP** (84 Oxford Road, Ferndale; tel: 011 792 4110; www.esp.co.za) and **The Town Hall** (66 Carr Street, Newtown; tel: 082 332 5772; www. facebook.com/thetownhall), is the best venue if you are looking for a party, expect lots of drum and base, house, electro, hip-hop, until the early hours; and the Town Hall street parties are also legendary. Check www.jhblive.co.za and www. iol.co.za/tonight for listings.

THEATRE

The large **Joburg Theatre Complex** (Loveday Street, Braamfontein; tel: 011 877 6800; www.joburgtheatre. com), whose three stages host imported musicals, ballet and opera, and community or supper theatres showing meaty plays or comedy. To find out what's on and book tickets, visit the Computicket desks in shopping malls or book online (www.computicket.co.za).

Market Theatre (Margaret Mcingana Street, Newtown; tel: 011 832 1641; www.markettheatre. co.za), a Johannesburg institution, was an important venue during apartheid for protest theatre.

The **Old Mutual Theatre on the Square** (Nelson Mandela Square, Sandton; tel: 011 883 8606; www. theatreonthesquare.co.za) is a good venue for comic plays, and eating in the square pre- or post-show makes for a good night out.

There are also several stages at the **Wits University Theatre Complex** (Jorissen Street, Braamfontein; tel: 011 717 1372; www.wits.ac.za/ witstheatre).

Mpumalanga & Limpopo

 **Little Treats**

Miners' Cottages
The best way to see the historic buildings lining **Pilgrim's Rest** (➤ 142) Main Street is on a donkey cart ride.

Victorian Gazebo
The outdoor Victorian Tea Gardens on Market Square in **Barberton** (➤ 146) serves English teas and light meals.

Picnic with Crocodiles
Nkhulu in the southern **Kruger National Park** (➤ 140) is one of the most beautiful places for a break; where else can you watch crocodiles as you *braai*?

Getting Your Bearings

Limpopo and Mpumalanga, the two northeastern provinces of South Africa, are areas traditionally settled by the Sepedi, Ndebele and Zulu. The land here is wild and unspoiled and that does not just apply to the Kruger National Park. There are also the breathtaking, mountainous landscapes of the Klein Drakensberg escarpment and the Blyde River Canyon. When it comes to exploring the national parks, a private vehicle is an advantage but you can also join one of the organized tours offered by the many tour operators and lodges.

Cheetah in the Wildlife Rehabilitation Centre at Moholoholo Lodge near Hoedspruit

Mbombela, the capital of Mpumalanga, lies on the Crocodile River in the subtropical lowveld. It is the gateway to the Kruger National Park and has good transport links (bus, train and plane). Here in the north nature in its purest form awaits the traveller: South Africa's largest wildlife reserve right next to the tremendous scenery of the acclaimed Blyde River Canyon, South Africa's own Grand Canyon. There are not enough superlatives to describe this beautiful region where you will encounter the passing show of Africa's legendary Big Five, stunning vistas of bizarre erosion sculptures, lush gorges and spectacular waterfalls. Polokwane, the largest city and the capital of Limpopo, is on the N1 highway north of Johannesburg, and serves as a good stopover en route to your safari.

TOP 10

Don't Miss

At Your Leisure

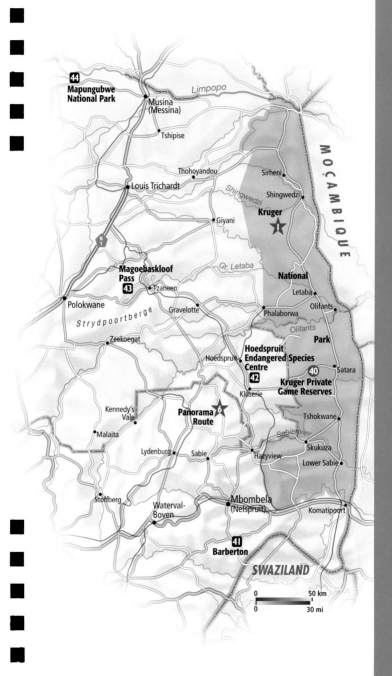

Mapungubwe National Park **44**

Limpopo

Musina (Messina)

Tshipise

MOÇAMBIQUE

Thohoyandou

Sirheni

Shingwedzi

Louis Trichardt

Shingwedzi

Giyani

Kruger

N 1

Gr. Letaba

Magoebaskloof Pass **43**

Tzaneen

National

Letaba

Polokwane

Gravelotte

Phalaborwa

Olifants

Strydpoortberge

Olifants

Zeekoegat

Park

Hoedspruit

Hoedspruit Endangered Species Centre **42**

40

Satara

Kruger Private Game Reserves

Klaserie

Kennedy's Vale

Panorama Route

Tshokwane

Malaita

Sabierivier

Lydenburg

Sabie

Skukuza

Hazyview

Lower Sabie

Stoffberg

Waterval-Boven

Mbombela (Nelspruit)

Komatipoort

Barberton 41

SWAZILAND

0   50 km

0   30 mi

137

Five Perfect Days

If you are not quite sure where to begin your travels, this itinerary recommends five practical and enjoyable days exploring Mpumalanga and Limpopo, taking in some of the best places to see. For more information see the main entries (➤ 140–147).

Day 1

Morning
Stop in the provincial capital **Mbombela** and stock up with provisions at the supermarkets in Riverside Mall. Continue along the N4 to Malelane.

Afternoon
Stop at **Buhlebethu** at the **Pestana Kruger Lodge** (R570, Malelane; tel: 013 790 2503), the restaurant overlooks the Crocodile River and you can view game drinking while you dine. Continue along the N4 and enter ★**Kruger National Park** (right; ➤ 140) at the southern corner at Crocodile Bridge.

Evening
Spend the late afternoon game viewing along the Sabie River. You may see herds of impala, waterbuck or elephant drinking at the water's edge. Stay overnight in self-catering accommodation in Lower Sabie.

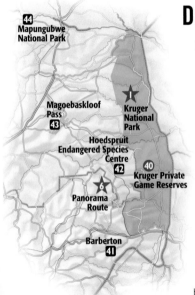

Day 2

Morning
Head out for an early-morning game drive when the animals are at their most active, or opt for a guided game walk booked through reception.

Afternoon
Back at camp have a picnic and relax for a couple of hours at the swimming pool. Watch out for game as you drive to Skukuza, Kruger's largest restcamp, which has a number of facilities.

Evening
Book into your chalet at Skukuza and enjoy an early-evening *braai* (barbecue) below the African night sky.

Day 3

Morning
Exit the park via the Paul Kruger or Phabeni gates to go sightseeing on the scenic ☆**Panorama Route** (► 142) and drive through the country towns of Hazyview and Graskop.

Afternoon
Eat lunch at **Harrie's Pancakes** (► 150) in Graskop and spend an hour or two exploring the miners' cottages along the single street of **Pilgrim's Rest** (► 142), a 19th-century gold-mining village.

Evening
Stay the night in one of the region's country lodges.

Day 4

Morning
Drive along the R532 and take in the sweeping views of the spectacular **Blyde River Canyon** (► 142) from the viewpoints. Visit the unusual rock formations at Bourke's Luck Potholes.

Afternoon and Evening
Head to one of the superb **40 Kruger Private Game Reserves** that run along the western border of Kruger. Ensure you are there in plenty of time for the guided afternoon game drive that is almost always included in the room rate.

Day 5

Morning
Enjoy a guided morning game drive and a late brunch at your lodge.

Afternoon
Return to Johannesburg or continue northeast on the R36 toward the **43 Magoebaskloof Mountains** (► 146).

★Kruger National Park

The 20,000km² (7,800mi²) park was established in 1898 and is one of Africa's largest reserves. The vast reserve (350km/217mi long, 90km/56mi at its widest) is bordered by Mozambique to the east, Zimbabwe to the north, and private game reserves to the west. In 2002 the park became a peace park when it linked to the Gonarezhou National Park in Zimbabwe and the Limpopo National Park in Mozambique, forming the Great Limpopo Transfrontier Park.

Named after the former president of the South African Republic, Paul Kruger (1825–1904), this park is one of the richest game reserves in southern Africa. Here you are almost guaranteed to see the Big Five – the 2016 census recorded 1,600 lions, 2,000 leopard 13,000 elephants, 40,000 buffalo and endangered rhino (data withheld due to poaching) – as well 250,000 antelope, 8,000 giraffes and 3,000 crocodiles. There are a total of 150 mammal species, 507 bird species and 114 species of reptiles. The park is also home to about 300 endangered African wild dogs, so if you spot a wild dog or one of the 150 cheetahs, you'll be very lucky.

Pretoriouskop's round huts seen through the bright flowers of a coral tree

The variety of flora is as equally impressive as the fauna with each region displaying different plants. Tracts of mopane woodlands characterize the northern half while

THE MOST POPULAR CAMPS

Lower Sabie: This restcamp is located on the Sabie River and in the early morning and evening attracts numerous hippos, buffaloes, elephants, warthogs and lions when they come to drink. There are various accommodation options; each camp space comes with its own water connection.

Pretoriouskop: One of the largest restcamps is set in a landscape of enormous granite outcrops. It is a particularly good place for spotting white rhino and it also boasts a lovely natural rock swimming pool.

Orpen: A simple restcamp (no restaurant) near the Orpen Gate that also has two attractive satellite camps, Maroela and Tamboti, hidden in the bush. The latter has tents on a high bank above the Timbavati River with views over the open plains.

Olifants: This restcamp is set on a high ridge overlooking the Olifants River. It offers spectacular views of the bushveld and the game viewing includes hippo, buffalo, giraffe, kudu, elephant and numerous birds. No campground.

Letaba: Slightly quieter than Olifants, but just as beautifully situated, the camp is on a bend above the Letaba River. The camp's Elephant Hall exhibits the powerful tusks of the Kruger's most famous elephants.

INSIDER INFO

- Kruger is considered a low-risk malaria region – take **malaria prophylactics**, use **insect repellent** and cover up at dusk when mosquitoes are at their most active.
- Avoid visiting during **South African school holidays** (Easter, end Jun–mid-Jul, end Sep–early Oct, early Dec–mid-Jan) when the restcamps can be horribly crowded.
- **Advance reservations are necessary** for accommodation, but once in the park you can swap your bookings to another restcamp if there is availability.
- The best time for hiking on the **Wilderness Trails** is Mar–Jul when it's dry and cool. These trails must be booked several months in advance (tel: 012 428 9111; www.sanparks.org). Maximum group size is eight people.
- Many **tour operators** in Johannesburg offer three- to five-day tours combining Kruger and the Panorama Route (➤ 142–143).

Insider Tip

Insider Tip

Above: Leopards can climb trees with a few leaps

Below: Burchell's zebra are the smallest of the zebra species and have the widest stripes

the southern region has open veld with scrub, buffalo grass and different species of acacia, coral and marula trees. The banks of the rivers (most flow through the park from west to east) feature reeds and riparian vegetation but, outside of the rainy season, most of these rivers are dry. The park's hot, rainy season is in the summer months from November to April, with a cool dry season in the winter. The best time for game viewing is during the dry season when the bush thins out and animals can easily be spotted congregating along the rivers or man-made waterholes; the malaria risk is also lower at this time. The southern part of the park, between **Sabie** and the **Olifants River**, is more geared towards tourism and has the most camps and lodges. Visitors can explore the park on self-drive tours (open vehicles, bicycles or motorcycles are prohibited) and it is worth noting that it is illegal (and dangerous) to get out of your car unless you are in a designated area. All visitors must leave the park before the gates close in order to allow enough time to travel to the restcamps.

Insider Tip

TAKING A BREAK

The twelve main restcamps have facilities such as shops, restaurants, petrol stations, laundromats, and even swimming pools. Each camp has their own selection of accommodation, which varies from campsites to huts, bungalows and safari tents (with shared kitchen and ablution facilities) and self-catering cottages.

✚ 203 E5 ☎ 012 428 9111; www.sanparks.org
🕐 Jan–Feb, Nov–Dec 5:30am–6:30pm; Mar, Oct 5:30am–6pm; Apr 6am–5:30pm; May–Aug 6:30am–5:30pm; Sep 6–6 🚗 R304

⭐6 Panorama Route

The Panorama Route winds its way along rugged mountain passes, past dramatic waterfalls, deep canyons and picturesque country towns surrounded by pine and eucalyptus forests. It offers fantastic views of the Kruger National Park's plains 1,000m (3,280ft) below.

Sabie and Graskop

Ringed by mountains and vast pine and eucalyptus plantations, **Sabie** was once a small gold mining town and today it's the centre for the largest man-made forest in the country, which supports an estimated 50 per cent of South Africa's timber needs. The interesting **Komatiland Forestry Museum** can organize day and overnight hikes and mountain biking in the forests. Near town, the **Sabie Falls**, **Bridal Veil Falls**, **Horseshoe Falls** and **Lone Creek Falls** are well worth a visit and 12km (7mi) of the Sabie River have been reserved for trout fishing. There are more waterfalls around **Graskop**, another forestry centre with a main street lined with restaurants and gift shops.

Pilgrim's Rest

To the east, the picturesque village of **Pilgrim's Rest** has been declared a national monument for its gold mining history: gold was discovered here in 1873. Today the single street of Victorian miners' cottages has been restored to its former glory, and it houses a number of interesting **museums** for which tickets can be bought at the tourist

Insider Tip office. At the **Diggings Site** you can watch a demonstration of gold panning and have a go yourself.

Blyde River Canyon

North of Graskop, en route to **Blyde River Canyon** are a number of viewpoints with names like "God's Window" and "Wonder View", which hint at views they offer over the lowveld running back towards the Kruger Park.

The Blyde River has its source in the Drakensberg Mountains south of Pilgrim's Rest

Even more spectacular is the Blyde River Canyon itself, which is one of the largest canyons in Africa at 26km (16mi) long and up to 800m (2,624ft) deep. Dense vegetation with moss and ferns fill the deep valleys, while the mountain tops are covered with vividly coloured lichen.

The **Pinnacle** is a single quartzite column jutting out from the canyon and the **Three Rondavels** are three huge domes of dolomite rock rising out of the far wall, so-named because they resemble traditional, circular African huts.

At **Bourke's Luck Potholes** a network of pathways and footbridges allow you to explore the potholes – strange cylindrical sculptures carved by swirling water at the confluence of the Blyde and Treur rivers. You can continue along the R532 and then the R36 to the bottom of the canyon where there are a number of attractions and places to stay along the way to **Hoedspruit** and Kruger's Orpen Gate.

The spectacular Bourke's Luck Potholes in the Blyde River Canyon, South Africa's own version of the Grand Canyon

TAKING A BREAK

Graskop is famous for its pancakes with sweet and savoury fillings. Try **Harrie's Pancakes** (➤ 150) on the main street.

✚ 203 E4

Komatiland Forestry Museum
✉ Ford Street, Sabie
☎ 013 764 3399; www.sabie.co.za
🕐 Mon–Fri 8–4:30, Sat 8–noon
💲 R20

Pilgrim's Rest Tourist Information
✉ Main Street, Pilgrim's Rest
☎ 013 768 10 60;
www.pilgrims-rest.co.za
🕐 Daily 9–12:45, 1:45–4

Diggings Site
✉ 1km (0.6mi) south of Pilgrim's Rest
🕐 Daily hour-long tours leave at 10, 11, noon, 2 and 3 💲 R12

Bourke's Luck Potholes
☎ 013 774 3617
🕐 Daily 7–5 💲 R30, vehicle R20

INSIDER INFO

■ The **best time** to view the Blyde River Canyon is in the cool dry winters, as it can often be misty in summer. By contrast the best time to see the waterfalls is in summer, when rain increases the surge of water.
■ There's a **visitors' centre** at Bourke's Luck Potholes outlining the geological history of the area.
■ For a **driving tour** of the region see ➤ 182.

㊵ Kruger Private Game Reserves

Wildlife moves freely between Kruger and the private game reserves in the wide lowveld plains of the southwest border of the park. Here, luxury lodges offer an exclusive safari experience, where you can game drive in a private vehicle with a knowledgeable guide, and enjoy fine cuisine and luxurious accommodation in the heart of the bush.

All game reserves have been sensitively built to blend in with the landscape. Most charge an **admission fee** (R100–R200 per person, R200–R400 per vehicle) and at some you may also have to pay a small conservation levy at the lodge. Game drives organized by the camps set off in the early morning and late afternoon, some also offer night drives. Headed by experienced safari guides, you will not only see many more animals, but also learn about the different species of birds and animals.

TAKING A BREAK
A normal day on safari begins with coffee and rusks at dawn before an early morning game drive. A late brunch is served back at the lodge and there's time to relax before afternoon tea, followed by a game walk or late afternoon game drive and a sumptuous dinner sometimes served out in the bush.

Opposite page clockwise: elephants and giraffe near Camp Satara, white rhino in the south of the park, hippos at Lower Sabie restcamp and a lion near Hoedspruit

✚ 203 E4

Sabi Sand Game Reserve ☎ www.sabisand.co.za
MalaMala Game Reserve ☎ www.malamala.com
Manyeleti Game Reserve ☎ www.manyeleti.co.za
Thornybush Game Reserve ☎ www.thornybushcollection.co.za
Kapama Game Reserve ☎ www.kapama.co.za
Klaserie Private Nature Reserve ☎ www.klaseriecamps.com
Timbavati Private Nature Reserve ☎ www.timbavati.co.za
Transfrontiers Walking Safaris ☎ 015 793 1350; www.transfrontiers.com

INSIDER INFO

You will get **much more out of your safari** if you take an interest in not only the Big Five, but the smaller species and birds too (left: a crested barbet at the lookout point near Olifants restcamp).

Insider Tip

At Your Leisure

41 Barberton

After the discovery of gold in
1884, a mining town instantly
sprang up here. Four years later
and Barberton's gold rush was
over and prospectors moved on
to the richer deposits of the
Witwatersrand. Today all that
remains of the glory days are
a few historical buildings, some
of which are open to the public.
The **Barberton Museum** has exhibits on gold, geology, mining and
the general history of the region.
🔟 203 E3 ℹ️ Market Square, Crown Street
☎ 013 712 2880; www.barberton.co.za
🕐 Mon–Fri 7:30–5, Sat 8–1

42 Hoedspruit Endangered Species Centre

The small town of **Hoedspruit**,
which lies just 30km northwest of
the Kruger National Park's Orpen
Gate, is home to several wildlife
rehabilitation centres, including the
Moholoholo Wildlife Rehab Centre
(www.moholoholo.co.za). One of
South Africa's leading breeding and
research centres for endangered

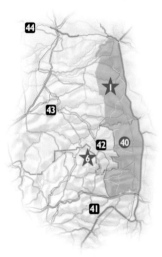

FOLLOW IN THE PAW PRINTS
In front of the Barberton town hall is a statue of Sir Percy Fitzpatrick's heroic dog Jock, immortalized in his children's book 📖 *Jock of the Bushveld*. Download the free Kindle Edition and delight your children with the true stories of plucky Jock and his owner, who was as an ox-cart driver in the area in the 1880s.

species, the **Hoedspruit Endangered
Species Centre**, is part of the
Kapama Game Reserve (➤ 144).
The project was initially established
to breed cheetah and more than
80 can be seen. The reserve is also
home to wild dog, young rhinos,
African wild cat, ground hornbills
and various antelope. Guided tours
depart on the hour: visitors travel
in open safari vehicles around the
animal enclosures. You can also
arrange an elephant ride at the
affiliated Camp Jabulani – if you
opt to stay overnight at the camp
there's the chance to ride an elephant in the dark!

Insider Tip

🔟 203 E4 ✉️ Off the R40, near Hoedspruit
☎ 015 793 1633; www.hesc.co.za
🕐 Tours daily 9, 11, 1 and 3 💳 R150

43 Magoebaskloof Mountains

From Tzaneen – the centre of a
lush agricultural region and a
popular stopover on the way to
the Kruger National Park – the
R71 heads southwest through the
Magoebaskloof Pass. The road
first runs parallel to the Magoebas
River valley then, after about 18km
(11mi) there is a right turn and
after another 3km (2mi) it takes
you to the remote **Debegeni Falls**.
The spectacular waterfall cascades
80m (260ft) down into a small lake,
where swimming is allowed. The
road continues to climb steeply

before reaching the summit (1,400m/ 4,600ft) and the Magoebaskloof Hotel. Further on is the Ebenezer Dam, an excursion area popular for picnics, birding, boating and fishing.

From here it is only 5km (3mi) to **Haenertsburg**, which is known for its trout and its Spring Festival in September. You can do the relatively easy Magoebaskloof Hiking Trail (starting at the Dokolewa Pools; tel: 013 764 2682, R20; permit required), a lesser-known hike that leads through lush, indigenous vegetation and picturesque

with grave goods from Arabia and Asia. Mapungubwe Hill revealed traces of a wealthy African trading kingdom that existed before the stone city of Great Zimbabwe, the oldest known southern African culture to date. It is believed that Mapungubwe was at its height from 1050 to the end of the 13th century and traded along the East African coast, where objects from Arabia and China were acquired. In 1994, the government declared the excavation site a national park; in 2002 the then-president, Thabo Mbeki, established the Order of

Baobab tree in Mapungubwe National Park, a UNESCO World Heritage Site since 2003

scenery. Six rustic huts along the route provide overnight accommodation).
🔢 203 D4 ✉ Haenertsburg ☎ 083 442 7429; www.magoebaskloooftourism.co.za
🕐 Mon–Fri 8–5, Sat, Sun 8.30–noon

44 Mapungubwe National Park
It is just an unassuming hill in the remote rocky border area of South Africa, Botswana and Zimbabwe, yet it has provided archaeologists with an entirely different view of the history of Africa. In 1932, archaeologists uncovered graves where the dead wore precious gold jewellery and were buried

Mapungubwe, South Africa's highest order, and awarded it to Nelson Mandela. In 2003, UNESCO declared the ruins and graves a World Heritage Site. Artefacts that were previously held by the University of Pretoria were returned to the new Interpretive Centre that opened on site in September 2011. Book a guided walking tour of the archaeological hill site at the park's central office. *Insider Tip*
🔢 203 D5
✉ 70km (42mi) west of Musina on the R572
☎ 015 534 7925; www.sanparks.org
🕐 Day visitors: Sep–Mar 6am–6:30pm; Apr–Aug 6:30am–6pm 🎫 R176

Mpumalanga & Limpopo

Where to...
Stay

Prices
Expect to pay per double room, per night
R under R1,500   **RR** R1,500–R2,500   **RRR** over R2,500

KRUGER NATIONAL PARK & PRIVATE GAME RESERVES

Camp Jabulani RRR
Under thatch with slate walls and contemporary African furnishings, the six elegant suites have slide-away walls for views of the bush, wooden decks and plunge pools.
🕂 203 E4
✉ Kapama Game Reserve
☎ 015 793 1265 (camp),
012 460 5605 (reservations);
www.campjabulani.com

MalaMala (Main Camp, Rattray's, Sable Camp) RRR
These are three camps in the 13,000ha (32,123-acre) MalaMala Game Reserve, South Africa's largest privately owned Big Five reserve, which shares open borders with Kruger to the east and Sabi Sand to the west. The game viewing here is reliably superb, with leopards being a particular speciality, and since traversing rights are limited to these camps, good sightings very seldom get oversubscribed.
🕂 203 E4
✉ MalaMala Game Reserve
☎ 011 442 2267; www.malamala.com

Ngala RRR
This game lodge has 20 thatched cottages decorated with exquisite antiques, sheltered by mopane trees and overlooking a waterhole and large swimming pool. Rates are all-inclusive of game activities and the guides are superb. Suitable

for families, though there's one deluxe honeymoon suite.
🕂 203 E4
✉ Timbavati Private Nature Reserve
☎ 011 809 4300;www.ngalasafarilodge.com,
www.andbeyond.com

Singita RRR
Singita is actually a group of luxury game lodges. Ebony and Boulders lodges are in the Sabi Sand Game Reserve, while Lebombo and Sweni are in a concessionaire part of Kruger near the border with Mozambique. All are design masterpieces using a combination of thatch, wood, glass and steel with bright furnishings and modern art. With fine food and wine, superb game guides and a spa, this is a top safari experience.
🕂 203 E4 (Sabi Sand) ✉ Various, see website for specific lodge details
☎ 021 683 3424; www.singita.co.za

Skukuza and Lower Sabie R
The largest of Kruger's restcamps, Skukuza overlooks the Sabie River in the game-rich south of the park. Excellent facilities include a restaurant, three swimming pools and a golf course. You can stay in self-catering units or camp. The smaller Lower Sabie camp nearby, also lies on the Sabie River.
🕂 203 F4 ✉ Near Paul Kruger Gate
☎ 013 735 4265; www.sanparks.org

PANORAMA ROUTE

Blyde River Canyon Lodge R
This intimate thatched lodge is on the road to the Blyde River Dam at

the bottom of the canyon. Set in calm, scenic grounds, the nine air-conditioned rooms are modern and comfortable, each with a garden terrace; there's a pool and zebra stroll across the lawns.

➕ 203 E4 ✉ Off the R531, 67km (41mi) from the Orpen Gate ☎ 015 795 5305; www.blyderivercanyonlodge.com

Cybele Forest Lodge RR–RRR

Accommodation at this upmarket lodge, hidden in a tract of forest, is in a converted 1800s hunting lodge. Rooms are in individual cottages, some in their own grounds with a pool. There's an excellent restaurant, a spa, and stables for horseback riding in the surrounding forest.

➕ 203 E4
✉ Off the R40 between Mbombela and Hazyview
☎ 013 764 9500; www.cybele.co.za

The Royal Hotel R

Imagine what life was like as an early gold prospector in this 1896 hotel in historic Pilgrim's Rest.

With original wooden walls and tin roofs, the rooms are in 10 buildings around the village and have been restored with reproduction antiques. There are no TVs but soak up the village's history from the memorabilia in the bar and restaurant.

➕ 203 E4 ✉ Main Street, Pilgrim's Rest ☎ 013 768 1100; www.pilgrimsrest.org.za/royal.htm

MAPUNGUBWE NATIONAL PARK

Leokwe Camp R

The largest camp in Mapungubwe National Park lies in the eastern section, in a valley surrounded by spectacular sandstone hills, a 15-minute drive from the main entrance gate. All units are self-catering. Facilities include a shared swimming pool and picnic area, as well as a treetop hide for bird-watching nearby.

➕ 203 D5
✉ 10km (6mi) north of main entrance gate
☎ 015 534 7923; www.sanparks.org

Where to...
Eat and Drink

Prices
Expect to pay for a two-course meal per person excluding drinks:
R under R150   RR R150–R300   RRR over R300

MBOMBELA

Kuzuri Restaurant RR

Set on a wooden deck overlooking the main waterfall in Mbombela's lush botanical garden, this tranquil place serves up a cosmopolitan à la carte menu with a good selection of Cape Malay dishes.

➕ 203 E3
✉ Lowveld National Botanical Garden
☎ 013 757 0907; www.kuzuri.co.za
🕐 Wed–Sat 8am–9pm, Sun–Tue 8–3

PANORAMA ROUTE

The Ant and Elephant RR

Nestling among mango and lychee plantations with knotted wild fig trees in the gardens, The Ant and Elephant has an extensive à la carte menu as well as chef's specials. The winner is the Hot Summer's Dream – pan-fried spicy calamari (squid).

➕ 203 E4 ✉ 6km (4mi) from Hazyview on the R536 towards Sabie

☎ 013 737 8172
🕐 Mon–Sat 6–late

Canimambo Restaurante RR

Spicy chicken *piri-piri*, grilled lemon butter prawns (shrimp) and other excellent seafood are the specialities at this popular Portuguese restaurant.

✚ 203 E4
✉ Corner Louis Trichardt and Hoof streets, Graskop ☎ 013 767 1868; www.facebook.com/canimambo.restaurant.graskop
🕐 Sat–Thu 11–9, Fri 12–9

Gum Treez Pub & Grill R–RR

This little complex, on the White River side of Casterbridge Centre under some huge gum trees, consists of a coffee shop for breakfasts or teas, a pub and a restaurant. The best place to sit is outside on the covered deck. The atmosphere is laid-back and relaxed and the menu features South African favourites (lots of meat dishes) but also fish and chips, curries and bunny chow.

✚ 203 E3
✉ Casterbridge Lifestyle Centre, White River
☎ 013 750 0334; www.facebook.com/gumtreezpubandgrill
🕐 Mon–Thu 10–9, Fri, Sat 9–9, Sun 9–2

Harrie's Pancakes R

Harrie's, which now has outlets countrywide, is renowned for its pancakes and there is a divine selection of fillings to choose from, including trout mousse, spicy butternut pumpkin, blue-cheese sauce, banana and caramel, and black cherries and liqueur.

✚ 203 E4
✉ Louis Trichardt Street, Graskop
☎ 013 767 1273; www.harriespancakes.com
🕐 Daily 8–5:30

The Wild Fig Tree RR

There is a wide veranda for alfresco eating at this friendly spot. Grab a coffee or light lunch during the day, or something more ambitious in the evening – crocodile, venison and trout, a local speciality, are all on the menu. The home-made cakes and desserts are legendary and there's a curio shop where you can browse while you eat. **Insider Tip**

✚ 203 E4
✉ Corner Main Road and Louis Trichardt Street, Sabie
☎ 013 764 2239; www.facebook.com/WildFigTreeSabie
🕐 Daily 8:30am–9pm

The Windmill Wine Shop R

Within the country's most northerly vineyard, this is a wine shop and deli with a selection of tables as well so you can stop off on your journey and dine. Make up your own platter of tapas, cheese, sliced meat, pickles and olives accompanied by freshly made, still-warm bread, all stacked on rustic wooden boards. Wine is available by the glass and locally brewed beer is on tap.

✚ 203 E4
✉ R536 between Hazyview and Sabie
☎ 082 930 6289; www.thewindmill.co.za
🕐 Mon–Sat 9–5

HOEDSPRUIT

Mad Dogz Café R

A well-worthy stop en route to Kruger's Orpen Gate and the private reserves, this delightful country café, with its shady terrace under thatch, serves up South African favourites such as *bobotie* (a type of shepherd's pie with a savoury custard topping), chicken livers, smoked trout and Cajun dishes. The farm breakfasts are a great way to start the day and the attached Monsoon Gallery is worth a browse. **Insider Tip**

✚ 203 E4
✉ R527, 28km (17mi) from Hoedspruit at the bottom of Blyde River Canyon
☎ 084 250 1233; www.bluecottages.co.za
🕐 Daily 7:30–4:30

The Hat & Creek RR

Although this restaurant is large and often busy, the staff are dedicated and attentive. The menu features traditional South African dishes – from the perfect steak to the classic burger – the food is excellent, the portions generous and the atmosphere pleasant and relaxed..

➕ 203 E4
✉ R527, Main Street, Hoedspruit
☎ 015 793 1135; www.thehatandcreek.co.za
🕐 Daily 10–1

MAGOEBASKLOOF PASS

The Iron Crown Pub and Grill R

Set amid the pretty Magoebaskloof Mountains, this country pub with a long wooden bar attracts families for Sunday lunch. It is popular for its meaty fare, such as prime steaks, ribs and chicken schnitzel, accompanied by a variety of sauces. Service is friendly and informal and there are big-screen TVs on which to watch important matches – don't expect a quiet drink.

➕ 203 D4
✉ Haenertsburg village on the R71
☎ 015 276 4755
🕐 Tue–Sat 11–late, Sun 9–4

Where to...
Shop

MBOMBELA

An abundance of citrus and other subtropical fruits, including mangoes, bananas, pawpaws and guavas, are grown in this region, as well as nuts. Buy these from the roadside or stop at one of the many country **farm stalls** (known as *padstal* in Afrikaans).

The provincial capital Mbombela has Mpumalanga's largest shopping mall, the **Riverside Mall**, (tel: 013 757 0080; www.riversidemall.co.za, Mon–Sat 9–6, Sun 9–3), which is 5km (3mi) out of town on the White River road; it has 140 shops, 15 restaurants, a cinema and casino. It's worth stopping here to stock up on food in the supermarkets if you're heading to self-catering accommodation in Kruger.

Casterbridge Lifestyle Centre (tel: 013 751 1540; www.casterbridge.co.za, Mon–Sat 9–4:30, Sun 9–4), 2km (1mi) beyond White River on the R40, is an attractive country shopping centre where there are also several restaurants and a cinema. Shops sell second-hand books, art, home-made food, jewellery and clothes.

This is also where you will also find the **Kruger Lowveld Tourist Information** (tel: 013 755 1988), a 30-room boutique hotel, fitness centre and spa.

In Casterbridge, **Rottcher Wineries** (tel: 013 751 3472) sells Avalencia, a wine-like drink made from fermented orange juice and cane sugar. It is produced on a working macadamia nut farm and the shop at Casterbridge sells nuts as well as orange and ginger liquors in stone jugs.

Across the road from the Casterbridge Farm, the **Bagdad Centre** is a small centre with shops selling African handicrafts and a delicatessen selling fresh trout, cheeses and jam.

PANORAMA ROUTE

Sabie and Graskop have plenty of curio shops and numerous roadside stalls aimed at tourists, and African carvings markets can be found in the car parks at the viewpoints at some of the waterfalls and Blyde River Canyon.

In Sabie, there's an excellent book shop called **The Bookcase**

(Woodsman Centre, Main Street; tel: 013 764 2014, Mon–Sat 8:30–5, Sun 8:30–3), which is stuffed full of new and used books including a very good section on South African history.

In Hazyview, **Perry's Bridge Trading Post** (Main Street; tel: 013 737 6929; www.perrys bridge.co.za, Mon–Fri 7:30–4) has a number of interesting shops including a deli, a shop selling imported chocolates, a tourist information office, *Insider Tip* a reptile park (www.perrysbridge reptilepark.com) and several restaurants.

The **Marula Market** (five minutes from Hazyview on the R535 toward Graskop; tel: 013 737 5804; www.shangana.co.za) at Shangana Cultural Village (► right) is a wide circle of huts surrounded by trees and is home to craftspeople from all over the region; it has been an important catalyst for enabling local artists to make a living.

The long single street in Pilgrim's Rest is lined with gift and curio shops as well as restaurants, many of them housed in restored miners' cottages.

HOEDSPRUIT

On the R527 at the bottom of Blyde River Canyon, as it goes towards Hoedspruit, are a couple of places worth venturing to.

Monsoon Gallery (R527, east of the junction with the R36; tel: 015 795 5114; http://bluecottages. co.za/monsoon-gallery) sells a wonderful selection of quality ethnic jewellery, pottery, rural art, embroidery, baskets and wildlife books. Some of the items are antique and the owner is an avid collector of tribal artefacts. It's next to the Mad Dogz Café.

Nearby, the **Bombyx Mori Silk Estate** (tel: 082 808 9203; www. goddingandgodding.com) is on the R531, 23km (14mi) south of Hoedspruit, which among other items, makes divinely luxurious silk duvets. You can go on a tour *Insider Tip* to learn how silk is made and about the lifecycle of a silkworm.

Where to...
Go out

Given that this region is famed for its bush and countryside, there is little in the way of nightlife. But there are plenty of outdoor activities in the area to entertain you.

The **Big Swing** (Panorama Gorge, on the R533 a few metres outside of Graskop towards Hazyview; tel: 013 767 1612; www.bigswing.co.za) is similar to a bungee jump but with more of an outward swing over the pretty Panorama Falls.

The region's rivers are ideal for **whitewater rafting** day trips and overnight trips can be arranged through a number of operators via Panorama Information and Central Reservations (tel: 013 767 1377; www.panoramainfo.co.za).

The Blyde River Canyon looks even more impressive from the air, and **helicopter trips** (Sunrise Aviation; tel: 083 625 6991; www.sunrisehelicopters.co.za) dramatically dip down into the canyon and the various waterfalls, or take an early morning **balloon ride** (Suncatchers; tel: 087 806 2097; www.sun catchers.co.za).

At **Shangana Cultural Village** 5km (3mi) from Hazyview on the R535 towards Graskop; tel: 013 737 5804; www.shangana. co.za) there are daily tours of the authentic village although the best time to go is for the evening festival.

Northwest & Central Regions

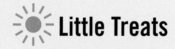 **Little Treats**

Spectacular Sunsets
Watch as the sky turn royal blue and the
sand dunes glow orange in the early evening
light of the dramatic **Kgalagadi Park** (➤ 164).

Join the Locals for a Sundowner…
…just outside **Clarens** (➤ 167) at the Ash
River Outfall point where water from Lesotho
transfers to Johannesburg's Vaal Dam.

Audi to Volvo
In the desert plains around **Upington** (➤ 168)
car manufacturers test-drive camouflaged
prototypes at top speed (legally) on the
region's dead-straight roads.

Getting Your Bearings

Few overseas visitors venture to the northern reaches of the country, and it's not always easy travelling. It can be hot in places, there are long distances to cover, and towns and settlements are few and far between. However, the region will appeal to the adventurer and there are some wonderful wildlife experiences to be had in the remote regions.

Boundless semi-desert plains and sculptural, craggy mountains characterize the Northern Cape. The secrets of the desert are its true treasures: succulents than store water in their stems and roots, seeds that explode into improbable carpets of flowers after a spattering of rain, and diamonds in the vents of its subterranean volcanoes. The Kalahari section is home to the San and the Nama, the last nomadic peoples of southern Africa, and despite the arid landscape, offers a diverse wildlife habitat. The largest wilderness is in Botswana and Namibia, on the border with South Africa, an area that forms the magnificent Kgalagadi Transfrontier Park. Not far from Johannesburg is the gambler's playground of Sun City, a world away from the adjoining wildlife sanctuaries of Pilanesberg and Madikwe. Inland is the Free State Province, dominated by endless wheat fields, while the mountains of the Eastern Highlands rise scenically on the eastern border to Lesotho.

Kalahari
BOTSWANA
Desert
47
Kgalagadi
Transfrontier Park

• Andriesvale

Upington
51
52
Augrabies Falls
National Park

• Kenhardt   • Marydale

NORTHERN CAPE
• Van Wyksvlei
PROVINCE

Flat-topped sandstone formations at Golden Gate National Park

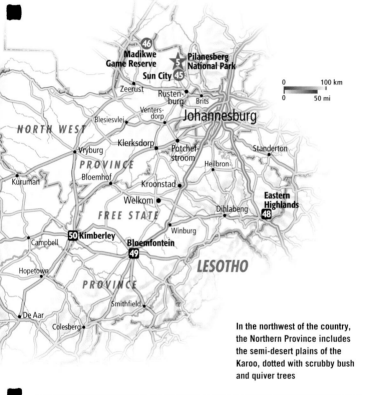

In the northwest of the country, the Northern Province includes the semi-desert plains of the Karoo, dotted with scrubby bush and quiver trees

Perfect Days in...

Seven Perfect Days

If you are not quite sure where to begin your travels, this itinerary recommends seven practical and enjoyable days in the northwest and central regions of South Africa, taking in some of the best places to see. For more information see the main entries (➤ 158–169).

Day 1

In the morning, head out to ㊹ Sun City (➤ 160), a two-hour drive from Johannesburg. Spend a leisurely afternoon, playing golf, frolicking in the wave pool and man-made beaches at the **Valley of the Waves** (➤ 160) or try some of the water sports on offer at Waterworld or at the Sun City Dam. Then dine at one of the fine restaurants in the evening, followed by a flutter in the casino.

Day 2

Enjoy an early-morning game drive or perhaps a hot air balloon ride in the ☆ **Pilanesberg National Park** (right: a Cape buffalo – one of the Big Five – at a waterhole; ➤ 158). After a late breakfast or early lunch, drive to ㊻ **Madikwe Game Reserve** (➤ 162) arriving in time for afternoon tea on the deck of your luxury lodge. Go on a late-afternoon game drive or perhaps a spotlight drive after dark and enjoy dinner back at your lodge.

Day 3

At dawn go on another guided game drive before a hearty brunch. Spend the rest of the day driving the 500–600km (310–372mi) to ㊿ **Kimberley** (➤ 168). Treat yourself to some quality pub food at **The Occidental Bar (The Ox)** (➤ 171).

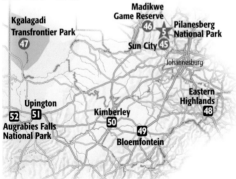

Day 4

Visit Kimberley's **Big Hole Complex** (➤ 168), one of largest man-made holes in the world, where you can ride a tram through a reconstruction of a 19th-century diamond-mining town.

In the afternoon, drive 377km (233mi) along the R64 and then the N10 to **51 Upington** (➤ 168). Stay overnight in Upington, and enjoy dinner and the friendly atmosphere at **Café Zest** (➤ 171).

Day 5

Drive the 120km (75mi) trip to the **52 Augrabies Falls National Park** (➤ 169) to see the falls crashing through the gorge. Spend the afternoon strolling along one of the many short walking trails through the park, or arrange to go rafting on the rapids upstream of the falls. In the evening, join a night drive in search of secretive nocturnal predators, then have a bush dinner or barbecue at camp.

Day 6

Return to Upington early, swap your saloon car for a four-wheel drive, and stock up on provisions and fuel. Drive the 260km (161mi) to the **47 Kgalagadi Transfrontier Park** (➤ 164). On arrival at your camp take a refreshing dip in the pool after the long dusty drive. Then in the mid-afternoon, head out for an exciting game drive, followed by a relaxed dinner at the restcamp restaurant.

Day 7

Head out early when the animals are at their most active and explore the dune belts and dry riverbanks. Rest up in the middle of the day when the heat is at its most intense. After a late afternoon game drive, cook a *braai* (barbecue), listen out for intriguing animal noises in the night and admire the vast canopy of stars over the Kalahari.

⭐5 Pilanesberg National Park

This national park is in the transition area between the dry Kalahari and the humid lowveld. Nestled in the eroded caldera of the long-extinct 1,687m-high (5,535ft) Pilanesberg volcano, the 570km² (220mi²) reserve is one of the largest and most popular wildlife sanctuaries in South Africa. In addition to the Big Five there are a wealth of other animals to see, including 300 bird species.

Established in the 1970s, it lies 150km (95mi) northwest of Johannesburg, adjacent to Sun City, making it a natural haven for weekend getaways. The park was stocked with animals from all over the country in the successful reintroduction project Operation Genesis. Today, it supports an estimated 7,000 large mammals representing about 25 species. It is a particularly good place for spotting white rhino and elephant, but black rhino, lion, leopard and buffalo are also present and seen with some regularity. Common herbivores include giraffe, plains zebra, blue wildebeest, warthog, impala and greater kudu. The park also hosts several antelope species that are absent or rare further east, including the black wildebeest, which are on the Red List of Threatened Species.

Set right in the centre of the park, **Mankwe Dam** is the habitat of crocodile, hippo and water-associated birds such as the handsome African fish eagle and various herons, storks and kingfishers. A hide overlooks the dam, and there are several other hides scattered at smaller watering points too.

INSIDER INFO

- **Guided game drives** to Pilanesberg depart regularly throughout the day from the Welcome Centre at Sun City.
- At **Kwa Maritane Lodge** there, a walk-in hide reached by a 180m (600ft) tunnel overlooks a waterhole where elephants and other animals regularly come to drink, providing excellent opportunities for close-up photography. Insider Tip
- All hotels and lodges around the Pilanesberg offer **night drives**, an opportunity to glimpse shy nocturnal creatures.

There are numerous lodges and camps within the park, and the main entrance gate is less than 5km (3mi) from Sun City. A thrilling way to see the landscape of the Pilanesberg National Park is to go game viewing from a hot air balloon. The views and animals are fantastic and the whole adventure takes about 5 hours (60 minutes of which is pure flight time).

Insider Tip

TAKING A BREAK

The park has five picnic areas the most attractive of which is **Fish Eagle**, which overlooks Mankwe Dam. There's also a quieter **coffee shop** at the Pilanesberg Centre in a converted old farmhouse north of Mankwe Dam.

✚ 202 B4 ✉ Off the R565
☎ 014 555 1600; www.pilanesbergnationalpark.org
🕐 Nov–Feb daily 5:30–7; Mar–Apr, Sep–Oct 6–6:30; May–Aug 6:30–6
💰 R110

Hot Air Balloon Safari/Mankwe Game Trackers
☎ 014 552 50 20; www.mankwegametrackers.co.za
💰 R4,500

A herd of black wildebeest grazing in the park's open savannah

㊺ Sun City

Tucked away in the lush rolling bush of the former homeland of Bophuthatswana is the Las Vegas of South Africa, a huge, brash entertainment resort that attracts 25,000 guests daily.

During apartheid gambling was illegal in South Africa but legal in the former black homelands where casino resorts were built. This explains the rather remote location of Sun City, which was built in 1979 in the homeland of Bophuthatswana, now all part of the Northwest Province. Today, now that casinos have been built in the cities, there's less emphasis on gambling at Sun City, though one casino remains open, and the complex is more geared to family entertainment. You can stay overnight or visit on a long day trip from Johannesburg or Pretoria. You'll not be short of things to do here; the whole complex can be explored from the Sky Train monorail that starts in the parking area, and you can pick up a map, and book activities in the **Welcome Centre**. The resort's extravagant recreational facilities include one of the world's largest casinos, numerous cinemas, nightclubs, a huge range of water sports and two internationally renown golf courses. The arena hosts sporting events and pop concerts.

> **🚸 FOR KIDS**
> While parents try their luck at the slot machines, children can enjoy the **Entertainment Centre's** large gaming arcade.

Sun City's Attractions

The fantasy complex is dominated by the **Lost City,** which symbolises a legend in African culture, one that actually never existed – a perfectly executed illusion. In the centre of the Lost City is the **Palace of the Lost City**, an African-themed luxury hotel created in an astonishing mixture of architectural styles with a 70m-high (230ft) tower and a 25m-high (82ft) hotel lobby that feels more like a cathedral.

Below the hotel, a 25ha (62-acre) tropical rainforest has been established with transplanted mature trees. The Valley of the Waves has meandering streams, a waterfall

Visitors to Sun City's Valley of the Waves enjoy its man-made beaches and wave pool

INSIDER INFO

- All accommodation at the Palace of the Lost City, Sun City Hotel, Cascades and the Sun City Cabanas must be booked through **Sun International Central Reservations** (tel: 011 780 7800; www.suninternational.com).
- The 25ha (62-acre) **man-made forest** has over 1.6 million plants and trees, and the intriguing pathways make a pleasant distraction from the rest of the Disney-like resort.

Sun City is Africa's answer to Las Vegas: pictured here is the luxurious Palace of the Lost City hotel

(16m/52ft) and walkways to the Roaring Lagoon, a pool area created using shipped in beach sand. The lagoon has mechanically generated waves so that water surges up the white sand beach. To create an "authentic" African experience, animal sounds are played on loudspeakers, and every now and then the ground trembles in a mock earthquake.

TAKING A BREAK

At the **Cultural Village** there's a *shebeen* (pub). It serves African cuisine and you can watch traditional singing and dancing.

Facilities at the Palace of the Lost City include two golf courses

🕂 202 B4   ✉ On the R565 north of Rustenburg
☎ 014 557 1000; www.suninternational.com
💷 R60 Sun City entrance fee, Valley of the Waves R120–R160

⓸⓺ Madikwe Game Reserve

In the far north of the country on the border with Botswana, a 750km² (290mi²) reserve was created in 1991, where the chances of seeing wild animals in their habitat is even higher than in the better-known Kruger National Park.

Closed to day visitors and self-drive safaris, Madikwe is serviced by 16 luxury lodges and guests explore the reserve in game drives led by highly knowledgeable guides. Madikwe safaris are not cheap, but worth the expense as the animals have become accustomed to the open four-wheel drive vehicles and don't see the game rangers – and their guests – as a threat. So your ranger may switch off the vehicle in the middle of a buffalo herd and not even the clicking of cameras will disturb the herd from their grazing. The rangers also communicate with each other via radio, so if one finds a family of lions resting under an acacia tree, they will let the other guides know.

The reserve was created from land previously used for agricultural purposes and while its primarily purpose was to protect endangered animals, it also created jobs for the local population. The area was previously completely isolation and had some of the province's poorest inhabitants. Scenically, the reserve consists of vast plains of open

Antelope and zebra near Jaci's Lodge, one of the 16 luxury lodges in Madikwe

A male southern masked weaver (*Ploceus velatus*) building a nest

woodlands and grasslands, a landscape that tends to be rather uniform in the east, but is dotted with rocky hills in the west, while the **Dwarsberg Mountains** lie close to the southern boundary. The most important river is the **Marico**, which flows along the eastern boundary.

Operation Phoenix

Similar to Operation Genesis, the Pilanesberg reintroduction project, Madikwe's Operation Phoenix ran from 1991 to 1998 when 28 different mammal species, and a total of 8,000 individual animals, were resettled here from other South African game reserves. All the animals, including elephant herds, were originally native to the region, but were almost completely wiped out by hunting and farming.

Birdlife

In addition to the Big Five, the reserve's open grassland is also one of the best places anywhere to see the endangered African wild dog. More than 350 varieties of bird have been recorded in the reserve, ranging from outsized grassland species such as ostrich and kori bustard (the world's heaviest flying bird) to striking Kalahari specials such as pied babbler and violet-eared waxbill, and an impressive selection of eagles and other raptors. The best time of the year for game viewing is from March to September.

Insider Tip

TAKING A BREAK

Enjoy lavish brunches and afternoon tea in the **luxury lodges** before and after game drives.

➕ 202 B4 ✉ Off the R49 north of Zeerust. No day visitors to the reserve
☎ 018 350 9931/2; www.tourismnorthwest.co.za
💵 Gate entrance fee R180, in addition to accommodation

INSIDER INFO

- You can drive from Johannesburg in about four hours. There are several **entrance gates**, and these are accessed from different routes, so confirm the best entry point and route for your specific lodge before you set off.

Insider Tip

- **Madikwe Charters** operates daily flights between Johannesburg and the reserve (tel: 011 805 4888; www.madikwecharters.com). The lodges pick up guests from the reserve's airstrip.
- Madikwe – like Pilanesberg National Park – ranks among the few top African safari destinations to be **completely free of malaria**.

④⑦ Kgalagadi Transfrontier Park

The vast 38,000km² (14,700mi²) cross-border Kgalagadi Transfrontier Park was created by the merger of Botswana's Gemsbok National Park and South Africa's Kalahari Gemsbok National Park. Two usually dry rivers, the Auob and the Nossob, cross the park from northwest to southeast and form the main arteries along which game drives take place.

The Kalahari basin stretches over a more than 1 million km² (385,000mi²), the largest area is in Botswana, the western region is in Namibia and only the southern tip is in South Africa. The vast arid plains are, on average, about 800–1,200m (2,600–3,900ft) above sea level and are covered by a layer of red, iron oxide sand, formed by the erosion of huge rock masses. The luminous, multi-shaded dune landscapes alternate with expanses of dry savannah.

Due to its inhospitable conditions, the Kalahari is a virtually untouched wilderness; only the San roam its endless expanses. It is a thirst land – as opposed to a waterless desert devoid of any life – and the part within South Africa receives an average rainfall of 200mm (8in) per annum, which allows for some vegetation. Plants that are well adapted to the dry conditions include

As a cross-border conservation area, the Kgalagadi Transfrontier Park is one of the peace parks

Gemsbok is one of the varieties of antelope common in the park

A well-camouflaged, sand-coloured ground squirrel

dwarf shrubs, grass tussocks and succulents. One of the few tree species is the white-barked shepherd tree, which has a shady canopy of evergreen leaves that provide a high protein food source. Beautiful camelthorn trees, which grow in dry river valleys, can grow up to 15m (50ft). After rain showers the desert landscape is briefly transformed by an array of grasses and flowers. There is no permanent surface water and although there are two riverbeds (the Auob and the Nossob) running through the park, they have only flowed a few times in the last century. Over millennia flash floods have nonetheless caused the rivers to carve out impressive valleys. About 80 windmills along the dry river valleys provide water for the park's animals. Another source of water is the Tsamma, a wild melon that is 90 per cent water, which is eaten by both animals and the nomadic San.

The Park's Wildlife

In addition to the gemsbok, found here in numbers, there are also numerous blue wildebeest, eland and harte-beest. More rarely seen are the park's black-backed jackals, spotted hyenas, caracals, leopards, impalas and kudus. Among the 200 varieties of birds are 50 raptors, including the Martial eagle, African hawk eagle and long-legged secretary birds. Game viewing is at its best in the dry valleys and around the waterholes.

Staying in Kgalagadi

There are 10 camps on the South African side. The largest is Twee Rivieren, which lies at the entrance gate, and is fenced with a shop, restaurant, swimming pool and petrol station. Mata-Mata and Nossob are also relatively large fenced camps with similar facilities. There are six unfenced wilderness camps, where you might hear the roar of a lion below the Kalahari night sky, while !Xaus Lodge is an isolated community-owned upmarket tented camp overlooking a saltpan.

Insider Tip

TAKING A BREAK

About 50km (30mi) before the park's gate, **Molopo Kalahari Lodge** (tel: 054 511 0008; www.molopolodge. co.za; R) is the last stop before the park. Enjoy a meal and a dip in the pool and there's a petrol station and bottle shop.

Kalahari lions are not a distinct species but have adapted well to their desert environment and can go without water for up to two weeks

➕ 189 E5

Kgalagadi Transfrontier Park
➕ 201 D4
✉ 385km (239mi) from Kuruman, 260km (161mi) from Upington
☎ 054 561 2000; www.sanparks.org
🕐 Twee Rivieren gate hours vary every month but are generally open 7–6:30
🚗 R304

INSIDER INFO

- Although not essential, it's recommended you use a **four-wheel drive vehicle** *Insider Tip* because of the gravel roads. These can be rented in Upington. Try Kalahari 4×4 (tel: 082 490 1937; www.kalahari4x4hire.co.za) or Desert 4×4 (tel: 054 332 1183; www.desert4x4.co.za).
- All parks **accommodation** must be booked in advance through South African National Parks (SANParks); tel: 012 428 9111; www.sanparks.org.
- If you don't want to self-drive, take a **tour**, also from Upington. Try Kalahari *Insider Tip* Safaris (tel: 054 332 5653; www.kalaharisafaris.co.za) or Kalahari Tours and Travel (tel: 054 338 0375; www.kalahari-tours.co.za).
- Ensure you **drink plenty of fluids** – up to 5 litres (1gal) of water a day – to avoid becoming dehydrated. Although the water in the park is safe to drink, it's salty; the shops sell bottled water.
- **Temperatures** vary greatly from -11°C (around 12°F) on cold winter nights to 42°C (108°F) in the shade on summer days when the temperature of the ground reaches a sizzling 70°C (158°F).

At Your Leisure

48 Eastern Highlands

In the middle of the country, the Free State Province is dominated by an undulating grassy plain with fields of corn and sunflowers. In the southeast, however, it abruptly rises to a highland area bordering Lesotho, where the **Golden Gate Highlands National Park** derives its name from the brilliant shades of gold cast by the sun on the park's sandstone cliffs. The grasslands and hills offer superb hiking and birdwatching, and there's a hotel

🧒 FOR KIDS

Spend the night with your children in the **Hobbit Boutique Hotel** (19 President Steyn Avenue, Westdene, Bloemfontein; tel: 051 447 06 63; www.hobbit.co. za; R) where all the rooms are named after characters from the *Lord of the Rings* trilogy.

and a restcamp. Just before the park's western gate, the **Basotho Cultural Village** gives an insight into the lives of the Basotho people where you can tour the village huts, watch craft workers and sample home-made beer.

Further west, the village of **Clarens** is an artists' refuge thanks to the pretty mountain scenery, and you can visit a number of galleries situated around the village square.

✚ 203 D2

Golden Gate Highlands National Park
☎ 058 255 1000; www.sanparks.org 💷 R176

Basotho Cultural Village
🕐 Daily 9–4 💷 Guided tour R70

Clarens Tourist Information
✉ Market Street, Clarens
☎ 058 256 1542; www.clarens.co.za
🕐 Daily 9–1, 2–5

49 Bloemfontein

Straddling the N1 highway, Bloemfontein, the capital of the Free State Province and part of the Mangaung Metropolitan Municipality, is a convenient overnight stop for motorists going between Johannesburg and Cape Town and there are scores of accommodation options. The city centre is home to some historical, tree-lined streets concentrated around **President Brand Street**, with some stately government buildings like the City Hall, the Old Presidency, the Anglican Cathedral, the twin-tower Dutch Reformed Church and the Supreme Court. The tourist office produces a map for a historical walking tour. The **National Museum** has displays on dinosaurs and natural history as well as a mock-up of an early street in Bloemfontein. To the northeast of the city centre is Naval Hill, which is worth driving up for the broad city views, and at the top is the **Franklin Game Reserve**, which is home to some springbok, eland and hartebeest and giraffe. Bloemfontein is where the author JRR Tolkien, creator of *The Hobbit* and *Lord of the Rings*, was born.

✚ 202 B1
🏠 60 Park Road
☎ 051 405 8489; www.mangaung.co.za, www.bloemfonteintourism.co.za
🕐 Mon–Fri 8–4:30, Sat 8–noon

Northwest & Central Regions

National Museum

✉ 36 Aliwal Street

☎ 051 447 9609; www.nasmus.co.za

🕐 Mon–Fri 8–5, Sat 10–5, Sun 12–5

💵 R5

50 Kimberley

Kimberley, the capital of the Northern Cape, is synonymous with diamonds. These were discovered here in 1871, attracting a rush of prospectors who collectively excavated the Big Hole, mining some 14.5 million carats before the Hole's closure in 1914. At the time, at 460m (1,500ft) wide (1.6km/1mi perimeter) and 1,100m (3,608ft) deep, it was the world's largest hand-dug hole. Today, the Big Hole Complex includes a museum dedicated to the diamond rush, when prospectors lit their cigars with banknotes and bathed in Champagne, and more millionaires – among them Cecil John Rhodes – met at the Kimberley Club than anywhere else in the world

✚ 191 D2

Kimberley's aptly named Big Hole

The Big Hole Complex

✉ Tucker Street

☎ 053 839 4600; www.thebighole.co.za

🕐 Daily 8–5 💵 R100

51 Upington

Upington is the most substantial town for hundreds of kilometres in any direction and the main gateway to the **Kgalagadi Transfrontier Park** (➤ 164), so you'll no doubt end up here if you tour the remote northwest. Here the Gariep River (formerly the Orange River) irrigates a narrow ribbon of fertile land where wine grapes are cultivated, and sultanas and raisins produced. Upington is home to the Orange River Wine Cellars Co-operative and the South African Dried Fruit Co-operative, so look out for these items for sale. The town developed from a mission station, founded in 1871, and the history can be seen in the little **Kalahari Oranje Museum**, which has the best view of the river in town. Upington is the country's hottest town; summer temperatures often rise to more than 40°C (104°F).

✚ 201 D2

At Augrabies Falls the Gariep River plunges dramatically into the valley below

Upington Information Centre
✉ Anton Lubowski Street ☎ 054 332 6064;
www.upington-information.co.za
🕐 Mon–Fri 8–5:30, Sat 9–12

Kalahari Oranje Museum
✉ Schröder Street
🕐 Mon–Fri 9–12:30, 2–5
💶 R30

52 Augrabies Falls National Park

The Augrabies Falls are where the Gariep (Orange) River drops 100m (328ft) over a series of cataracts before thundering through a small gap in an explosion of white water into the 18km (11mi) Orange River Gorge. For good reason the Khoi people called it Aukoerebis, meaning "place of great noise". The best time to see the falls is in late summer when the river carries a lot of water: additional waterfalls form on the side walls of the gorge and the air is full of spray. Surrounding the gorge is a lunar-like landscape of eroded rock, and the rest of the park is semi-desert and home to a number of small mammals and some reintroduced

Insider Tip

black rhino. The most characteristic plant in the park is the giant aloe called *kokerboom* (quiver tree), which gets its name from the Bushmen (San) who use the soft branches to make quivers for their arrows. The Augrabies Restcamp, managed by South African National Parks (SANParks), has a good range of simple self-catering accommodation and a campsite with swimming pools, and there's a restaurant and bar. Reservations for night drives can be made at reception.

Insider Tip

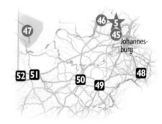

🕂 200 C2
✉ 120km (74mi) west of Upington
☎ 054 452 9200; www.sanparks.org
🕐 Daily 7:30–6:30 💶 R176

Where to...
Stay

Prices
Expect to pay per double room, per night
R under R1,500   **RR** R1,500–R2,500   **RRR** over R2,500

Kimberley Country House RR

Conveniently located in the middle of town, close to all the attractions, this 10-bedroom guest house offers Victorian era charm with modern amenities (WiFi, air conditioning). The team of staff are friendly and helpful, the breakfast is excellent and when it gets too hot you can cool off in the swimming pool.

✚ A202 A2
✉ 6 Carrington Road (Belgravia), Kimberley
☎ 076 388 0756; www.kchouse.co.za

Kwa Maritane/Tshukudu RRR

Kwa Maritane is in the southeast of Pilanesberg National Park, right next to an entrance gate, with a hide overlooking a busy waterhole, yet only a 10-minute drive from Sun City. Under the same management, the more exclusive Tshukudu lies deep within the park, perched on a rocky outcrop offering superb views over the plains. There are just eight thatched chalets here, and rates include game drives. Both lodges have a swimming pool.

✚ 202 B4 ✉ Pilanesberg Game Reserve
☎ 011 806 6800; www.legacygroup.co.za

Makanyane Safari Lodge RRR

Set on private land on the eastern border of Madikwe Game Reserve, this stunning lodge consists of eight large suites overlooking the Marico River. Top-notch guides lead the game drives and the reliably good wildlife sightings are complemented by fine cuisine and a good wine list. Facilities include a swimming pool, spa and gym.

✚ 202 B4 ✉ Access via Makanyane Gate on the dirt road between Sun City and Derdepoort
☎ 014 778 9600; www.sanctuaryretreats.com

Le Must River Residence and Le Must River Manor R–RR

Le Must River Residence is a 5-star guest house in the theme of an Italian-style villa with 11 individual rooms overlooking a pool and the river. The Manor is a very comfortable 3-star guest house with 6 rooms with contemporary African art.

✚ 201 D2 ✉ 14 Butler Street and 12 Murray Avenue, Upington
☎ 054 332 3971; www.lemustupington.com

Tuningi Safari Lodge RRR

This 5-star lodge lies in the western half of Madikwe Game Reserve, in a hilly area renowned for its game viewing. The eight spacious villas come with every possible comfort and there are two swimming pools and a spacious dining/lounge/bar area.

✚ 202 B3 ✉ Access via the R49 from Zeerust
☎ 011 805 9995; www.seasonsinafrica.com

Twee Rivieren R

This is Kgalagadi's administrative headquarters and largest rest-camp, and is at the entrance of the park. It's also the only camp that has cell-phone reception and 24-hour electricity. There's a pool (essential in this region), campsite, restaurant and petrol station. The air-conditioned cottages are equipped for self-catering groups of up to six.

✚ 201 D4 ✉ Kgalagadi Transfrontier Park
☎ 021 428 9111; www.sanparks.org

Where to…
Eat and Drink

Prices
Expect to pay for a two-course meal per person excluding drinks:
R under R150   **RR** R150–R300   **RRR** over R300

The Occidental Bar (The Ox) RRR

This saloon bar in the Big Hole Complex is headed up by Chef Daniel Williams who is well known beyond the borders of Kimberley. Together with his crew he prepares top-quality South African pub food including steaks, chicken, venison, prawns, gourmet burgers and sandwiches. The diamond rush era atmosphere makes it a very nice place to spend an evening, and in the summer, there is an outside area with long tables and benches.

➕ 202 A2
✉ Big Hole Complex, Tucker Street, Kimberley
☎ 053 831 1296
🕐 Mo–Thu 10–10, Fri, Sat 10–2am, Sun 10–3

Clementine's RR

Don't be put off by the corrugated iron exterior because inside this popular restaurant close to Clarens's central square is a well-stocked bar, neat candlelit tables and an affordable menu. Opt for steak with a delicious sauce or grilled fish, followed by imaginative desserts such as chocolate crème brûlée or butternut cheesecake. There's a patio overlooking the mountains.

➕ 202 D2 ✉ Church Street, Clarens
☎ 058 256 1616; www.clementines.co.za
🕐 Tue–Fri 12–3, 6–late, Sat, Sun 11–3

Café Zest RR

This casual, tastefully decorated restaurant has a café in the front, an attractive courtyard and a dining area at the rear section. The menu features locally sourced meaty fare, such as whole Kalahari lamb shank but also includes hearty fish, chicken and pasta dishes.

➕ 201 D2
✉ 49 Schroder Street, Upington
☎ 054 332 1413; www.facebook.com/cafezestupington
🕐 Daily 9am–10pm

De Oude Kraal Country Estate RRR

Locals travel a long way to get to this delightful farmhouse, especially for the Sunday lunch and six-course gourmet evening meals. Surrounded by vines and blue gum trees the restaurant has high ceilings, wooden floors and there's a veranda for alfresco dining. Food is beautifully presented and the wine cellar has some rare vintages. Accommodation is also available and overnight guests can tour the cellar to pick their own wine for dinner.

➕ 202 A1
✉ 35km (22mi) south of Bloemfontein, take the Riversford exit off the N1
☎ 051 564 0733; www.oudekraal.co.za
🕐 7:30am–9:30pm

Seven on Kellner RR–RRR

This award-winning restaurant, set in a historic mansion in Bloemfontein, has a globetrotting menu with something for everybody, ranging from spicy Moroccan stew to tasty pizzas cooked in a wood-fired oven.

➕ 202 B1
✉ 7 Kellner Street, Bloemfontein
☎ 051 447 7928; www.sevenonkellner.co.za
🕐 Mon–Fri noon–2, Mon–Sat 6–10

Where to...
Shop

Given that this is a region of wide open spaces, it's not known for its shopping. However, you should be able to pick up curios at shops in lodges, and the small towns have supermarkets and bottle shops to top up provisions.

Sun City has a shopping mall and shops in the entertainment complexes and its hotels have excellent amenities.

The village of **Clarens** in the Eastern Highlands has galleries and craft shops gathered around the village square.

The **Windmill Centre** (www.clarenswindmillcentre.co.za) has a shop selling home-made body products and sandstone gifts plus a cafés, and the **Johan Smith Gallery** (tel: 058 256 1620; www.johansmith.co.za) specializes in paintings and ceramics and has a café.

The **Clarens Meander** is a small shopping mall on the approach to the village.

The two premier shopping malls in Bloemfontein are the **Mimosa Mall** (corner of Nelson Mandela and Parfitt streets; tel: 051 444 6914; www.mimosamall.com), and **Loch Logan Waterfront** (Henry Street; tel: 051 448 3607; www.lochlogan.co.za), an outdoor mall arranged around a boardwalk overlooking a lake in King's Park.

Kimberley's major shopping mall is **Diamond Pavilion** (Bloemfontein Road; tel: 053 832 9200; www.diamondpavilion.co.za).

Insider Tip

Upington is the last stop for travellers going to the Kgalagadi Transfrontier Park so take advantage of the supermarkets.

Where to...
Go Out

Nightlife is restricted to dinner in a *boma* (African hut), a glass of wine in a hotel bar, or a beer while you barbecue at the grill outside your chalet. There are, however, a number of outdoor pursuits.

SPORT

Sun City (tel: 014 557 1000; www.suninternational.com) is a premier destination for **golfers**, with two 18-hole, par 72 courses.

In the Eastern Highlands near Clarens, **Outrageous Adventures** (tel: 083 485 9654; www.outrageousadventures.co.za, Oct–Mar) organizes **whitewater rafting** day trips on the Ash River with an optional 35m (115ft) abseil down a nearby cliff.

Umkulu Safari and Canoe Trails offer multi-day **rafting trips** on the Gariep (Orange) River along the South African-Namibian border. An adventurous way of seeing the area's wild animals and unique landscape, and you can opt to sleep under the stars or in a tent before returning by bus (http://umkuluadventures.com).

FESTIVALS

The 10-day **Macufe** (www.macufe.co.za) is held in Bloemfontein in September. One of the biggest festivals in the country, it celebrates African arts and culture.

Connoisseurs of the amber nectar should head to Clarens in February for the **Craft Beer Festival** (www.clarenscraftbeerfest.com), which showcases the country's top artisanal breweries.

In Kimberley, there's the **Gariep Arts Festival** (www.gariepfees.co.za, Aug–Sep).

Walks & Tours

Walks & Tours

1 CAPE TOWN CITY
Walk

DISTANCE Approximately 1.5km (1mi) **TIME** 1.5 hours
START/END POINT Cape Town Tourism, corner of Castle and
Burg streets ➕ 206 C2

A short walk in Cape Town's centre
will take you through lively streets
and busy shopping thoroughfares
with both impressive older buildings
and modern high-rises.

🄁–🄂

From the **tourist office** walk along
Strand Street to the Golden Acre
shopping complex and turn right
on to Adderley Street. On the
left is the aromatic and colourful
flower market in Trafalgar Place and
next door is the Standard Bank, a
good example of late 19th-century
architecture. Further up on the
other side of the road is the First
National Bank designed in 1933
by architect Sir Herbert Baker who
is responsible for many of South
Africa's finest buildings. Opposite
and on the corner of Adderley and
Wale streets is the **Slave Lodge**
(➤ 50), built in 1679 as accommodation for slaves from Indonesia
and India-Ceylon and one of the
oldest buildings in South Africa.

🄂–🄃

Opposite the Slave Lodge is the
Anglican **St George's Cathedral**,
designed by Sir Herbert Baker and
where Archbishop Desmond Tutu,
who received the Nobel Peace
Prize in 1984, made many of his
sermons against apartheid.

🄃–🄄

Next to the cathedral is the start
of Government Avenue, where
you can stroll among the oak
trees, lawns and hedges known

> ### TAKING A BREAK
> Head to one of the wonderfully atmos-
> pheric local restaurants, such as the
> **Savoy Cabbage**. In the restaurant
> section you can try delicacies such
> Tian of Chevre or Twice-baked Cheese
> Soufflé or you can just opt for a glass
> of champagne at the bar (101 Hout
> Street, tel: 021 424 2626; www.
> savoycabbage.co.za, Mon–Fri noon–
> 2:30, 7–10:30, Sat 7–10:30; RR).

as **Company's Garden** after the
Dutch East India Company who
first settled in the Cape in the
17th century. The site was originally
used to grow vegetables to sell to
passing ships. The grey squirrels
in the trees were introduced from
America by Cecil Rhodes when
he was Prime Minister of the Cape
(1890–96). In the garden are a
number of museums, the **National
Library of South Africa** – which
opened in 1818 and was one of
the first libraries in the world offering free loans of books – and the
Houses of Parliament, built in 1884
with a statue of Queen Victoria out
front. Today it's the seat of both
the houses of the South African
Parliament, while **De Tuynhuys**
("the garden house" in Afrikaans)
is the Cape Town office of the
president.

🄄–🄅

Return to the cathedral and left
into Wale Street, then turn right
into St George's Mall, a pedestrian

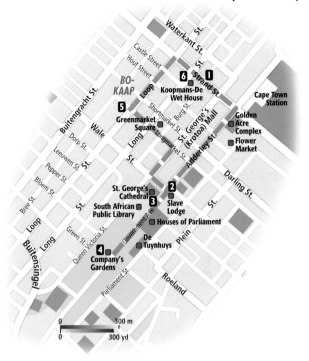

precinct and then left along Longmarket Street to **Greenmarket Square**, the oldest square in the city. Continue along Longmarket and cross Long Street, which is alive with trendy shops, cafés and nightclubs.

5–6

Another block takes you to Loop Street, where on the right-hand corner you'll find Heritage Square, a lovingly restored block of 18th- to 19th-century town houses with bars, restaurants and the Cape Heritage Hotel cluster around a courtyard, which is home to the oldest vine in South Africa planted in 1781. Walk north along Loop Street for two blocks, crossing Castle Street and turn right on to Strand Street. Cross Long Street

again and on your right is the **Koopmans-De Wet House**, which has been restored with 18th-century furnishings and has stables and slave quarters. Turn right on to Burg Street and you're back at the tourist office.

The Houses of Parliament, the seat of the National Assembly

2 CAPE PENINSULA

Drive

DISTANCE Approximately 180km (112mi)
TIME 1 day
START/END POINT Central Cape Town ✚ 204 B3

The ruggedly beautiful Cape Peninsula is dominated by the mountains of Table Mountain National Park running down its spine. On both sides are pretty fishing villages, clutches of luxurious houses, winding roads that hug the cliffs and ever-present ocean views where you may spot whales in season. A leisurely day's drive takes in the highlights, which are only a few kilometres apart and you can do this route in either direction.

❶–❷

From **Cape Town** follow the coast road south through the suburbs of Green Point and Sea Point before it snakes its way through the up-market residences of Clifton and its famous beaches. Next is im-

possibly trendy **Camps Bay**, where a stunning swathe of white sand beach is lined by a fashionable row of restaurants and bars, and is backed by the Twelve Apostles. This is one of the most beautiful beaches in the world and very popular for sunbathing, although you won't see many people in the ocean – the Atlantic's too cold to swim in.

Insider Tip

❷–❸

After Camps Bay, the mansions stop and the road follows the rocky coast through to **Hout Bay**, passing the Twelve Apostles Hotel and the upmarket village of **Llandudno**. Hout Bay is a historical fishing harbour with another fine beach favoured by dog walkers. You can eat fresh seafood at Mariner's

The surfers' paradise of Muizenberg on the Cape Peninsula

Wharf, wander around the brightly painted fishing boats or visit the fish market. From the harbour, sightseeing boats depart throughout the morning (and more occasionally in the afternoon) taking passengers to see the Cape fur seal colony on **Duiker Island**.

3–4

The next section of road is the stunning 15km (9mi) **Chapman's Peak Drive**, perhaps one of the world's most scenic drives. Now a toll road, it's carved in the rock 600m (1,970ft) above the crashing waves. In recent years giant nets have been constructed above the road to catch falling boulders and it has been fortified, so in places the road cuts into the mountainside and forms an overhang. As you pass Chapman's Peak the view opens up to the vast stretch of beach in **Noordhoek**.

Insider Tip

4–5

The 8km-long (5mi) beach is Noordhoek's greatest attraction, popular for horseback riding, and there are a number of equestrian centres. The road then heads inland to Sun Valley where you turn right on to the M65 to **Kommetjie**, where the beach is always busy with surfers, and **Scarborough**, a scattering of holiday homes. The road continues on to the entrance to the Cape of Good Hope sector of **Table Mountain National Park (Cape of Good Hope Sector)** and en route you can stop at an ostrich farm to learn about the giant birds or visit the large souvenir market at the entrance to the park.

5–6

Roughly 65km (40mi) from Cape Town, the **Table Mountain National Park** protects the wild flora and fauna of the southern quarter of the Cape Peninsula. You may spot an ostrich, or antelope such as bontebok or giant eland. The fynbos (fine bush) vegetation is made up of over 1,400 indigenous plant species including proteas and heather. However, it is not the wildlife, vegetation and wonderful isolated beaches that attracts hundreds of thousands of visitors to the very southwestern tip of Africa but rather the awe-inspiring landscape and the sense of being in a significant spot. At Cape Point, on the southern tip of the peninsula, there is a parking area and a visitor centre with a pricey gift shop and

Cape of Good Hope

Walks & Tours

a restaurant. From here, a steep paved footpath and a less demanding funicular railway ascend to the cliff-top **Cape Point Lighthouse**, which offers sweeping ocean views back along False Bay and out to the southern horizon. The 249m-high (817ft) lighthouse dates from 1860, its powerful light has a range 67km (42mi) in clear weather but as it was often shrouded in dense fog, a new lighthouse was built (1919) almost 100m (330ft) lower down. It safeguards the more than 20,000 ships that use the Cape route every year. The first European to sail round the headland was Bartolomeu Dias in 1488 and he named it the Cape of Storms, which is apt as there is often a strong wind blowing.

6–7

Once back out of the park, the M4 goes back to Cape Town on the eastern coast of the peninsula along False Bay, so named by sailors who confused the bay with Table Bay to the north. Stop at **Boulders Beach**, a lovely string of sandy beaches surrounded by massive boulders and home

to a colony of African penguins. To protect their natural habitat the area has been fenced but there are boardwalks so visitors can get close to the penguins.

Next along the M4 is **Simon's Town**, a still-working naval base, which rather surprisingly was in the hands of the British until as recently as 1957. The Quayside Centre is a pleasant place to stop for refreshment.

7–8

Continue through **Fish Hoek** with its good beach and colourful row of brightly painted beach huts, and then on to **Kalk Bay** with its bustling fishing harbour and bohemian atmosphere thanks to the antique and bric-a-brac shops and trendy cafés along the main street. The road then winds its way through to **Muizenberg**, the last settlement on False Bay, which has long been a popular bathing spot due to its lovely white sand beach, pounding surf and colourful beach huts. As great white sharks patrol this stretch of False Bay, Muizenberg has shark spotters who raise the alarm if swimmers and surfers are at risk. From Muizenberg it's a short 30-minute drive along the M3 back to central Cape Town.

Insider Tip

Table Mountain National Park (Cape of Good Hope Sector)
🕂 204 B2 ☎ 021 780 8204; www.sanparks.org
🕐 Oct–Mar daily 6–6; Apr–Sep 7–5
💶 R135

Cape Point Ostrich Farm
🕂 204 B2 ✉ M65, 400m from the entrance to the Table Mountain National Park
☎ 021 780 9294; www.capepointostrichfarm.com
🕐 Daily 9:30–5:30 💶 R55

Boulders Beach
🕂 204 B2 ✉ Boulder Visitor Centre, Bellevve Sreet, Simon's Town
☎ 021 786 2329; www.sanparks.org
🕐 Dec–Jan 7–7:30; Feb–Mar, Oct–Nov 8–6:30; Apr–Sep 8–5 💶 R70

3 ROUTE 62
Drive

DISTANCE 613km (380mi) **TIME** Allow 2 days
START POINT Cape Town ✚ 196 A2
END POINT Oudtshoorn ✚ 197 D2

Characterized by the wide open spaces of the Karoo and defined by the dramatic mountains dividing the dry interior from the wetter coastal regions, Route 62 is a quieter alternative to the N2 between Cape Town and the Garden Route.

❶–❷

From **Cape Town** drive 50km (30mi) up the N1 to **Paarl** in the Winelands where you can visit the scenic estates along Main Street, which is the longest street in the country. From here it's a short 9km (6mi) drive along the R303 through more **wine estates** to the town of **Wellington**, which is also an important region for the production of dried fruit.

❷–❸

From Wellington follow the R303 over the switchbacks of the spectacular **Bain's Kloof Pass**. Opened

in 1853, this is one of South Africa's greatest engineering feats, set in a truly dramatic mountain setting. Once over the pass and 29km (18mi) from Wellington, turn left on the R43 and drive 42km (26mi) to **Tulbagh** via Wolseley. Tulbagh is steeped in 300 years of history and has an impressive selection of old Cape Dutch buildings. These were extensively damaged in an earthquake in 1969 but were restored to their former glory and most are now listed as National Monuments. Park the car and stroll up Church Street.

❸–❹

Retrace the R43 and after 27km (17mi) turn left on the R303 and continue for 9km (6mi) to **Ceres**, the capital of South Africa's most important fruit growing region, which is aptly named after the Roman goddess of agriculture.

Lush vineyards in the Cape Winelands region

Walks & Tours

TAKING A BREAK
You'll be spoilt for choice of excellent
country restaurants along Route 62.
Perhaps the oddest place to stop is
the famous **Ronnie's Sex Shop** (tel:
028 572 1153; www.ronniessexshop.
co.za; R), a simple roadside pub
between Ladismith and Barrydale
where the **Road Kill Café** serves pub
meals – hopefully they are joking
about the roadkill ingredients!

thatched cottages, it's today home
to a number of artists.

🖪–🖬

From Robertson, stay on the R60
to go straight to Ashton and
Montagu or go on another detour
to **Bonnievale**, 35km (22mi) along
the R317, which is known for
its wine and cheese; tastings
are available locally. Loop back
round to **Montagu** and the R62
for about 25km (16mi) via the

Drive south on the R303 for 24km
(15mi) and you'll come to a
turn-off back to the R43 to
Worcester. Visit the KWV
House of Brandy here,
the largest cellar of
its kind in the world,
for a cellar tour and
brandy tasting. You
could also visit the
**Karoo National
Botanical Garden**
and the local
museum where
outdoor displays
preserve the
old-fashioned
farming methods
of the Cape.

🗗–🖪

Head southeast of
Worcester on the R60
where there are many wine
cellars to visit along the fertile
Breede River Valley, sheltered by
the Langeberg Mountains. This is
a pretty drive and there are many
farm stalls where you can buy
fresh produce. **Robertson**, 53km
(33mi) from Worcester, has neat
streets lined with jacaranda trees
with some good restaurants and
craft shops, and it is surrounded
by more than 20 wine estates.

From Robertson you can
choose to go on a short detour
to **McGregor**, 25km (16mi) away.
A beautiful 19th-century village
of picture-perfect whitewashed

unassuming village of Ashton and
the Kogmanskloof Pass. Montagu
is famous for its brandy, wine, fruit
and natural hot springs (43°C/
109°F); day visitors are welcome in the several pools in
the **Avalon Springs Resort** or you
could stay overnight here in comfortable self-catering apartments
or hotel-style rooms (tel: 023 614
1150; www.avalonsprings.co.za).
The resort has a good restaurant
and the pools stay open late.

6–7

Follow the R62 another 60km (37mi) to **Barrydale**, which is dotted with more vineyards and fruit orchards. From Barrydale there's the option of taking a shorter way to the Garden Route via the R324 and Tradouw's Pass, the R322 to Heidelberg and the N2 to Mossel Bay. Alternatively, stay on the R62, for another 77km (48mi) to the **Ladismith** region, which produces cheese and butter.

London and Paris and worth their weight in gold. Get a map from the tourist office and stroll among the lovely old sandstone buildings. There's also a string of ostrich farms along the R328 on either side of Oudtshoorn where you can learn all about ostriches, feed one and even ride one.

Insider Tip

A 28km (17mi) drive north from Oudtshoorn on the R328 are the **Cango Caves**. Sculptured by nature through the ages, the caves have fascinating limestone formations. There's a choice of two tours – the standard one takes you through the larger caverns and the adventure one leads you through tight crevices and up and down 400 stairs.

🛈 www.route62.co.za

KWV House of Brandy
🏠 196 B2
✉ Church Street, Worcester
☎ 023 342 0255; www.kwv.co.za
🕐 Mon–Fri 9–4:30; tours 10, 2

Avalon Springs Resort
🏠 196 C2 ✉ Uitvlucht Street, Montagu
☎ 023 614 1150; www.avalonsprings.co.za
🕐 Daily 8am–11pm
💵 R55, R100, R120 depending on the day

Oudtshoorn Tourist Office
🏠 196 D2 ✉ 80 Voortrekker Street
☎ 044 279 2532; www.oudtshoorn.com
🕐 Mon–Fri 8–6, Sat 8:30–1

After another 49km (30mi), you'll reach **Calitzdorp**, famous for its port, which can be tasted on a couple of estates, and after another 50km (30mi) you'll get to Oudtshoorn, the ostrich capital of the world.

7–8

Oudtshoorn witnessed an ostrich-feather boom in the late 19th and early 20th centuries when the feathers were fashionable in

Cango Caves
🏠 197 D2 (Oudtshoorn) ✉ R328
☎ 044 272 7410; www.cango-caves.co.za
🕐 Daily tours every hour 9–4
💵 R100 and R150 depending on tour

Walks & Tours

4 PANORAMA ROUTE
Drive

DISTANCE 127km (80mi)	**TIME** 1 day
START POINT Sabie ✚ 203 E4	
END POINT Blyde River Canyon ✚ 203 E4	

The mountainous Panorama Route (► 142) rises over low-lying regions known as the lowveld and southern Kruger and a drive through the scenic country roads makes for a refreshing change from the heat of the bush. Take your time in the shops and restaurants along the route and simply pull over to admire the sweeping views.

1–2

Drive along the R532 from **Sabie**, the centre for the largest man-made forest in the country, for 29km (18mi) to Graskop where there are a series of waterfalls to visit. Most charge a small fee to park and all are clearly signposted off the road. The Sabie Falls plunge 73m (240ft) down Sabie Gorge and the 65m (213ft) **Mac Mac Falls** drop into a series of refreshing pools that you can splash around in. Once in **Graskop**, a 1.5km (1mi) detour on the R533 toward Hazyview takes you to the Panorama Gorge and Falls, the location of the Big Swing (► 152).

2–3

From Graskop follow the R533, 15km (9mi) to **Pilgrim's Rest**. The village is a living museum dedicated to the gold mining days. Park in the top parking area (you'll see the tour buses) and explore the single street of restored miners' cottages, duck into the museums, *Insider Tip* have a go at gold panning or visit the shops and restaurants.

3–4

Retrace your steps back through **Graskop** and follow the R532 again, north toward the **Blyde River Canyon**. **Pinnacle Rock**, a 30m (98ft) free-standing quartzite buttress, and **God's Window**, the first of several viewpoints, are 6km (4mi) and 9km (6mi) respectively north of Graskop on the R534, a

Lisbon Falls, the highest waterfall in the region

scenic loop off the R532. God's Window offers unparalleled views from the edge of the escarpment over the lowveld and Kruger 900m (2,950ft) below, and a little further

The Three Rondavels, distinctive circular peaks capped with green, in Blyde River Canyon

on, **Wonder View** has another sweeping view.

4–5

Where the R534 rejoins the R532, turn left back toward Graskop for 800m (872 yards) and then right on to a gravel road for 2.2km

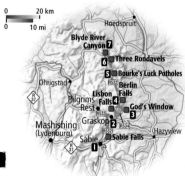

(1.4mi) to the 92m (302ft) **Lisbon Falls**, the highest waterfall in the region. Head north again on the R532 and 2km (1mi) after the R534 turn-off, turn left to reach the car park for the 45m (148ft) **Berlin Falls**.

5–6

Next are the **Bourke's Luck Potholes**, 35km (22mi) north of Graskop at the confluence of the Blyde and Treur rivers where waterborne sand and rock have scoured out huge cylindrical potholes into the river bed. There's a visitor centre and a series of walkways and bridges to watch the water swirl around below.

6–7

Another 20km (12mi) brings you to the **Three Rondavels** viewpoint with spectacular views of the 26km-long (16mi) canyon – the highlight of this tour. The **Blyde River** snakes its way down to sparkling Blydespoort Dam at the bottom with the shimmering lowveld plains beyond. From here you can retrace your steps back to Graskop or Sabie or continue on to the bottom of the canyon to the region around Hoedspruit.

TAKING A BREAK

Stop at any of the pancake houses along Graskop's main street, or grab home-made pies, bread, jams and pickles at the delis and bakeries along the main street in Pilgrim's Rest.

Walks & Tours

5 SWAZILAND
Drive

DISTANCE 200km (124mi) **TIME** 2 days
START POINT Ngwenya/Oshoek Border Post on the N17,
Mpumalanga ✚ 203 E3 **END POINT** Lavumisa Border Post
11km (7mi) from the N2, KwaZulu-Natal ✚ 203 F2

The smallest country in the southern hemisphere and still ruled by a royal family, the tiny autonomous kingdom of Swaziland lies almost entirely within South Africa, the landscape is dominated by bush and mountains. If you travel to Swaziland from South Africa in a rental car you will need a letter of authorization from your car rental company (some also charge a cross border fee) as proof of insurance. You can use South African Rand in Swaziland, and you will be required to produce a passport when you enter and exit the kingdom.

❶–❷
At the border crossing at **Ngwenya/Oshoek**, formalities should take no longer than 30 minutes. Stop at Ngwenya Glass (daily 9–4; www. ngwenya glass.co.sz) in Motjane, 5km (3mi) from the border, where you can buy hand-blown items such as glasses, vases and statues of African animals and watch glass-blowing. A number of other crafts are for sale too. From here

it's a short 18km (11mi) drive to the country's sleepy capital, Mbabane.

❷–❸
There's not much to see in **Mbabane's** busy grid of modern concrete buildings, but do stop at the Swazi Market at the end of Allister Miller Street for its colourful display of fresh produce and

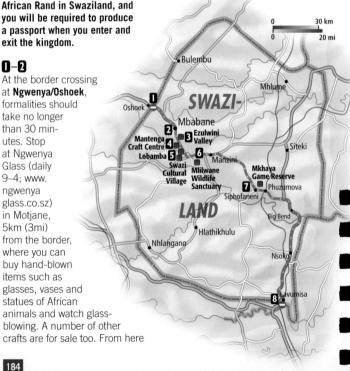

A panoramic view of the landscape near Mbabane

curios. The main road leaves town on a dramatic and giddy descent down into the **Ezulwini Valley** where the road winds in a series of sweeping curves for approximately 10km (6mi).

3–4

At the bottom, take the first main exit on to the old Ezulwini Valley road. The valley is 28km (17mi) long, and is home to a number of hotels, restaurants, bars, night-clubs and attractions. Opposite the Ezulwini Sun hotel is the Swazi Health and Beauty Studio (tel: 268 416 1164; daily 6–6), best known for its large outdoor pool fed by a warm spring known as the Cuddle Puddle. About 4km (3mi) further on is the **Mantenga Craft Centre**, which is an attractive purpose-built village of craft shops where you'll also find a tourist information desk and a desk for Swazi Trails, which can arrange white-water rafting, caving, hiking and safaris into the parks.

4–5

Just past the craft centre is the entrance to the small **Mantenga Nature Reserve** with picnic spots and walking paths to the 95m (312ft) Mantenga Falls. Also within

the reserve is the **Swazi Cultural Village**, which is a living, working reconstruction of a 19th-century Swazi village with traditional grass beehive huts, where you may see food being prepared, crafts being made, and livestock wandering around. The entrance fee to the village includes local guides to show you around.

5–6

In the heart of the valley at **Lobamba** and 20km (12mi) from **Mbabane**, are Swaziland's Houses of Parliament and the royal residence of Ludzidzini, home to King Mswati III and his Queen Mother, or *Ndlovukazi*, meaning "she-elephant". These can't be visited but next door is the National Museum, which covers the history of Swaziland and the royal family and there are some wonderful old photographs.

6–7

Take the right turning from the Ezulwini Valley road just after Ludzidzini and after 3.5km (2mi) on a dirt road is the entrance gate to **Mlilwane Wildlife Sanctuary**. You can go on guided game drives, mountain-bike trails, horseback rides or simply walk through the

Walks & Tours

A traditional beehive hut at the Swazi Cultural Village

grasslands that are home to white rhino, antelope, buffalo, hippo, crocodile and many species of

reserve, so aim to get to the gate by 10am to park and meet your guide for the 6-hour excursion into the reserve. Game drives and a generous lunch are included and it's essential to pre-arrange this tour. From Mkhaya it's 91km (56mi) to the border post at **Lavumisa** and Maputaland (➤ 98) in KwaZulu-Natal.

Insider Tip

Mantenga Nature Reserve
✉ Mantenga Craft Centre
☎ 268 416 1151 ✋ R100

National Museum
✉ Lobamba ☎ 263 416 1516; www.sntc.org.sz
🕐 Mon–Fri 8–1, 2–3:45, Sat, Sun 10–1, 2–3:45
✋ R100

Zebra making their way across the grasslands of Mlilwane Wildlife Sanctuary

birds. Stay overnight here, as there's a variety of accommodation to choose from and a delightful restaurant overlooking a hippo pool where the staff entertains with singing and dancing each evening.

7 – 8

From Mlilwane, drive on the new highway 19km (12mi) to Manzini, but don't linger in the dull and scruffy town, just continue straight through. After 8km (5mi) the road splits, so take the right-hand turning and continue for 44km (27mi) to the gate of the **Mkhaya Game Reserve**, home to rhino, elephant and numerous antelope. Private cars are not allowed into the

Mlilwane Wildlife Sanctuary
☎ 268 528 3943; www.biggameparks.org
✋ R40

Mkhaya Game Reserve
☎ 268 528 3943; www.biggameparks.org
🕐 Daily 10–4 ✋ R650 day safari

TAKING A BREAK
The **Maguga Viewpoint Restaurant** (near Piggs Peak at the Maguga Dam, 40km (25mi) north of Mbabane; tel: 268 668 6637; R) is a good place to stop on the scenic loop road. The terrace has lovely views over the water and the food (snacks and few main dishes) is freshly prepared.

Insider Tip

Practicalities

Practicalities

WHAT YOU NEED

		UK	USA	Canada	Australia	Ireland	Netherlands
● Required ○ Suggested ▲ Not required	Your passport should be valid for six months beyond the intended date of exit from South Africa. Kruger and its immediate environs are a low-risk malarial area at some times of year and prophylactics are advised.						
Passport/National Identity Card		●	●	●	●	●	●
Visa (for less than three months)		▲	▲	▲	▲	▲	▲
Onward or Return Ticket		●	●	●	●	●	●
Health Inoculations (tetanus and polio)		○	○	○	○	○	○
Health Documentation (▶ 192, Health)		○	○	○	○	○	○
Travel Insurance		○	○	○	○	○	○
Driving Licence (national) for car hire		●	●	●	●	●	●

WHEN TO GO

Cape Town

High season   Low season

JAN	FEB	MAR	APR	MAY	JUN	JUL	AUG	SEP	OCT	NOV	DEC
26°C	26°C	25°C	23°C	20°C	18°C	17°C	18°C	19°C	21°C	23°C	25°C
79°F	79°F	77°F	73°F	68°F	64°F	62°F	64°F	66°F	70°F	73°F	77°F

☀ Sun   🌧 Wet   ⛅ Sunshine and showers

The Western and Eastern Capes generally have dry, warm summers and cool, wet winters. The Indian Ocean coast along KwaZulu-Natal is tropical with relatively warm temperatures all year, while inland Johannesburg and the north have mild dry winters and wet summers. The temperatures given above are the average daily maximum for each month in Cape Town. Do note, however, that while temperatures follow a similar pattern around the country, with November to February being the warmest months and June, July and August the coolest, the rainfall patterns for the interior and east coast are reversed, with most of the rain falling between November and April. Book well in advance for the long summer school holidays over December as this is the most popular month for local tourism.

GETTING ADVANCE INFORMATION

- Cape Town & Western Cape:
  www.tourismcapetown.co.za
- Eastern Cape:
  www.visiteasterncape.co.za
- Tourism KwaZulu-Natal:
  www.zulu.org.za
- Mpumalanga:
  www.mpumalanga.com
- Limpopo:
  www.golimpopo.com
- Gauteng:
  www.gauteng.net
- Johannesburg:
  www.joburg.org.za
- Northwest Province:
  www.tourismnorthwest.co.za
- Northern Cape:
  http://experiencenortherncape.com

GETTING THERE

By Air South Africa has international airports in Johannesburg, Cape Town and Durban, which are served by over 40 airlines. Most of the other larger cities are connected by domestic flights.

From the UK Carriers include British Airways (www.britishairways.com), Virgin (www.virgin-atlantic.com), and South African Airways (www.flysaa.com).

From the rest of Europe Carriers include Air France, TAP Portugal, Alitalia, Austrian Airlines, Iberia, Lufthansa, KLM, and Swiss International. There are also indirect flights from other airlines such as Kenya Airways, Ethiopian Airlines, Air Namibia and Emirates.

From the US and Canada Delta and South African Airways both fly directly between the USA and South Africa. American Airlines code shares with British Airways on flights to South Africa via London.

From Australia and New Zealand Qantas code shares with South African Airways from Sydney and Perth, Singapore Airlines flies from Sydney and Wellington via Singapore, and Malaysia Airlines flies from several Australian cities and Auckland in New Zealand via Kuala Lumpur.

TIME

 South Africa Standard Time (SAST) is two hours ahead of Greenwich Mean Time (GMT+2). Between March to October, when daylight saving is observed in the UK, South Africa is only one hour ahead of the UK.

CURRENCY & FOREIGN EXCHANGE

Currency South Africa's currency is the Rand, denoted with an R on banknotes and price tags. Coins are issued in denominations of 5, 10, 20 and 50 cents, R1, R2 and R5. Notes (bills) are R10, R20, R50, R100 and R200. Try to avoid accumulating R200 notes as many forgeries are in circulation and an increasing number of retailers refuse to take them. A maximum of R5,000 in South African notes can be imported or exported.

Exchange Traveller's cheques and cash can be exchanged in any bank where you can also withdraw cash from a credit card. Transactions are subject to a commission charge. Branches of American Express and Rennies (local agent for Thomas Cook) can be found in the large shopping malls and airports.

Credit and debit cards ATMs are prolific in banks, petrol stations and shopping malls in the urban areas, but less so in remote areas. Cards are widely acceptable in shops, restaurants and hotels, and a credit (not debit) card is essential if you are renting a car. The exception is petrol (gas), which can often only be paid for in cash. Many petrol (gas) stations have ATMs but this cannot always be relied upon. Increasingly the chip-and-pin system is being used for foreign credit cards.

SOUTH AFRICAN TOURISM: www.southafrica.net

UK & Ireland
6 Alt Grove, Wimbledon,
London SW19 4DZ
☎ 0870-1550-044
info.uk@southafrica.net

In the US
500 Fifth Avenue, Suite 2200,
New York, NY10110
☎ 212-730-2929
info.us@southafrica.net

In Australia
Level 1, 117 York Street,
Sydney, NSW 2000
☎ 02-9261-5000
info.au@southafrica.net

Practicalities

NATIONAL HOLIDAYS

1 January	New Year's Day	16 June	Youth Day
21 March	Human Rights Day	9 August	Women's Day
March/April	Good Friday	24 September	Heritage Day
March/April	Family Day (Easter Mon)	16 December	Day of Reconciliation
27 April	Freedom Day	25 December	Christmas Day
1 May	Workers' Day	26 December	Day of Goodwill

Opening Hours

- ○ Shops
- ● Offices
- ● Banks
- ● Main Post Offices
- ● Pharmacies
- ● Museums/Monuments

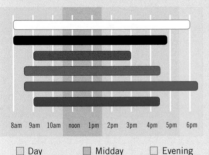

8am 9am 10am noon 1pm 2pm 3pm 4pm 5pm 6pm

☐ Day ☐ Midday ☐ Evening

Shops In towns, shops usually open Sat morning until 1pm. Shopping malls are usually open daily and close between 6 and 9pm. Supermarkets are open Mon–Sat 8:30am–6pm (9pm in cities and malls), and Sun 8:30am–1pm.
Banks Banks also open Sat 9–11:30am but close on Sun.
Pharmacies Most pharmacies open longer hours than regular shops. All the large towns and cities have late-night openings somewhere.

TIPS/GRATUITIES

Tipping is expected and is widespread. Car guards in the street are tipped to watch your car and it's usual to tip petrol station attendants.

Taxis	5–10 per cent
Restaurants/cafés	10 per cent
Tour guides	10–15 per cent
Room service	R10–20 per day
Porters	R10 per bag
Car guards	R2 in the day; R5 at night
Petrol station attendants	R2–R3

ELECTRICITY

 The power supply in South Africa is 220/230 volts. Sockets accept three-prong round-pin plugs.

An international adaptor is needed for two-prong or three-prong flat-pin plugs, you can either buy one locally or ask at the hotel front desk.

TIME DIFFERENCES (Nov–March)

South Africa (SAST)
12 noon

 →
London (GMT)
10am

 ←
New York (EST)
5pm

 ←
Los Angeles (PST)
2am

 →
Sidney (AEST)
9pm

STAYING IN TOUCH

Post offices are identified by a red, white and blue envelope sign and post boxes are usually red pillar boxes. Opening hours are Mon–Fri 9–3:30 and Sat 9–11 (longer in the shopping malls and airports). Postage rates can be found at www.postoffice.co.za

Public Telephones: Card and coin phones are widely available, and you can dial direct internationally from them. Phone cards are available from supermarkets and small shops. If not using roaming on your cell phone, pay-as-you-go SIM cards are available from phone shops or supermarkets. You will need to bring an adaptor for your cell phone charger. All telephone numbers in South Africa are composed of a three digit area code and a seven digit number. You must always use the area code, even if phoning from the same area.

International Dialling Codes
Dial 00 followed by
South Africa	27
UK:	44
USA / Canada:	1
Irish Republic:	353
Australia:	61
New Zealand:	64

Cell phone providers and services: MTN, Vodacom and Cell C provide network coverage in urban areas and along most trunk routes, but not in the more remote game reserves. If you expect to phone or text home regularly, consider buying a local SIM card, as call rates are much cheaper than for international roaming.

WiFi and internet: Inexpensive internet cafés can be found in all towns, although they may close over weekends, and most hotels and lodges catering to international visitors have ADSL and/or WiFi access.

PERSONAL SAFETY

South Africa's cities in particular have a problem with theft and isolated incidents of car-jacking. Tourists may be specifically targeted so keep an eye on who's around you and avoid trouble spots.

- Carry money in a slim belt under your clothes.
- Make use of hotel safes for valuables.
- Don't flash your wealth and leave expensive jewellery at home.
- Avoid walking at night.
- Don't leave bags or other items visible in your car.
- Drive with windows closed and doors locked.
- Be careful when drawing money at ATMs. Assume that anybody who comes too close or offers to help you has sinister motives.
- On shopping or other excursions, carry only as much cash as you are likely to need for the day.
- Make a note of your credit and debit card details and any emergency numbers and keep this separate from the actual cards.

Police assistance:
☎ 10111 from any phone

EMERGENCY NUMBERS
POLICE	10111
EMERGENCY CALL CENTRE (MOBILE)	112
AMBULANCE	10177

Practicalities

HEALTH

 Insurance Medical treatment in South Africa must be paid for and you will be asked to show proof of payment before treatment. Travel insurance is essential and should include repatriation to your home country.

 Dental Services Regular and cosmetic dentistry is of a very high standard and costs less than other countries. Ensure that your insurance covers at least emergency dentistry.

 Weather Even in winter the sun can be very intense, so bring sunglasses, hat and high-factor sunscreen. Use mosquito repellent in the bush and talk to your doctor about malaria prophylactics.

 Medication Staff in pharmacies can offer medical advice, though for prescriptions you will need to visit a doctor. Bring sufficient supplies of regular medication or note down the generic name as it may be sold under another brand in South Africa.

 Safe Water Tap water is safe to drink and bottled water is widely available and reasonably priced.

CONCESSIONS

Children Most hotels offer adjoining rooms or discounts for children sharing their parents' room and there is plenty of family self-catering accommodation, especially in the parks. There are discounts to museums and attractions though age ranges vary.
Students Holders of an International Student Identity Card (ISIC) or a Youth Hostel Association (YHA) card can get reductions on long-distance buses, the Baz Bus (hop-on-hop-off backpackers' bus) and some backpackers' hostels. Cards are not broadly recognised elsewhere but it's always worth asking.
Senior Citizens Discounts on entry fees and transport are offered to the over-60s. Proof of age required.

TRAVELLING WITH A DISABILITY

Facilities and access for wheelchair-bound visitors are generally good. Many hotels have specially adapted rooms, most public buildings have disabled parking at the entrance, newer tourist attractions have been developed with disabled visitors in mind, and several tour operators offer tours designed for visitors with disabilities.

CHILDREN

Children are welcomed everywhere. Baby changing facilities are available in shopping malls and the newer attractions. Special attractions for children are marked out in this book with the logo shown above.

RESTROOMS

Usually modern and clean, these can be found in all public buildings.

CUSTOMS

Duty-free allowances are up to R3,000 worth of gifts, 50ml of perfume, 250ml eau de toilette, 2 litres of wine or 1 litre spirits, and 200 cigarettes, 20 cigars or 250g of tobacco.

EMBASSIES & HIGH COMMISSIONS

UK
☎ (012) 421 7500

USA
☎ (012) 431 4000

Canada
☎ (012) 422 3000

Ireland
☎ (012) 452 1000

Australia
☎ (012) 423 6000

USEFUL WORDS AND PHRASES

South Africa has 11 official languages: Sepedi, Sesotho, Setswana, siSwati, Tshivenda, Xitsonga, Afrikaans, English, isiNdebele, isiXhosa and isiZulu. English is generally spoken by everyone but a simple hello or thank you in the local language of the region you're travelling through goes a long way. After English, the three most commonly used languages are Afrikaans (countrywide), isiZulu (predominantly KwaZulu-Natal) and isiXhosa (predominantly Eastern Cape). Speakers of these also live in the large cities. All are generally spoken as they are written, though isiXhosa and isiZulu have letters that are represented by various "clicks" – made by slapping the tongue against various parts of the inside of the mouth.

GETTING STARTED

I'm just a beginner at isiZulu	**Ngisaqala ukufunda isiZulu**
I only speak a little Xhosa	**Ndithetha isiXhosa kancinci nje**
I am trying to learn Afrikaans	**Ek probeer tans Afrikaans leer,**
but I cannot speak it yet	**maar ek kan dit nog nie praat nie**

USEFUL PHRASES

ENGLISH	ISIZULU	ISIXHOSA	AFRIKAANS
Hello	Sawubona	Uphila njani?	Hallo
How are you?	Kunjani?	Uphila njani?	Hoe gaan dit?
Fine, thanks	Ngiyaphila	Ndiphilile, enkosi	Goed dankie
Yes	Yebo	Ewe	Ja
No	Cha	Cha	Nee
Please	Ngiyakucela	Nceda	Asseblief
Thank you	Ngiyabonga	Enkosi	Baie dankie
Excuse me	Uxolo	Uxolo	Verskoon my
What is your name?	Ngubani igama lakho?	Ngubani igama lakho?	Wit is jou naam?
My name is...	Igama lami ngu...	Igama lam ngu...	My naam is ...
Where do you live?	Uhlalaphi?	Uhlala phi?	Waar woon jy?
I come from...	Ngiphuma e...	Ndivela...	Ek kom vanaf...
How much does it cost?	Kuyimalini lokhu?	Ixabisa malini?	Hoeveel kos dit?
Where is...?	Ihpi ...?	Ihpi ...?	Waar is ...?
What is this/that?	Yintoni le/leyo?	Yini le/leyo?	Wat is dit/daardie?
I would like...	Ngifuna...	Ndingathanda...	Ek wil graag ...hê
What time is it?	Yisikhathisini manje?	Ngubani ixesha?	Hoe laat is dit?
I am looking for...	Ngifuna i...	Ndikhangela i...	Ek is opsoek na die...
I am sorry	Ngiyaxolisa	Ndiva mtoembi	Ek is jammer
I don't know	Angazi	Andazi	Ek weet nie
I don't understand	Andiqondi	Andiqondi	Ek verstaan nie
Do you speak English?	Uyakwazi ukuk– huluma isiNgisi?	Uyakwazi ukut– hetha isiNgesi?	Praat jy Engels?
See you later	Sizobonana	Sobe sibonane	Sien jou later
Goodbye	Uhambe kahle/ Usale kahle	Sala sentle	Totsiens

Useful Words and Phrases

NUMBERS

	IsiZulu	IsiXhosa	Afrikaans
1	ukunye	nye	een
2	isibili	mbini	twee
3	kuthathu	ntathu	drie
4	okune	ne	vier
5	isihlanu	ntlanu	vyf
6	isithupha	ntandathu	ses
7	isikhombisa	xhenxe	sewe
8	isishiyagalombili	bhozo	agt
9	isishiyagalolunye	lithoba	nege
10	ishumi	lishuymi	tien
11	ishumi nanye	ishumi elinanye	elf
12	ishumi nambili	ishumi elinesibini	twaalf
13	ishumi nantathu	ishumi elinesithathu	dertien
14	ishumi nane	elinesine	veertien
15	ishumi nesihlanu	elinesihlanu	vyftien
20	amashumi amabili	amashumi amabini	twintig
50	amashumi amahlanu	amashumi amahlanu	vyftig
100	ikhulu	ikhulu	(een) honderd
1,000	inkulungwane	iwaka	(een) duisend

USEFUL WORDS IN AFRIKAANS

Afternoon	**Middag**	Ice cream	**Roomys**
Airplane	**Vliegtuig**	Information	**Inligting**
Airport	**Lughawe**	Left	**Links**
Arrival	**Aankoms**	Low-lying lake/swamp	**Vlei**
Bank	**Bank**	Lunch	**Middagete**
Barbecue	**Braai**	Market	**Mark**
Bed-and-breakfast	**Bed en ontbyt**	Menu	**Spyskaart**
Beach	**Strand**	Milk	**Melk**
Bill	**Rekening**	Morning	**Oggend**
Border	**Grens**	Night	**Nag**
Borough	**Burg**	Petrol	**Brandstoff**
Bread	**Brood**	Pharmacy	**Apteek**
Breakfast	**Ontbyt**	Police	**Polisie**
Cheap	**Goedkoop**	Post office	**Poskantoor**
Cheque	**Tjek**	Pub/bar	**Kroeg**
Chips	**Skyfies**	Right	**Regs**
Church	**Kerk**	Sausage	**(Boere)wors**
City	**Stad**	Station	**Stasie**
Credit card	**Kredietkaart**	Ticket	**Kaartjie**
Departure	**Vertrek**	Today	**Vandag**
Dinner	**Aandete**	Tomorrow	**Môre**
Evening	**Aand**	Town centre	**Middestad**
Expensive	**Duur**	Traveller's cheque	**Reisigerstjek**
Exit	**Uitgang**	Village	**Dorp**
Field	**Veld**	Wine	**Wyn**
Good/nice	**Lekker**	Yesterday	**Gister**

Road Atlas

For chapters: See inside front cover

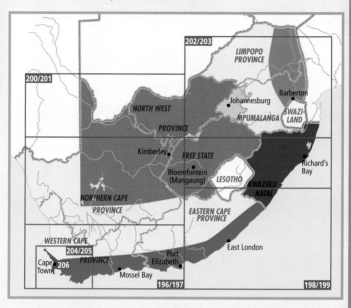

Key to Road Atlas

Motorway	International airport; airfield
Dual carriageway	Point of interest
Main Road	Monument; Waterfall
Secondary road	Archaeological site; Cave
Unpaved road	Peak; Geodetic point; Pass
Railroad	Spring; Surf spot
Ferry	(Swimming) beach
International border	TOP 10
Provincial/state border	Don't Miss
National Park, natural preserve	At Your Leisure
Restricted area	

196-203

1 : 4.200.000

0   50   100 km

0   25   50 mi

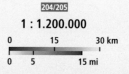

204/205

1 : 1.200.000

0   15   30 km

0   5   15 mi

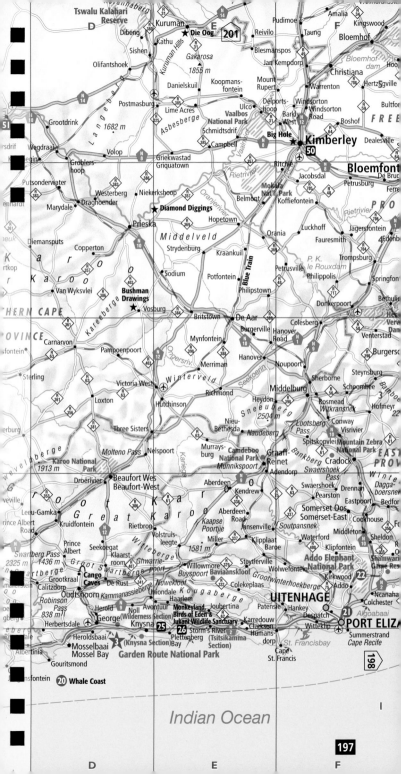

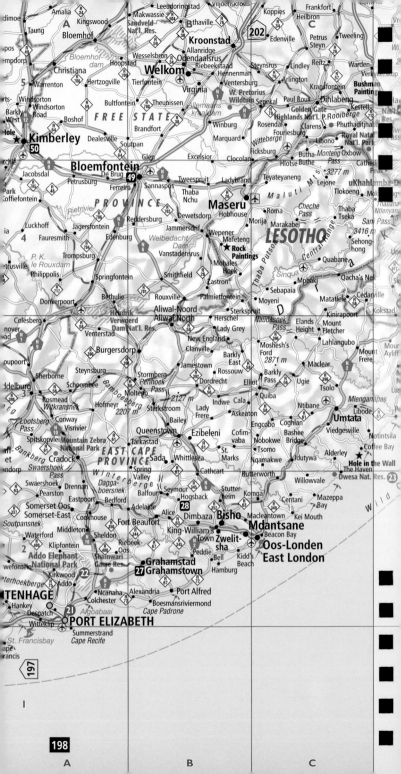

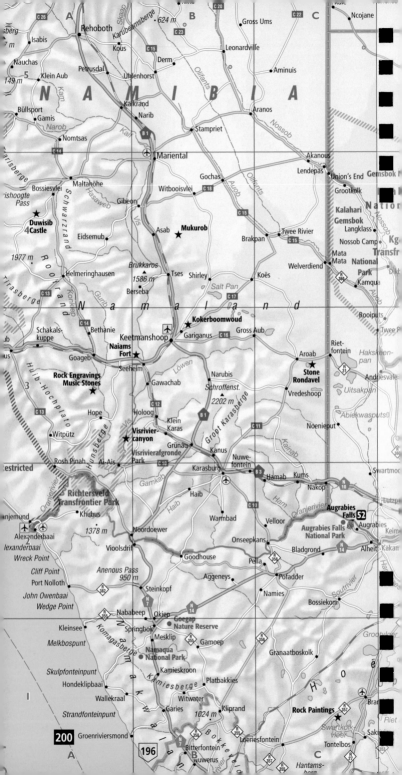

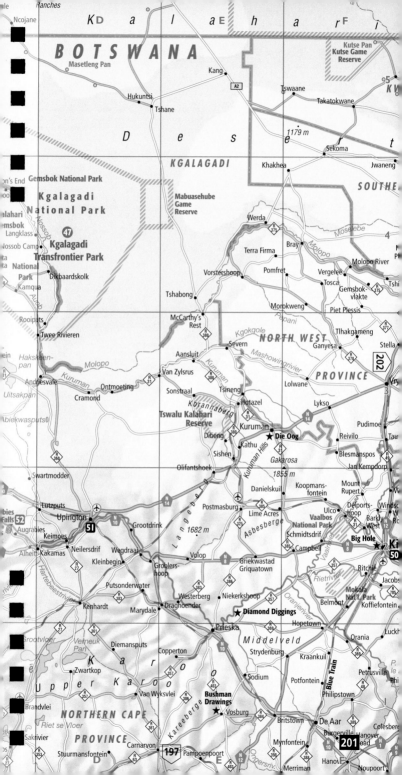

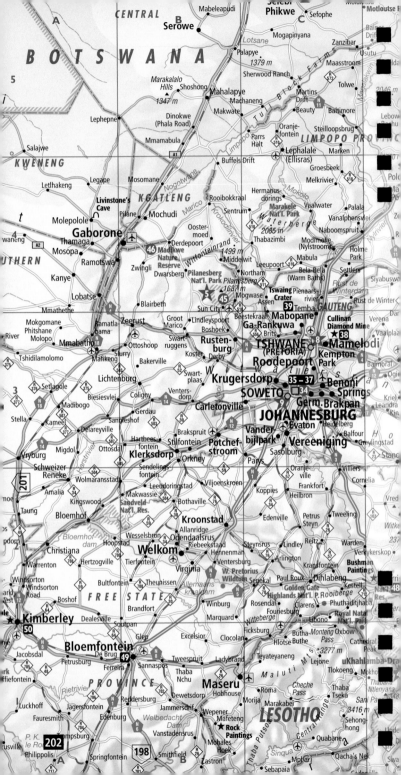

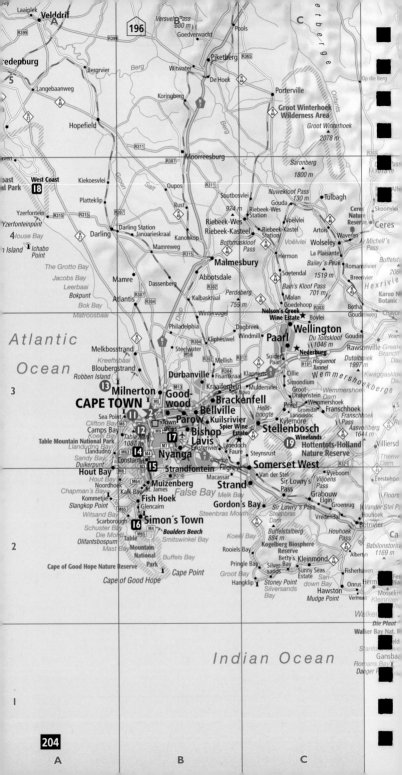

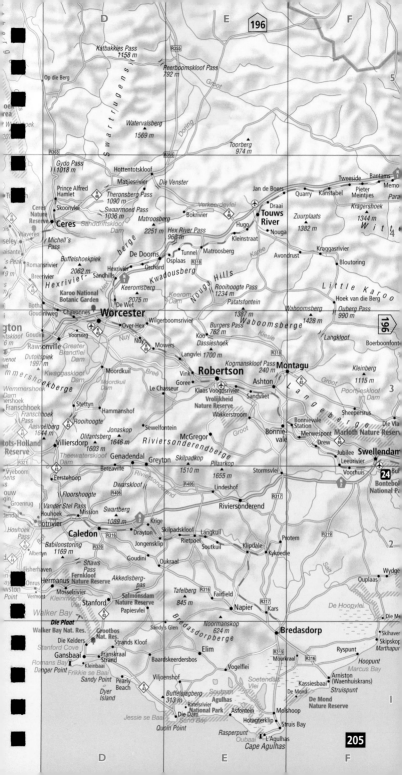

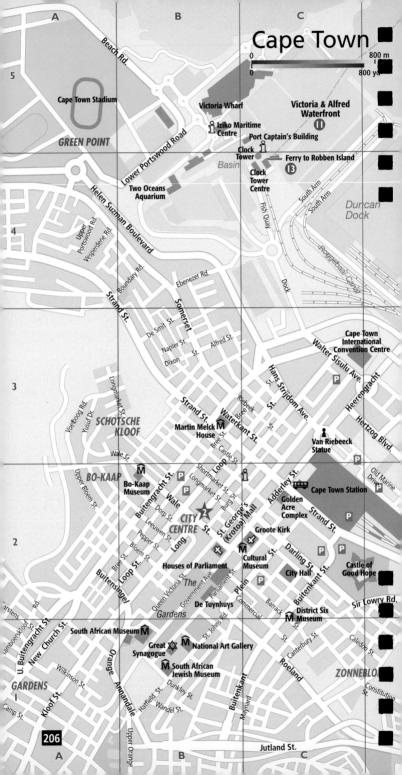

Cape Town

0   800 m
0   800 yd

GREEN POINT

Cape Town Stadium

Beach Rd.

Lower Portswood Road

Helen Suzman Boulevard

Upper Portswood Rd.
Vesperdene Rd.

Strand St.

Boundary Rd.

Victoria Wharf

Iziko Maritime Centre

Port Captain's Building

Clock Tower

Victoria & Alfred Waterfront

Ferry to Robben Island

Clock Tower Centre

Basin

Two Oceans Aquarium

Fish Quay

South Arm
South Arm

Dock

Duncan Dock

Roggebaai Canal

Ebenezer Rd.

Somerset

De Smit St.

Napier St.

Dixon St.

Alfred St.

Cape Town International Convention Centre

Walter Sisulu Ave.

Heerengracht

Hertzog Blvd.

Voetboog Rd.

Yusuf Dr.

Longmarket St.

SCHOTSCHE KLOOF

Wale St.

Strand St.

Martin Melck House

Waterkant St.

Riebeek St.

Bree St.

Hans Strijdom Ave.

St.

Van Riebeeck Statue

Old Marine Drive

BO-KAAP

Upper Bloem St.

Bo-Kaap Museum

Buitengracht St.

Dorp St.

Leeuwen St.

Pepper St.

Bloem St.

Bree St.

Loop St.

Wale

Shortmarket St.

Longmarket St.

Burg St.

Castle St.

Loop

CITY CENTRE

St. George's (Krotoa) Mall

Long

Adderley St.

Cape Town Station

Golden Acre Complex

Strand St.

Groote Kirk

St.

Darling St.

City Hall

Buitenkant St.

Castle of Good Hope

Sir Lowry Rd.

Houses of Parliament

Cultural Museum

Plein St.

The

Queen Victoria St.

Government Ave.

Parliament St.

Commercial

Barrack

De Tuynhuys

Gardens

St. Johns Rd.

District Six Museum

Canterbury St.

Roeland

U. Buitengracht St.

Karstens Rd.

Rainboekskloof Rd.

New Church St.

Wilkinson St.

South African Museum

Orange

Annandale

Great Synagogue

National Art Gallery

South African Jewish Museum

Buitenkant

Maynard

Caledon St.

ZONNEBLO

Constitution St.

GARDENS

Kloof St.

Camp St.

Hatfield St.

Dunkley St.

Wandel St.

Upper Orange

Jutland St.

206

Index

Index

Index

Index / Picture Credits

Picture Credits

1st Edition 2017

Worldwide Distribution: Marco Polo Travel Publishing Ltd
Pinewood, Chineham Business Park
Crockford Lane, Chineham
Basingstoke, Hampshire RG24 8AL, United Kingdom.
© MAIRDUMONT GmbH & Co. KG, Ostfildern

Authors: Lizzie Williams, Daniela Schetar and Friedrich Köthe
Translation and revised editing: Margaret Howie, www.fullproof.co.za
Program supervisor: Birgit Borowski
Chief editor: Rainer Eisenschmid

Cartography: © MAIRDUMONT GmbH & Co. KG, Ostfildern
3D-illustrations: jangled nerves, Stuttgart

Printed in China

Despite all of our authors' thorough research, errors can creep in.
The publishers do not accept any liability for this. Whether you
want to praise us, alert us to errors or give us a personal tip –
please don't hesitate to email or post to:

MARCO POLO Travel Publishing Ltd
Pinewood, Chineham Business Park
Crockford Lane, Chineham
Basingstoke, Hampshire RG24 8AL
United Kingdom
Email: sales@marcopolouk.com

10 REASONS
TO COME BACK AGAIN

1. One visit is rarely enough to experience all of South Africa's **rich wildlife**.

2. Fascinating **museums** span all the eras from early hominids through to the present day.

3. **Festivals** and events are spread throughout the year – enough to keep you coming back.

4. The **wines** are very good and they taste the best under warm African skies.

5. No other country offers the **cultural diversity** of the Rainbow Nation.

6. You need more than just one visit to do justice to the wide variety of **remarkable landscapes**.

7. South Africa is developing rapidly – there is always **something new** to discover.

8. Where else can you enjoy **5-star luxury** while on safari?

9. The starry beauty of the **night sky** is so breath-taking that you'll want to see it again.

10. The **exchange rate** is excellent so you can experience a great deal and stretch your travel budget.